AUG - / 2010
NO LONGER PROP
SEATTL

ID824565

JACKSON
LANZING

COLLIN
KELLY

MARCUS
TO

IRMA
KNIIVILA

JOYRIDE™

BOOM!
STUDIOS

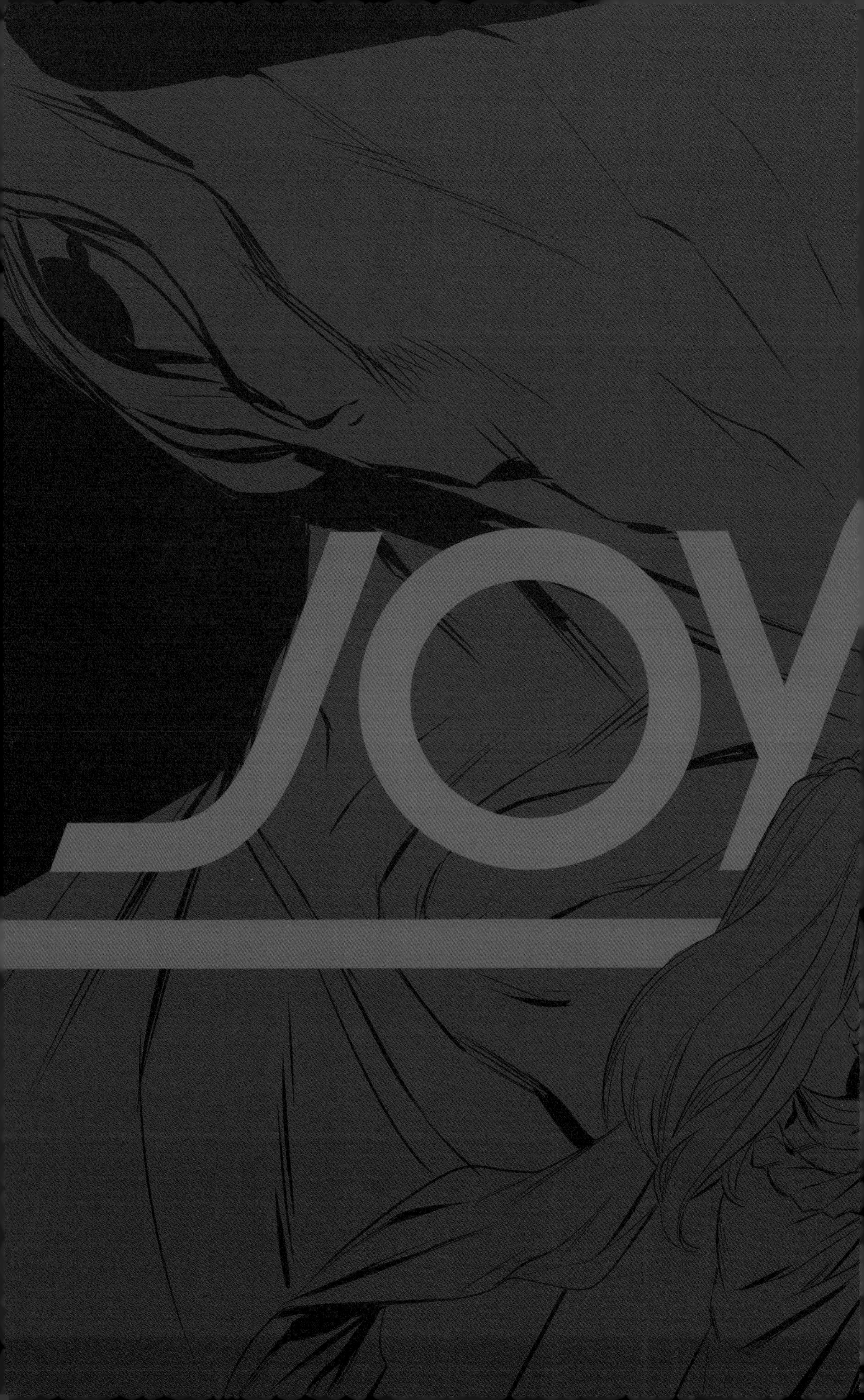
JOY

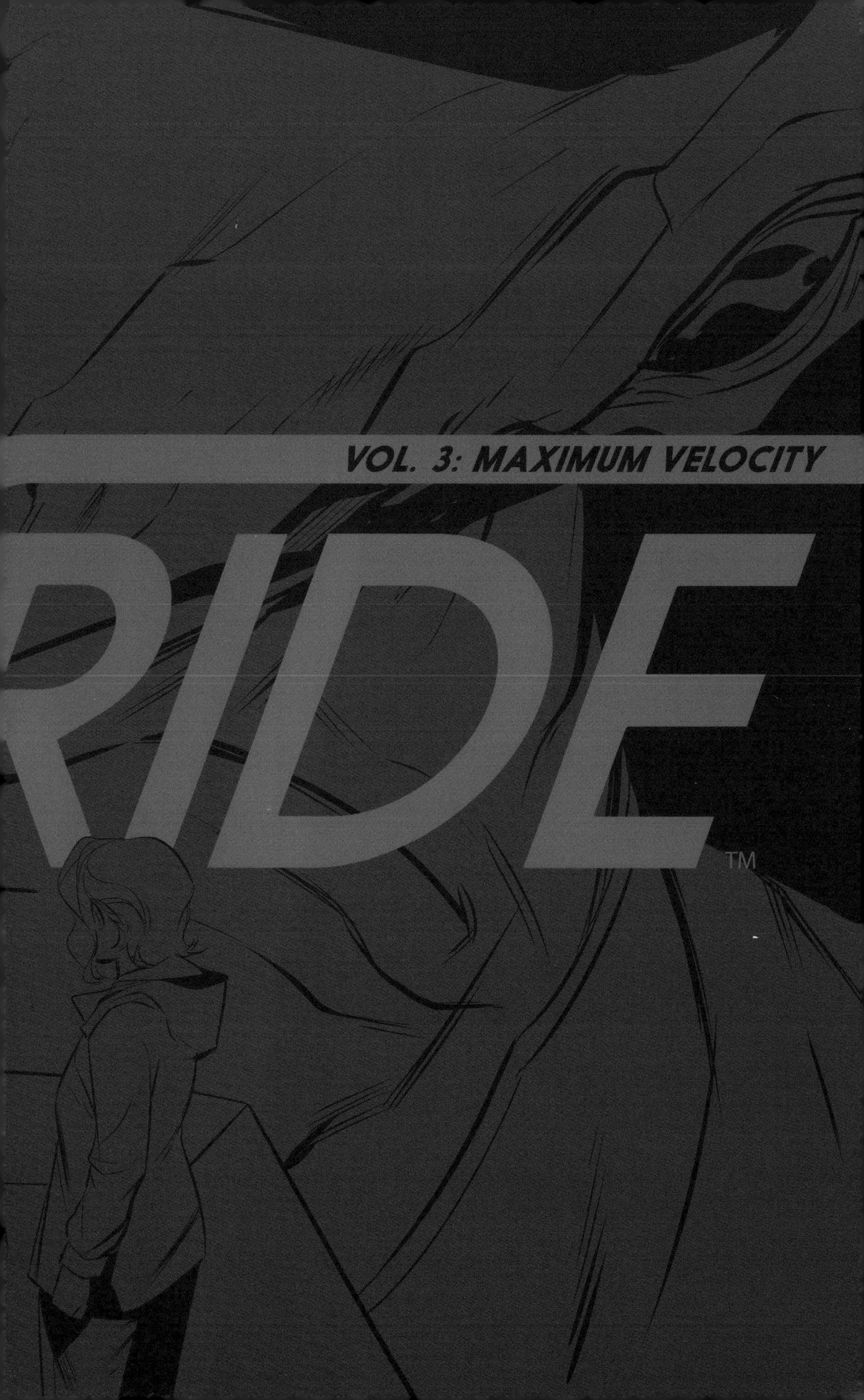

RIDE™

VOL. 3: MAXIMUM VELOCITY

Moon No. **77425981-TM1**
Classification: **Theta-Minor One**
Marker: **5-983-334-55515**

Planet No. **16489005-SP**
Classification: **Beta-Prime**
Marker: **5-983-741-11470**

Planet No. **77425981-TP**
Classification: **Theta-Prime**
Marker: **5-983-334-19848**

Moon No. **54978215-SM1**
Classification: **Sigma-Minor One**
Marker: **5-983-787-24892**

Planet No. **84971059-OP**
Classification: **Omega-Prime**
Marker: **5-983-667-31587**

Planet No. **54978215-SP**
Classification: **Sigma-Prime**
Marker: **5-983-787-16497**

Moon No. **54978215-SM2**
Classification: **Sigma-Minor Two**
Marker: **5-982-787-24778**

ROSS RICHIE CEO & Founder
MATT GAGNON Editor-in-Chief
FILIP SABLIK President of Publishing & Marketing
STEPHEN CHRISTY President of Development
LANCE KREITER VP of Licensing & Merchandising
PHIL BARBARO VP of Finance
ARUNE SINGH VP of Marketing
BRYCE CARLSON Managing Editor
MEL CAYLO Marketing Manager
SCOTT NEWMAN Production Design Manager
KATE HENNING Operations Manager
SIERRA HAHN Senior Editor
DAFNA PLEBAN Editor, Talent Development
SHANNON WATTERS Editor
ERIC HARBURN Editor
WHITNEY LEOPARD Editor
CAMERON CHITTOCK Editor
CHRIS ROSA Associate Editor
MATTHEW LEVINE Associate Editor
SOPHIE PHILIPS-ROBERTS Assistant Editor
AMANDA LaFRANCO Executive Assistant
KATALINA HOLLAND Editorial Administrative Assistant
JILLIAN CRAB Production Designer
MICHELLE ANKLEY Production Designer
KARA LEOPARD Production Designer
MARIE KRUPINA Production Designer
GRACE PARK Production Design Assistant
CHELSEA ROBERTS Production Design Assistant
ELIZABETH LOUGHRIDGE Accounting Coordinator
STEPHANIE HOCUTT Social Media Coordinator
JOSÉ MEZA Event Coordinator
HOLLY AITCHISON Operations Coordinator
MEGAN CHRISTOPHER Operations Assistant
RODRIGO HERNANDEZ Mailroom Assistant
MORGAN PERRY Direct Market Representative
CAT O'GRADY Marketing Assistant
LIZ ALMENDAREZ Accounting Administrative Assistant
CORNELIA TZANA Administrative Assistant

VISUAL RESEARCH ASSISTANT
DANI V

DESIGNER
SCOTT NEWMAN

EDITORS
CAMERON CHITTOCK
& **DAFNA PLEBAN**

JOYRIDE Volume Three, February 2018. Published by BOOM! Studios, a division of Boom Entertainment, Inc. Joyride is ™ & © 2018 Jackson Lanzing, Collin Kelly & Marcus To. Originally published in single magazine form as JOYRIDE No. 9-12. ™ & © 2017 Jackson Lanzing, Collin Kelly & Marcus To. All Rights Reserved. BOOM! Studios™ and the BOOM! Studios logo are trademarks of Boom Entertainment, Inc., registered in various countries and categories. All characters, events, and institutions depicted herein are fictional. Any similarity between any of the names, characters, persons, events, and/or institutions in this publication to actual names, characters, and persons, whether living or dead, events, and/or institutions is unintended and purely coincidental. BOOM! Studios does not read or accept unsolicited submissions of ideas, stories, or artwork.

BOOM! Studios, 5670 Wilshire Boulevard, Suite 450, Los Angeles, CA 90036-5679. Printed in China. First Printing.

ISBN: 978-1-68415-117-2, eISBN: 978-1-61398-856-5

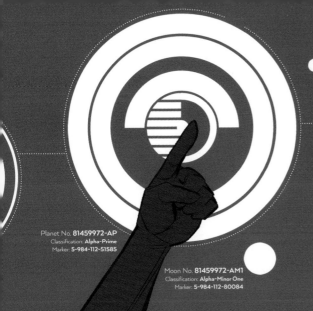

Planet No. **81459972-AP**
Classification: **Alpha-Prime**
Marker: **5-984-112-51585**

Moon No. **81459972-AM1**
Classification: **Alpha-Minor One**
Marker: **5-984-112-80084**

[WARNING]
UNCHARTED SPACE

SCRIPT BY
JACKSON LANZING & COLLIN KELLY

ART BY
MARCUS TO

COLORS BY
IRMA KNIIVILA

LETTERS BY
JIM CAMPBELL

COVER BY
MARCUS TO
WITH COLORS BY **IRMA KNIIVILA**

CREATED BY
MARCUS TO, JACKSON LANZING & COLLIN KELLY

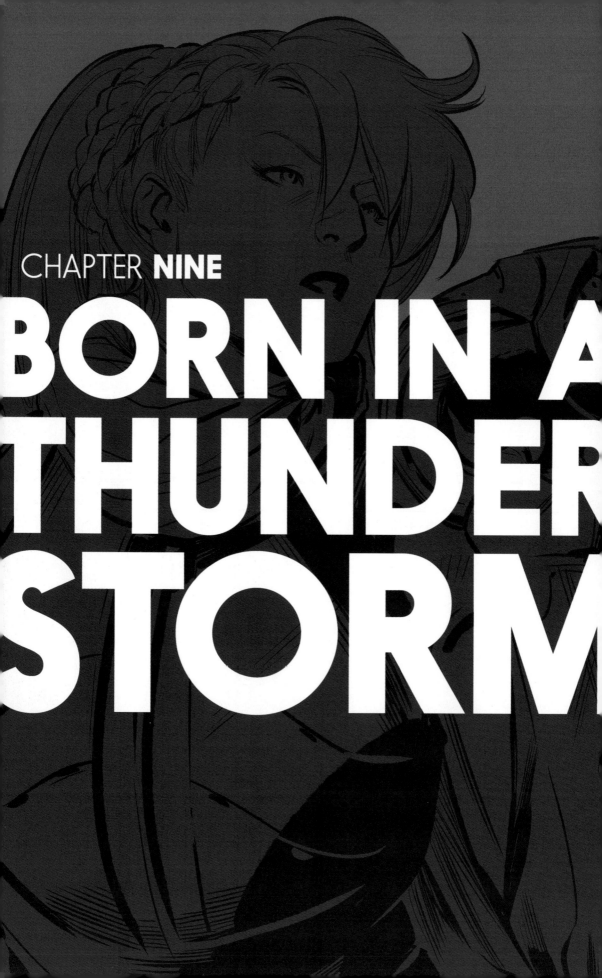

CHAPTER **NINE**

BORN IN A THUNDER STORM

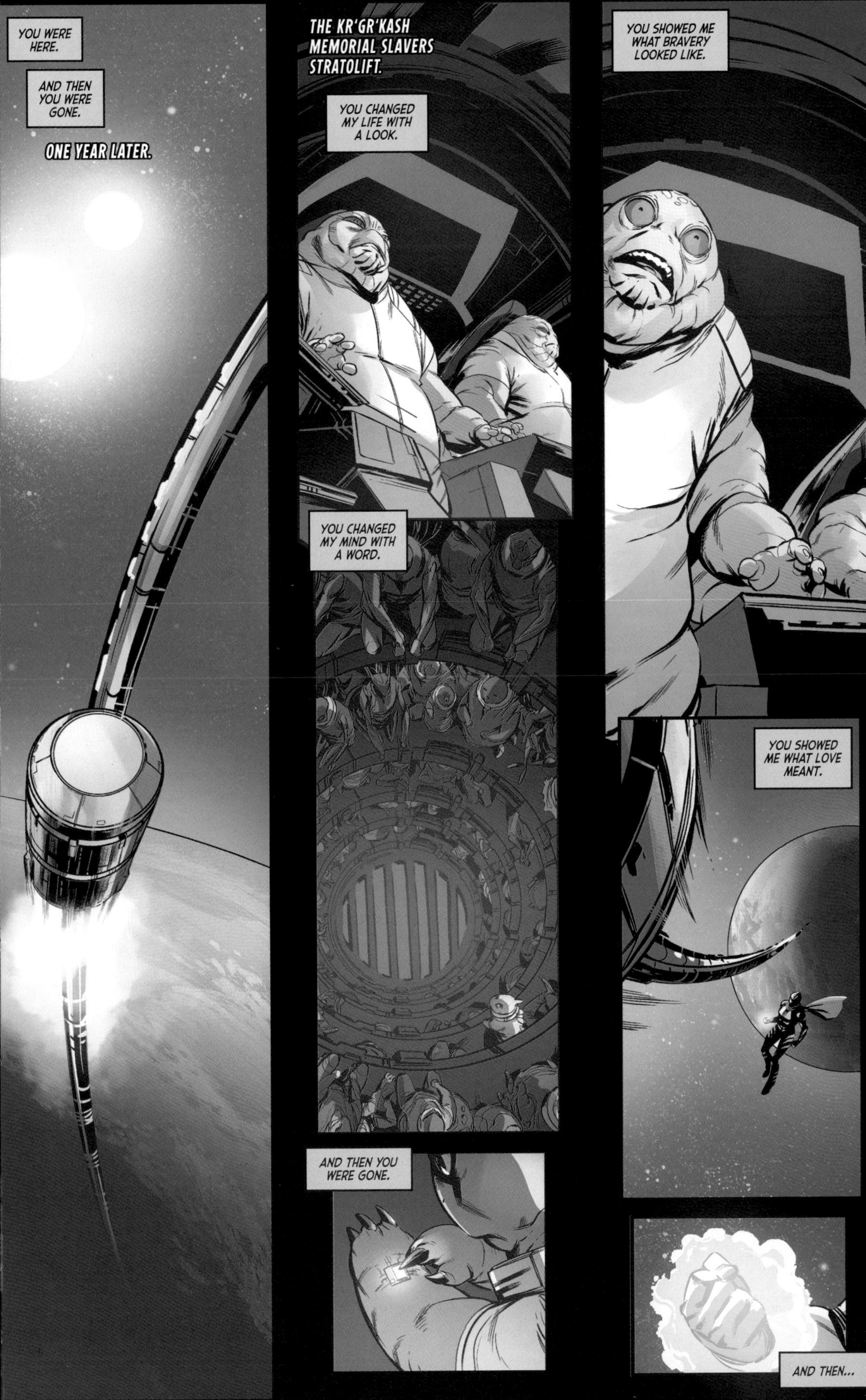
YOU WERE HERE.
AND THEN YOU WERE GONE.
ONE YEAR LATER.
THE KR'GR'KASH MEMORIAL SLAVERS STRATOLIFT.
YOU CHANGED MY LIFE WITH A LOOK.
YOU SHOWED ME WHAT BRAVERY LOOKED LIKE.
YOU CHANGED MY MIND WITH A WORD.
YOU SHOWED ME WHAT LOVE MEANT.
AND THEN YOU WERE GONE.
AND THEN...

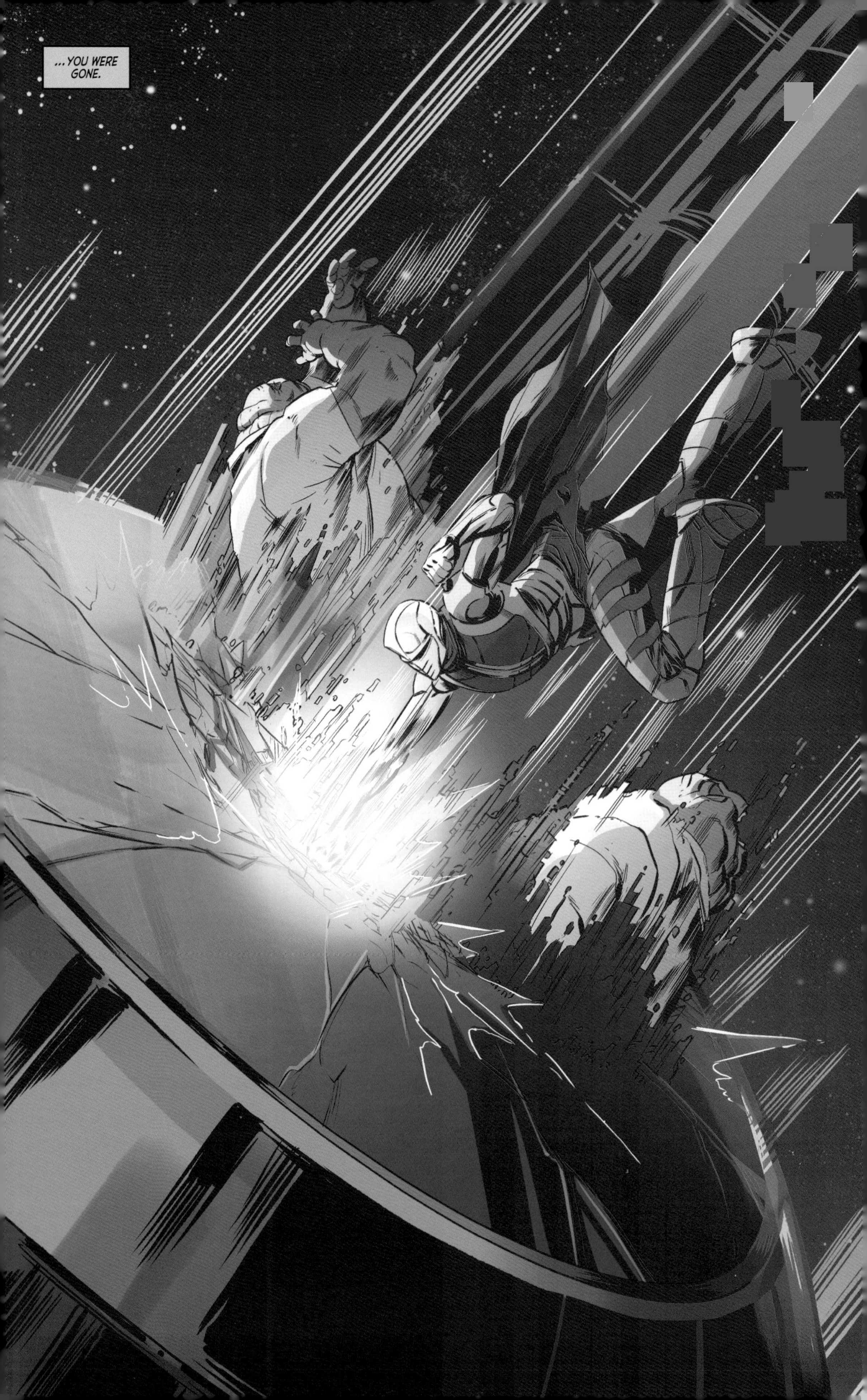
...YOU WERE GONE.

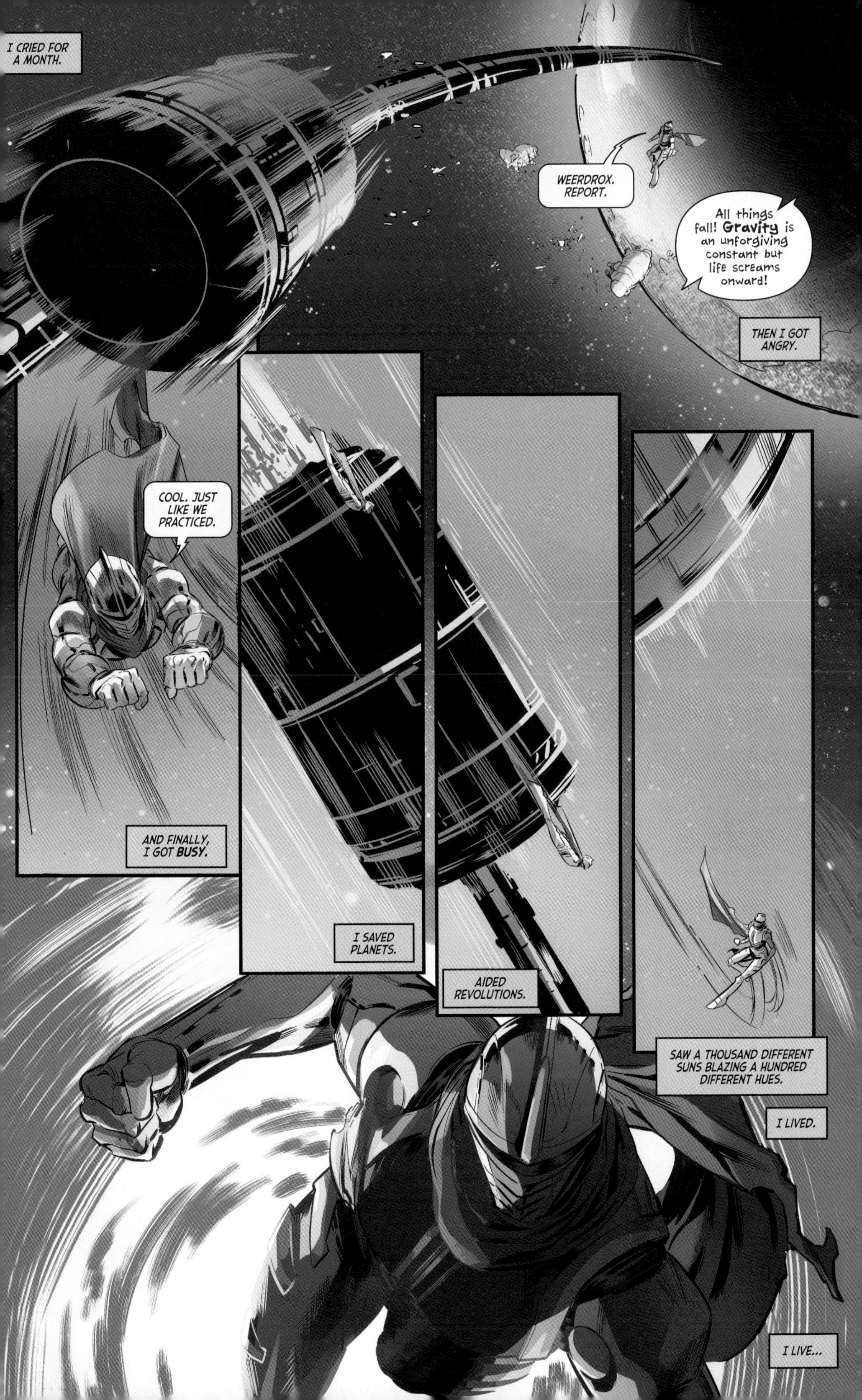
I CRIED FOR A MONTH.
WEERDROX. REPORT.
All things fall! Gravity is an unforgiving constant but life screams onward!
THEN I GOT ANGRY.
COOL. JUST LIKE WE PRACTICED.
AND FINALLY, I GOT BUSY.
I SAVED PLANETS.
AIDED REVOLUTIONS.
SAW A THOUSAND DIFFERENT SUNS BLAZING A HUNDRED DIFFERENT HUES.
I LIVED.
I LIVE...

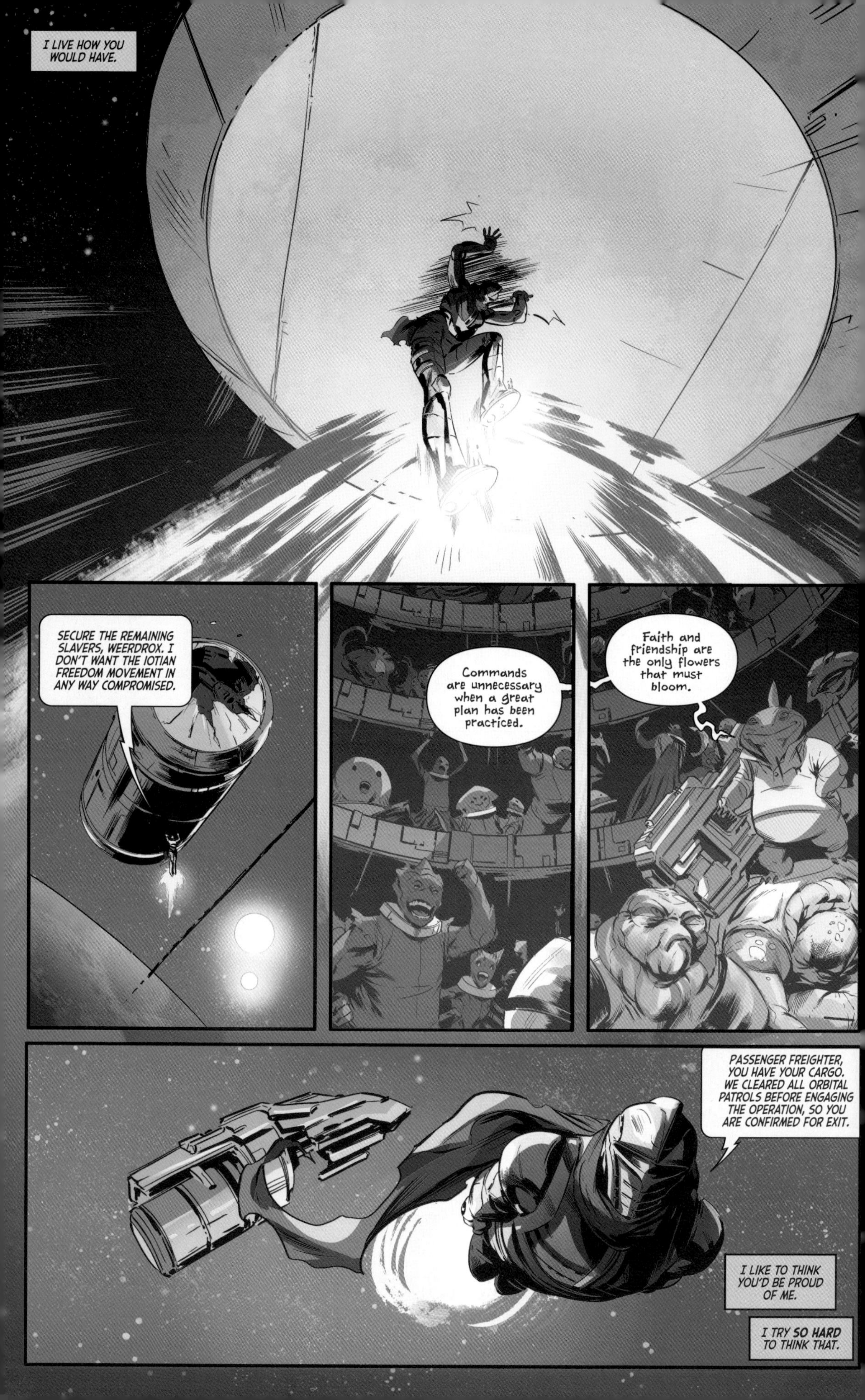

I LIVE HOW YOU WOULD HAVE.
SECURE THE REMAINING SLAVERS, WEERDROX. I DON'T WANT THE IOTIAN FREEDOM MOVEMENT IN ANY WAY COMPROMISED.
Commands are unnecessary when a great plan has been practiced.
Faith and friendship are the only flowers that must bloom.
PASSENGER FREIGHTER, YOU HAVE YOUR CARGO. WE CLEARED ALL ORBITAL PATROLS BEFORE ENGAGING THE OPERATION, SO YOU ARE CONFIRMED FOR EXIT.
I LIKE TO THINK YOU'D BE PROUD OF ME.
I TRY SO HARD TO THINK THAT.

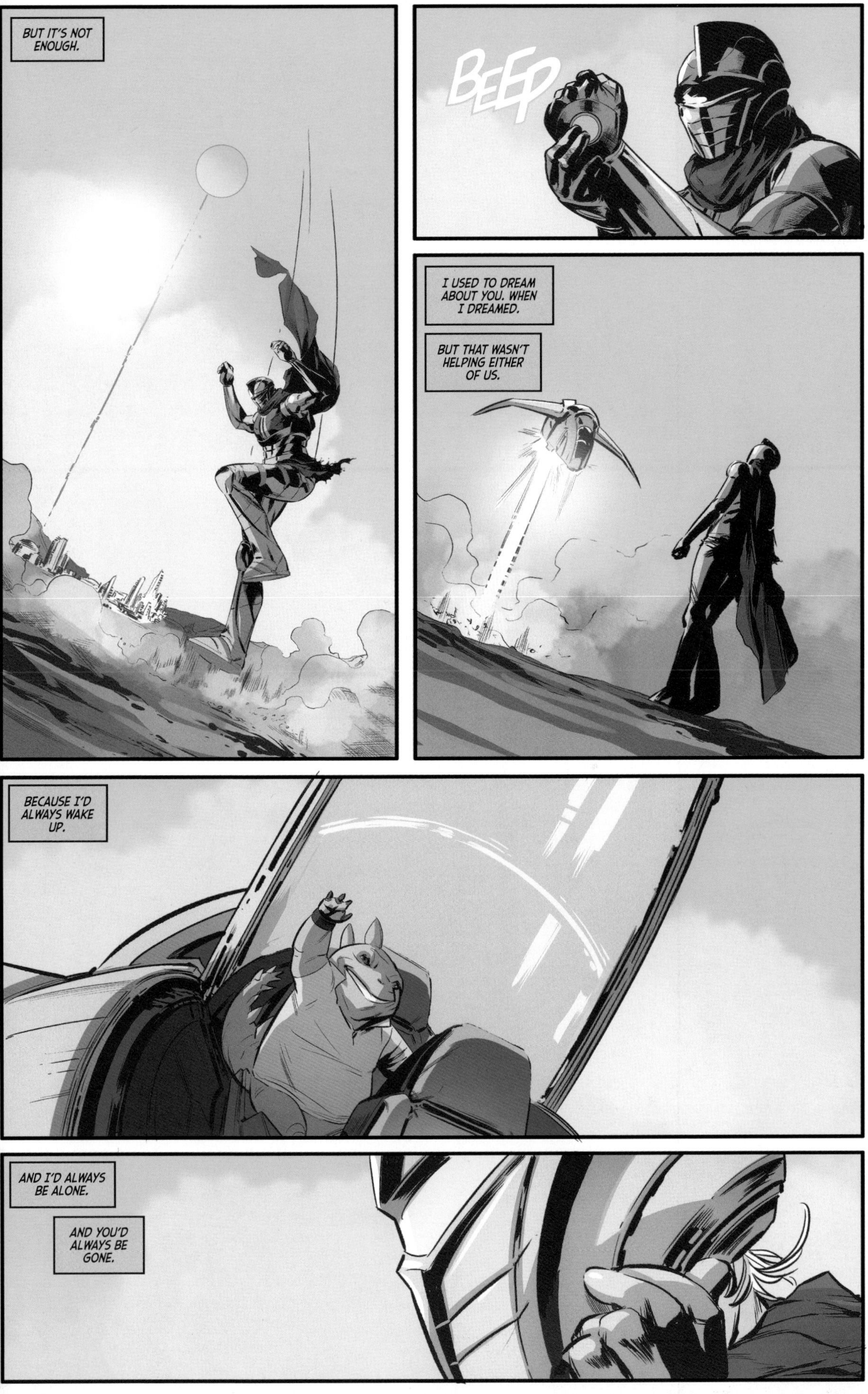
BUT IT'S NOT ENOUGH.
BEEP
I USED TO DREAM ABOUT YOU. WHEN I DREAMED.
BUT THAT WASN'T HELPING EITHER OF US.
BECAUSE I'D ALWAYS WAKE UP.
AND I'D ALWAYS BE ALONE.
AND YOU'D ALWAYS BE GONE.

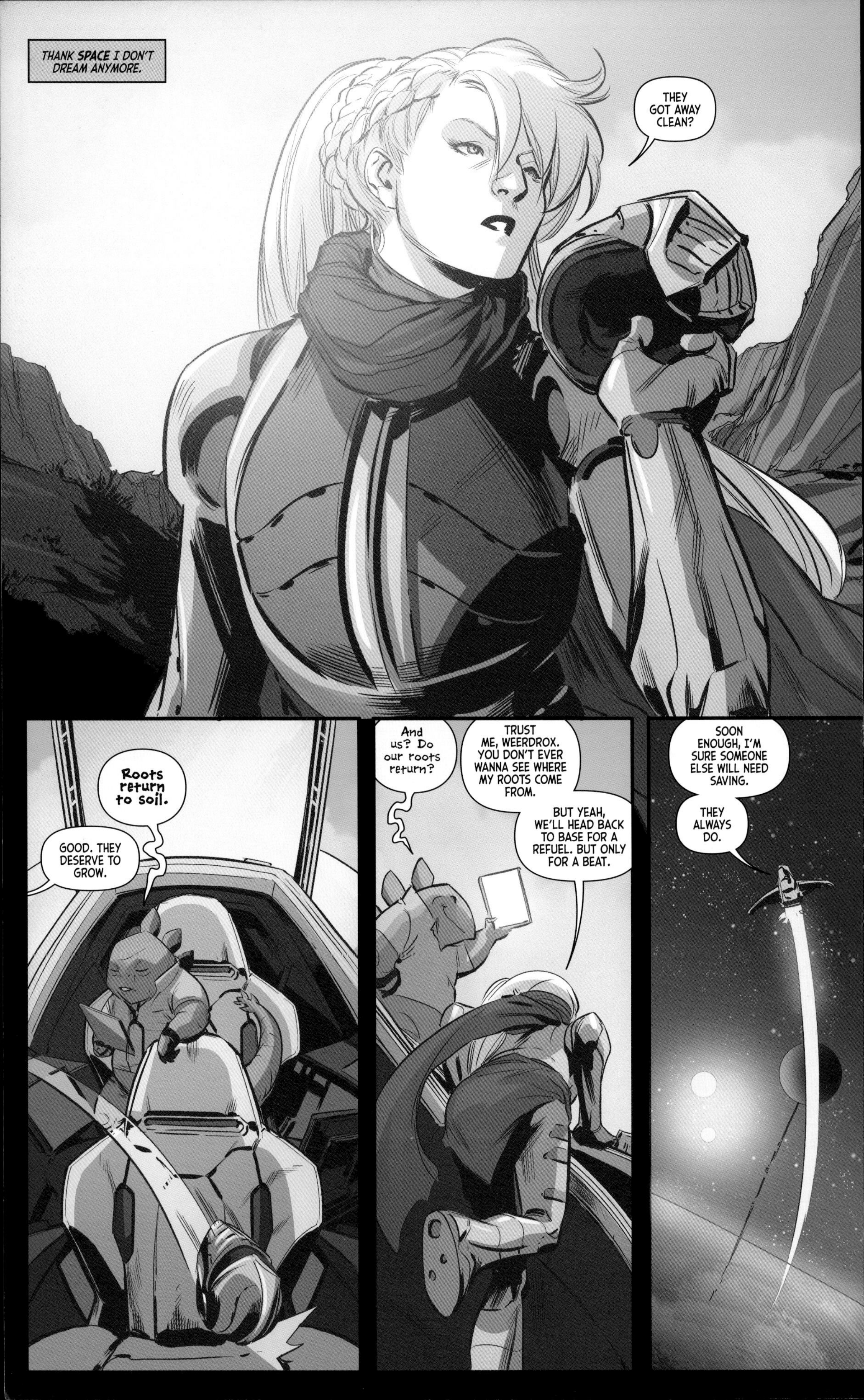
THANK SPACE I DON'T DREAM ANYMORE.
THEY GOT AWAY CLEAN?
Roots return to soil.
GOOD. THEY DESERVE TO GROW.
And us? Do our roots return?
TRUST ME, WEERDROX. YOU DON'T EVER WANNA SEE WHERE MY ROOTS COME FROM.
BUT YEAH, WE'LL HEAD BACK TO BASE FOR A REFUEL. BUT ONLY FOR A BEAT.
SOON ENOUGH, I'M SURE SOMEONE ELSE WILL NEED SAVING.
THEY ALWAYS DO.

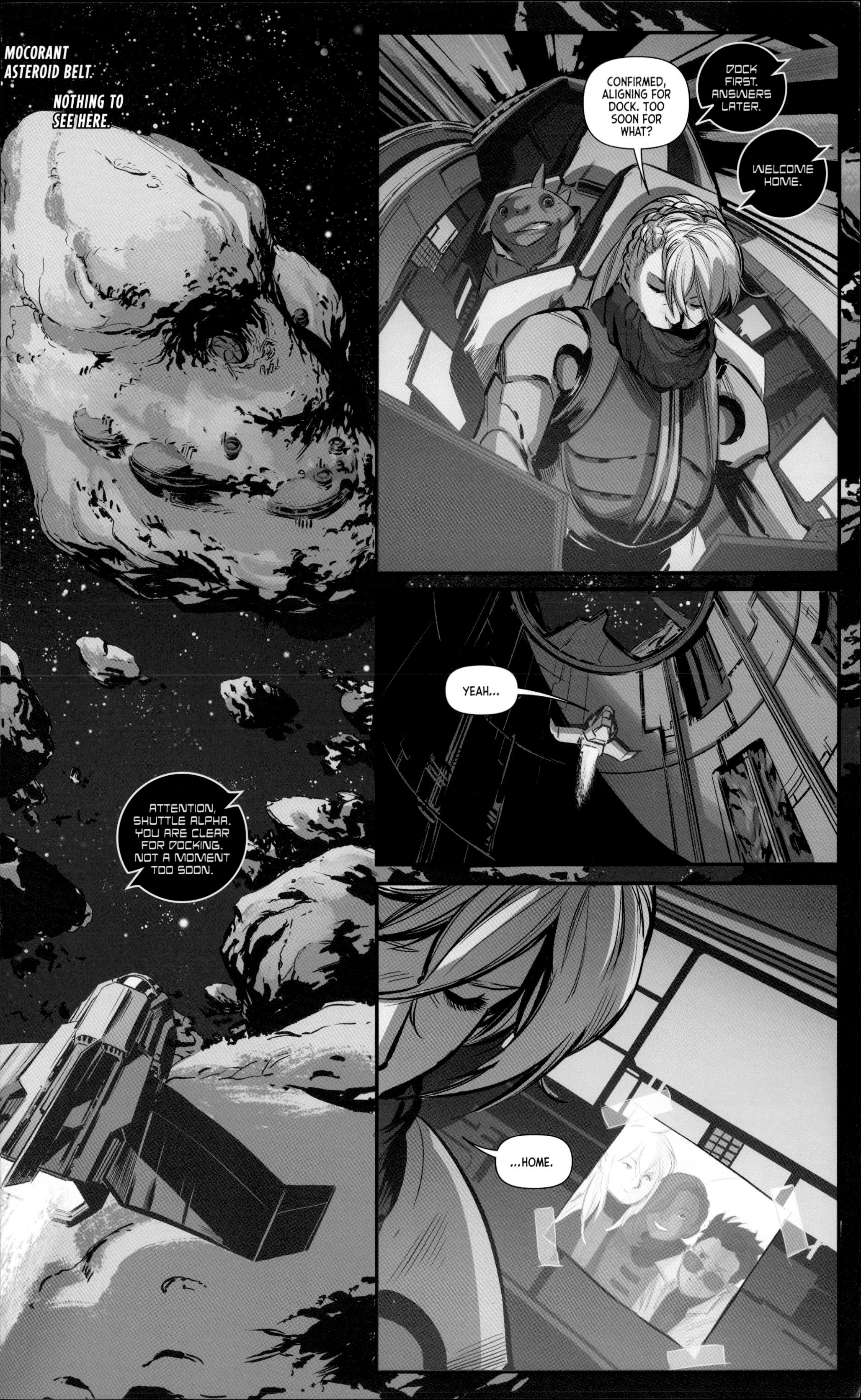
MOCORANT ASTEROID BELT.
NOTHING TO SEE HERE.
ATTENTION, SHUTTLE ALPHA. YOU ARE CLEAR FOR DOCKING. NOT A MOMENT TOO SOON.
CONFIRMED, ALIGNING FOR DOCK. TOO SOON FOR WHAT?
DOCK FIRST. ANSWERS LATER.
WELCOME HOME.
YEAH...
...HOME.

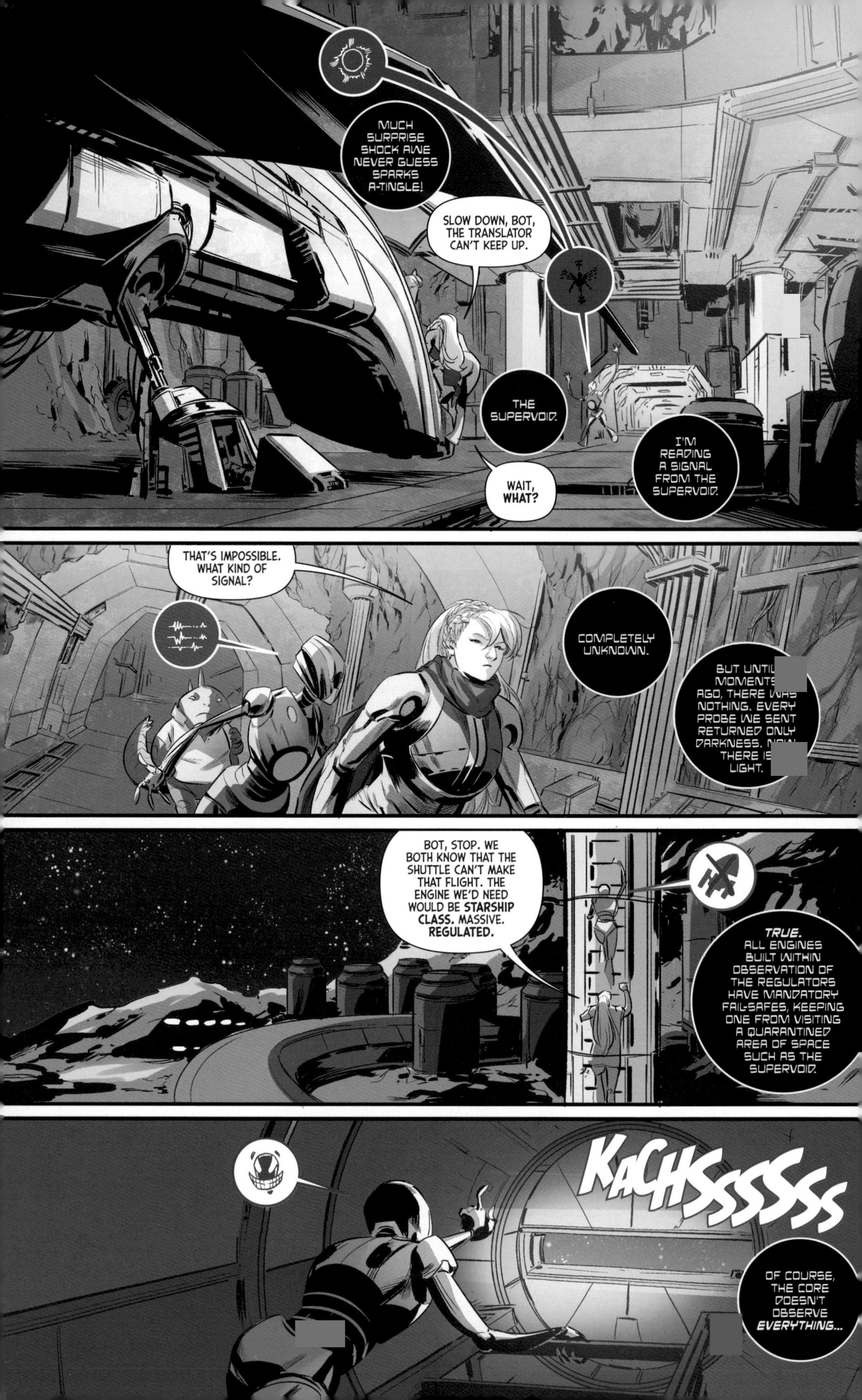
MUCH SURPRISE SHOCK AWE NEVER GUESS SPARKS A-TINGLE!
SLOW DOWN, BOT, THE TRANSLATOR CAN'T KEEP UP.
THE SUPERVOID.
WAIT, **WHAT?**
I'M READING A SIGNAL FROM THE SUPERVOID.
THAT'S IMPOSSIBLE. WHAT KIND OF SIGNAL?
COMPLETELY UNKNOWN.
BUT UNTIL MOMENTS AGO, THERE WAS NOTHING. EVERY PROBE WE SENT RETURNED ONLY DARKNESS. NOW THERE IS LIGHT.
BOT, STOP. WE BOTH KNOW THAT THE SHUTTLE CAN'T MAKE THAT FLIGHT. THE ENGINE WE'D NEED WOULD BE **STARSHIP CLASS.** MASSIVE. **REGULATED.**
TRUE. ALL ENGINES BUILT WITHIN OBSERVATION OF THE REGULATORS HAVE MANDATORY FAIL-SAFES, KEEPING ONE FROM VISITING A QUARANTINED AREA OF SPACE SUCH AS THE SUPERVOID.
KACHSSSSSS
OF COURSE, THE CORE DOESN'T OBSERVE ***EVERYTHING...***

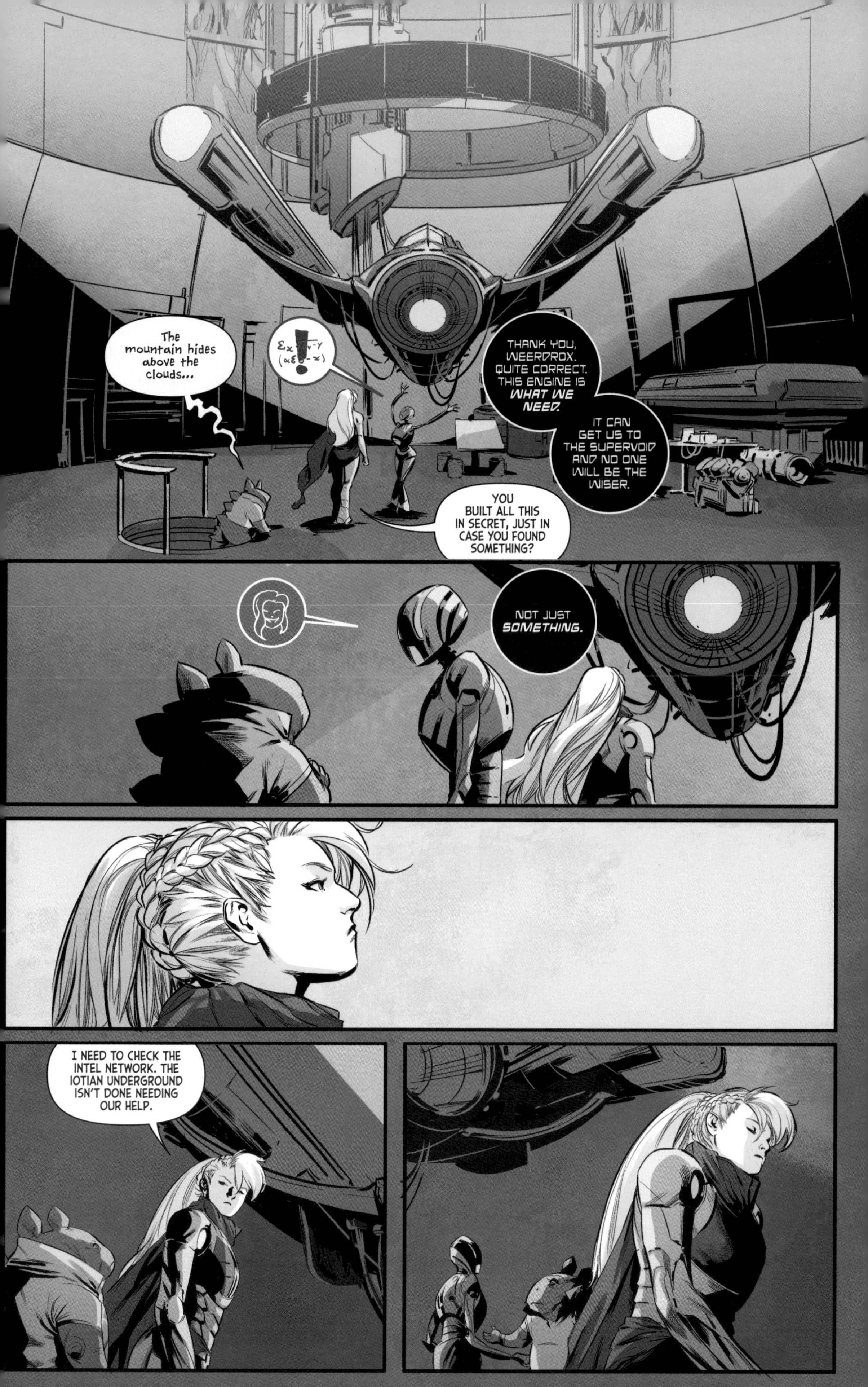
The mountain hides above the clouds...
THANK YOU, WEERDROX. QUITE CORRECT. THIS ENGINE IS *WHAT WE NEED.*
IT CAN GET US TO THE SUPERVOID AND NO ONE WILL BE THE WISER.
YOU BUILT ALL THIS IN SECRET, JUST IN CASE YOU FOUND SOMETHING?
NOT JUST *SOMETHING.*
I NEED TO CHECK THE INTEL NETWORK. THE IOTIAN UNDERGROUND ISN'T DONE NEEDING OUR HELP.

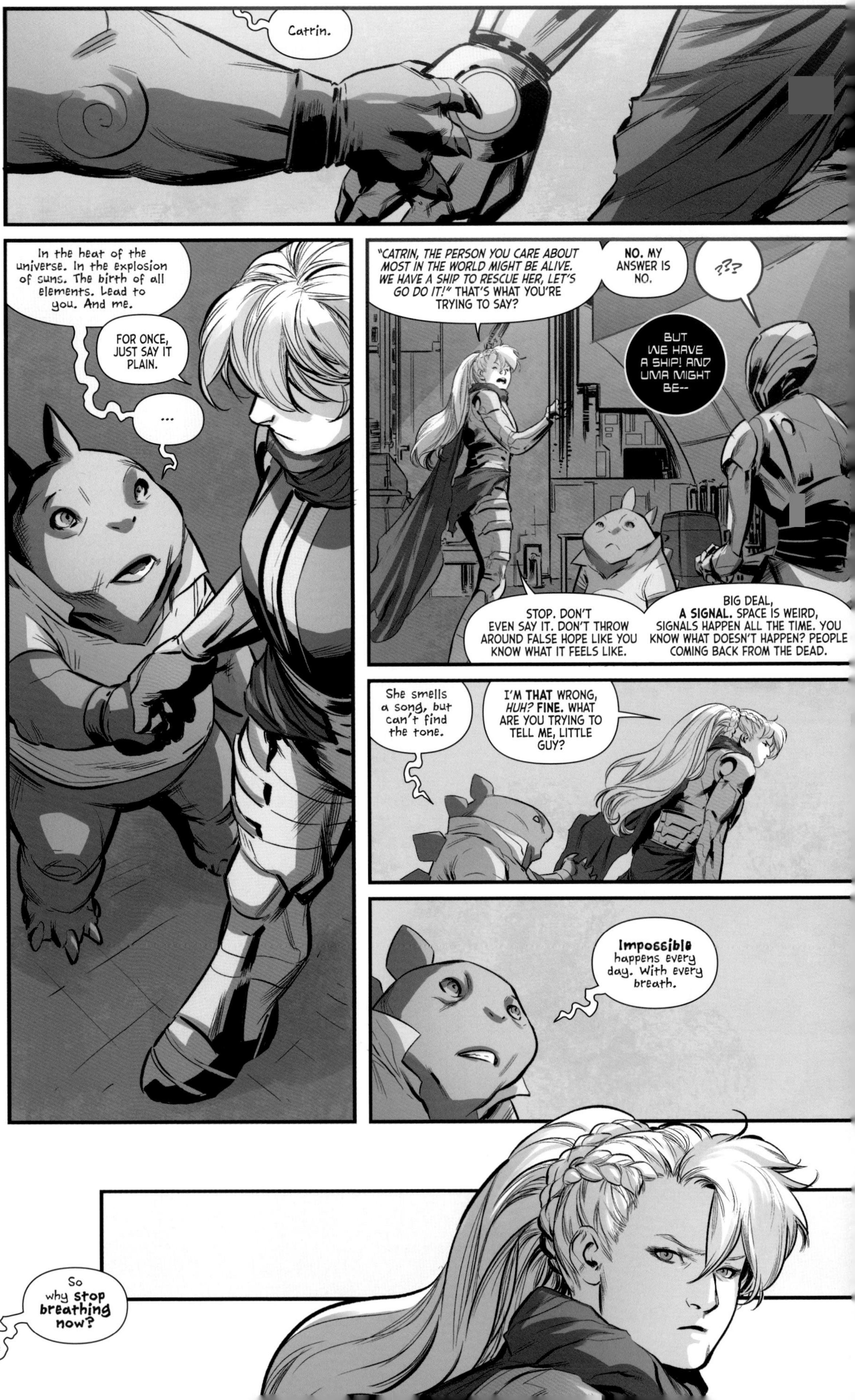
Catrin.
In the heat of the universe. In the explosion of suns. The birth of all elements. Lead to you. And me.
FOR ONCE, JUST SAY IT PLAIN.
...
"CATRIN, THE PERSON YOU CARE ABOUT MOST IN THE WORLD MIGHT BE ALIVE. WE HAVE A SHIP TO RESCUE HER, LET'S GO DO IT!" THAT'S WHAT YOU'RE TRYING TO SAY?
NO. MY ANSWER IS NO.
???
BUT WE HAVE A SHIP! AND UMA MIGHT BE--
STOP. DON'T EVEN SAY IT. DON'T THROW AROUND FALSE HOPE LIKE YOU KNOW WHAT IT FEELS LIKE.
BIG DEAL, A SIGNAL. SPACE IS WEIRD, SIGNALS HAPPEN ALL THE TIME. YOU KNOW WHAT DOESN'T HAPPEN? PEOPLE COMING BACK FROM THE DEAD.
She smells a song, but can't find the tone.
I'M THAT WRONG, HUH? FINE. WHAT ARE YOU TRYING TO TELL ME, LITTLE GUY?
Impossible happens every day. With every breath.
So why stop breathing now?

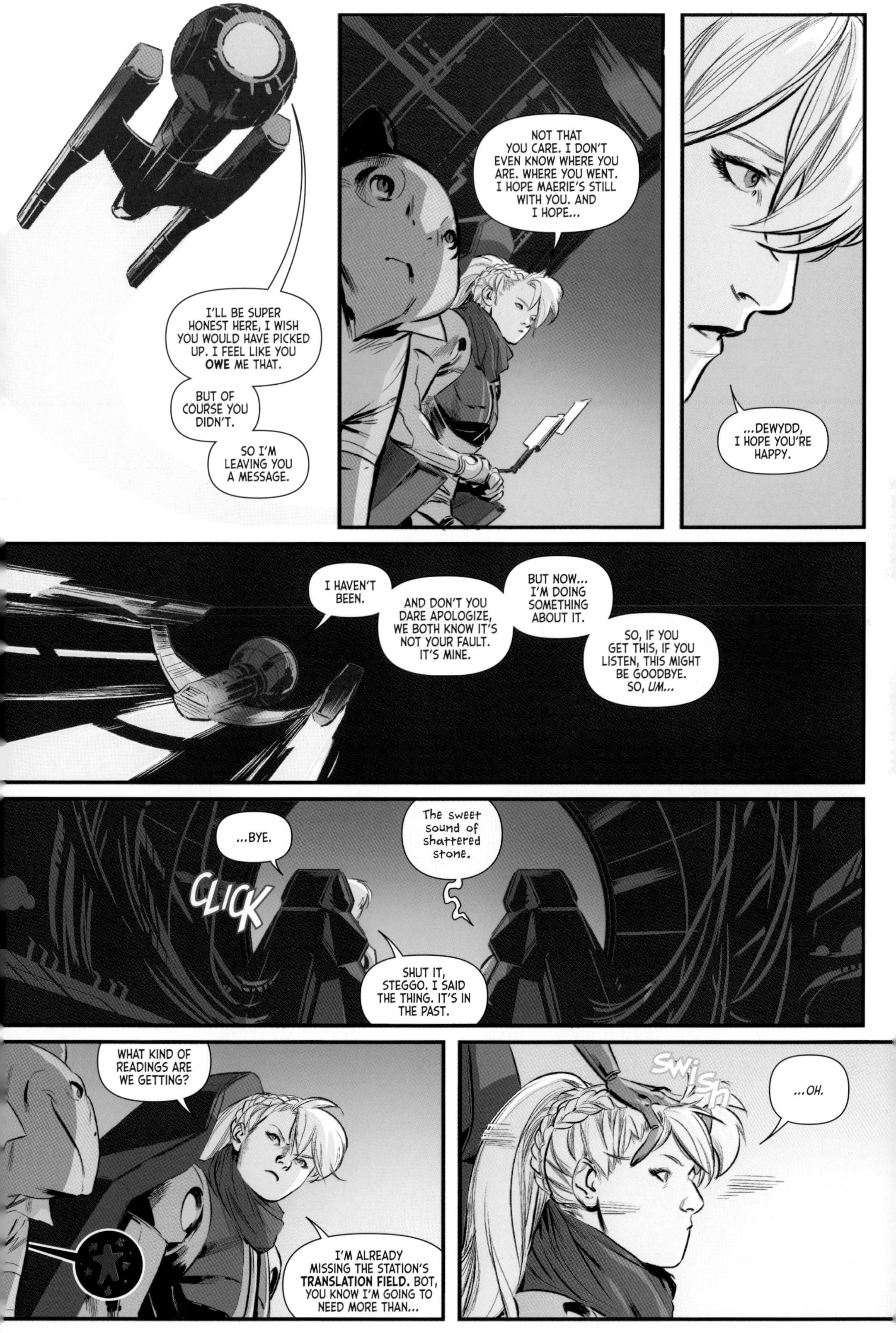
I'LL BE SUPER HONEST HERE, I WISH YOU WOULD HAVE PICKED UP. I FEEL LIKE YOU **OWE** ME THAT.
BUT OF COURSE YOU DIDN'T.
SO I'M LEAVING YOU A MESSAGE.
NOT THAT YOU CARE. I DON'T EVEN KNOW WHERE YOU ARE. WHERE YOU WENT. I HOPE MAERIE'S STILL WITH YOU. AND I HOPE...
...DEWYDD, I HOPE YOU'RE HAPPY.
I HAVEN'T BEEN.
AND DON'T YOU DARE APOLOGIZE, WE BOTH KNOW IT'S NOT YOUR FAULT. IT'S MINE.
BUT NOW... I'M DOING SOMETHING ABOUT IT.
SO, IF YOU GET THIS, IF YOU LISTEN, THIS MIGHT BE GOODBYE. SO, *UM*...
...BYE.
CLICK
The sweet sound of shattered stone.
SHUT IT, STEGGO. I SAID THE THING. IT'S IN THE PAST.
WHAT KIND OF READINGS ARE WE GETTING?
I'M ALREADY MISSING THE STATION'S **TRANSLATION FIELD.** BOT, YOU KNOW I'M GOING TO NEED MORE THAN...
SWISH
...OH.

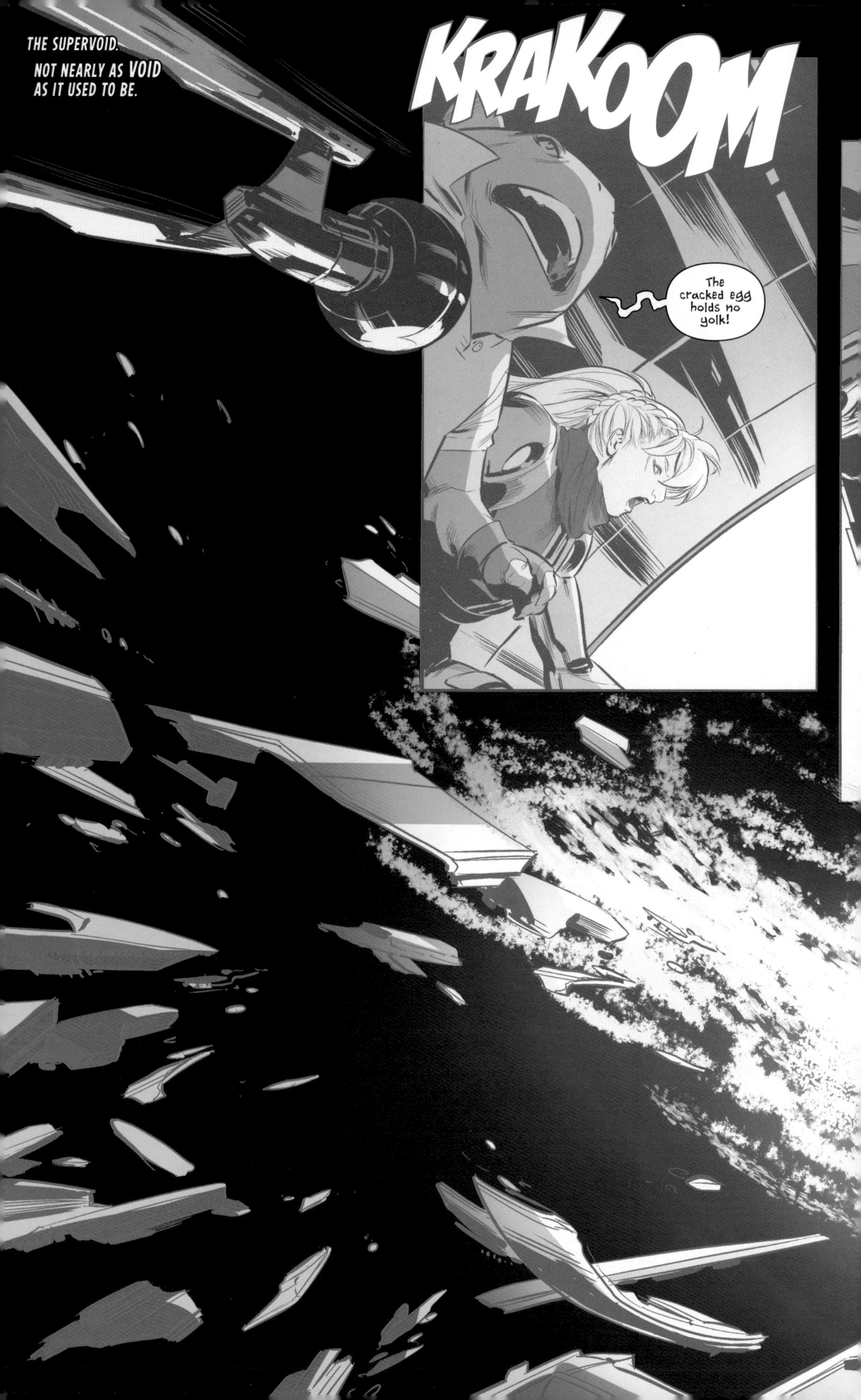
THE SUPERVOID.
NOT NEARLY AS VOID AS IT USED TO BE.
KRAKOOM
The cracked egg holds no yolk!

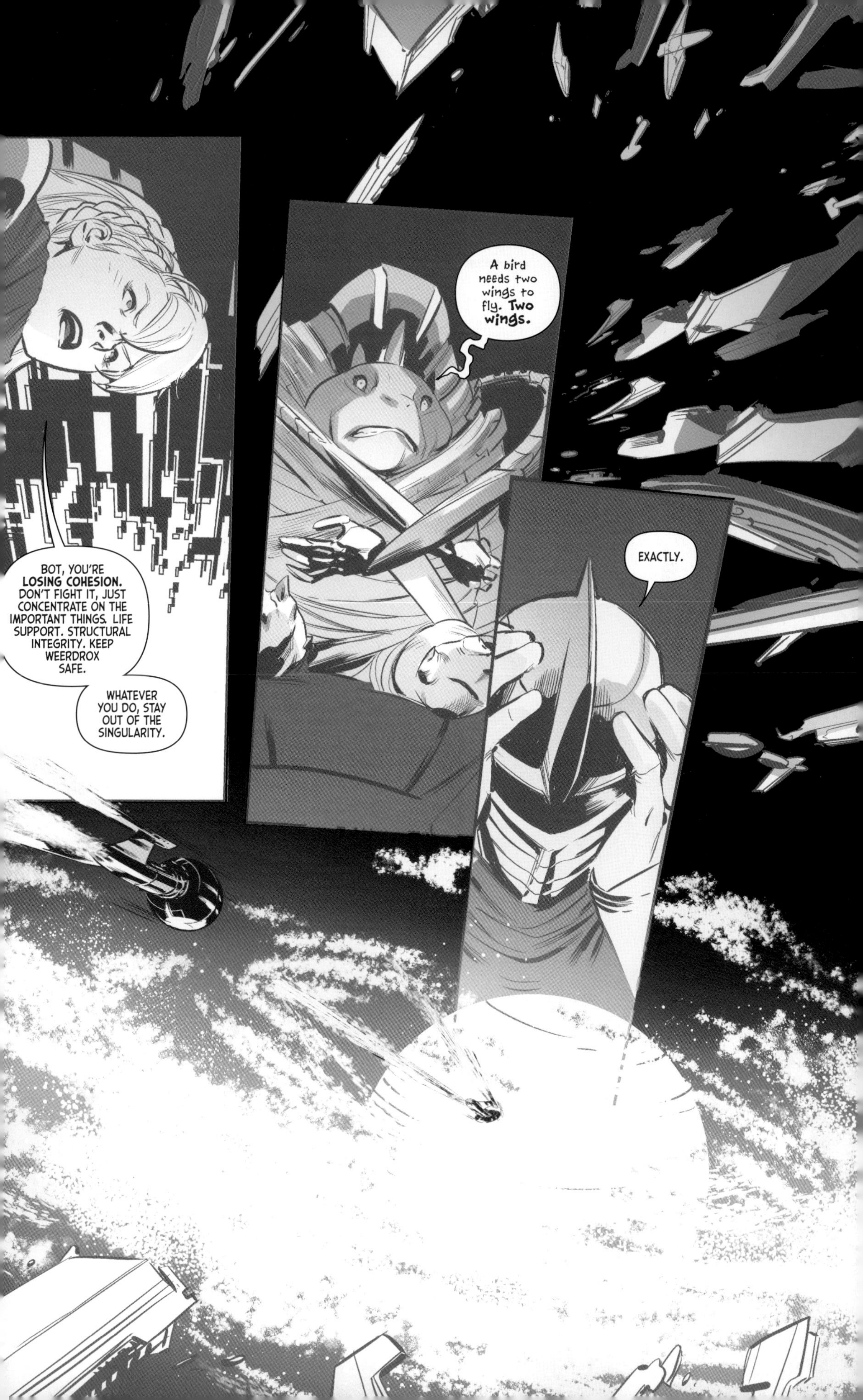
BOT, YOU'RE **LOSING COHESION.** DON'T FIGHT IT, JUST CONCENTRATE ON THE IMPORTANT THINGS. LIFE SUPPORT. STRUCTURAL INTEGRITY. KEEP WEERDROX SAFE.
WHATEVER YOU DO, STAY OUT OF THE SINGULARITY.
A bird needs two wings to fly. **Two wings.**
EXACTLY.

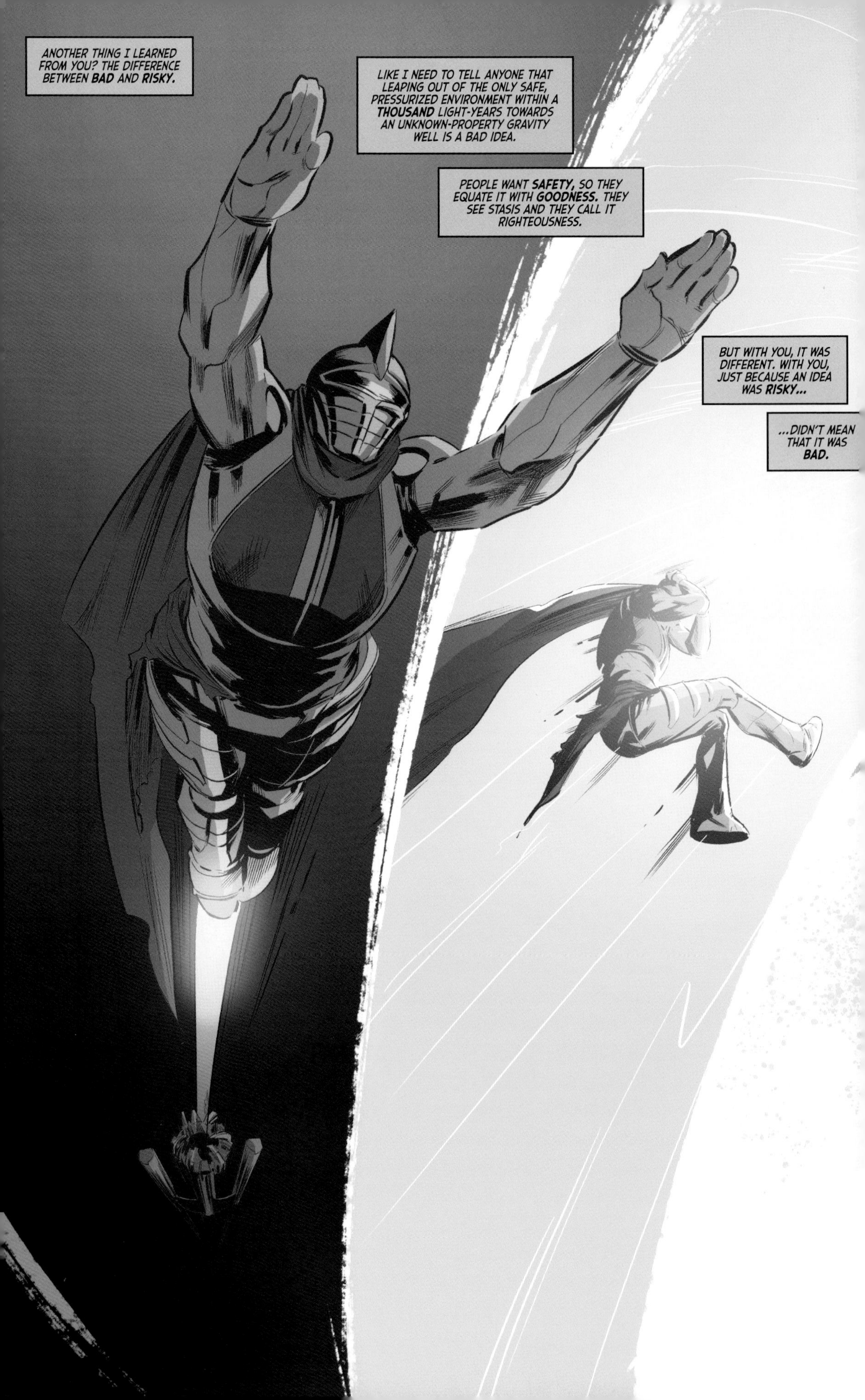
ANOTHER THING I LEARNED FROM YOU? THE DIFFERENCE BETWEEN BAD AND RISKY.
LIKE I NEED TO TELL ANYONE THAT LEAPING OUT OF THE ONLY SAFE, PRESSURIZED ENVIRONMENT WITHIN A THOUSAND LIGHT-YEARS TOWARDS AN UNKNOWN-PROPERTY GRAVITY WELL IS A BAD IDEA.
PEOPLE WANT SAFETY, SO THEY EQUATE IT WITH GOODNESS. THEY SEE STASIS AND THEY CALL IT RIGHTEOUSNESS.
BUT WITH YOU, IT WAS DIFFERENT. WITH YOU, JUST BECAUSE AN IDEA WAS RISKY...
...DIDN'T MEAN THAT IT WAS BAD.

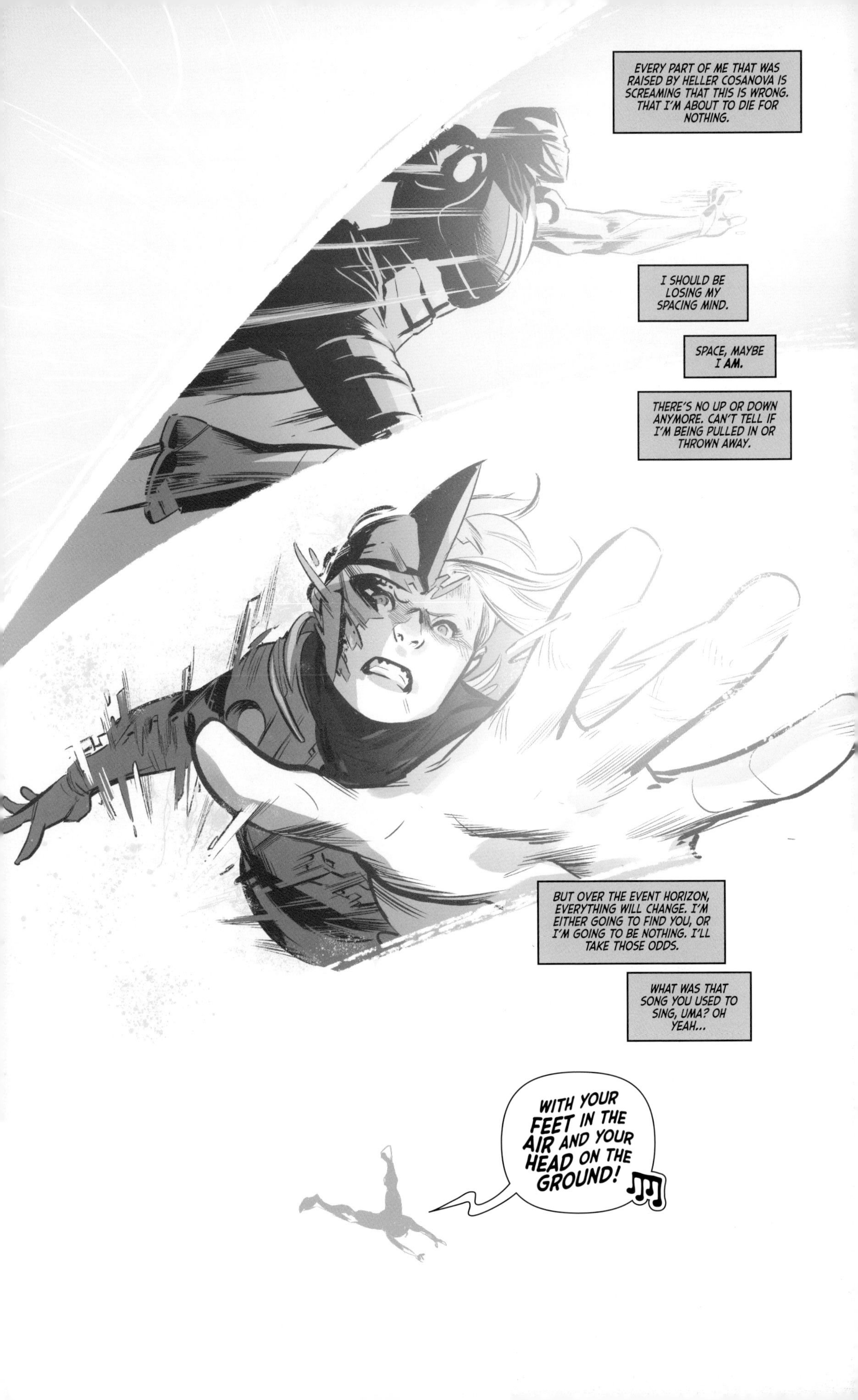
EVERY PART OF ME THAT WAS RAISED BY HELLER COSANOVA IS SCREAMING THAT THIS IS WRONG. THAT I'M ABOUT TO DIE FOR NOTHING.
I SHOULD BE LOSING MY SPACING MIND.
SPACE, MAYBE I AM.
THERE'S NO UP OR DOWN ANYMORE. CAN'T TELL IF I'M BEING PULLED IN OR THROWN AWAY.
BUT OVER THE EVENT HORIZON, EVERYTHING WILL CHANGE. I'M EITHER GOING TO FIND YOU, OR I'M GOING TO BE NOTHING. I'LL TAKE THOSE ODDS.
WHAT WAS THAT SONG YOU USED TO SING, UMA? OH YEAH...
WITH YOUR FEET IN THE AIR AND YOUR HEAD ON THE GROUND!

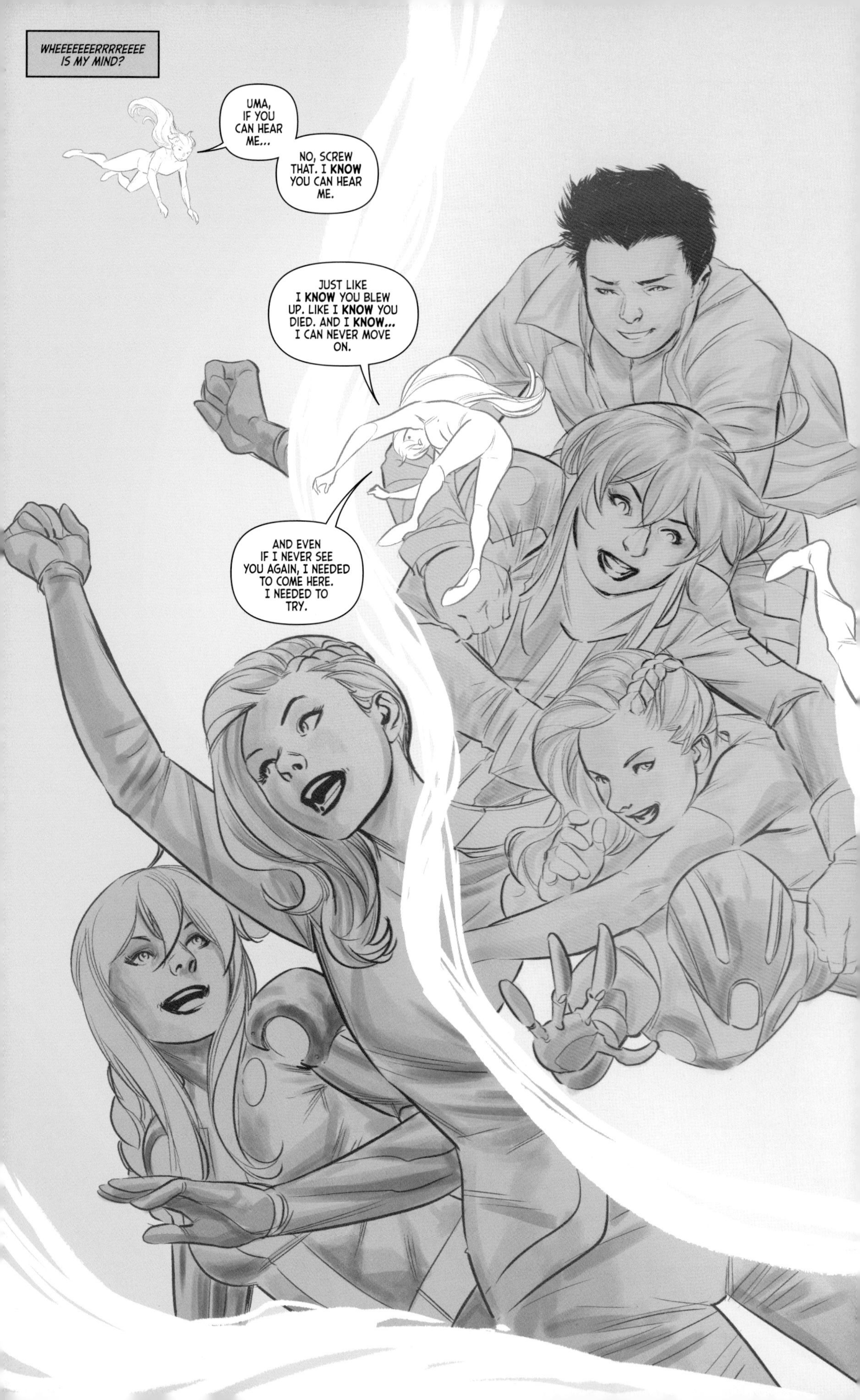
WHEEEEEEERRRREEEE IS MY MIND?
UMA, IF YOU CAN HEAR ME...
NO, SCREW THAT. I **KNOW** YOU CAN HEAR ME.
JUST LIKE I **KNOW** YOU BLEW UP. LIKE I **KNOW** YOU DIED. AND I **KNOW...** I CAN NEVER MOVE ON.
AND EVEN IF I NEVER SEE YOU AGAIN, I NEEDED TO COME HERE. I NEEDED TO TRY.

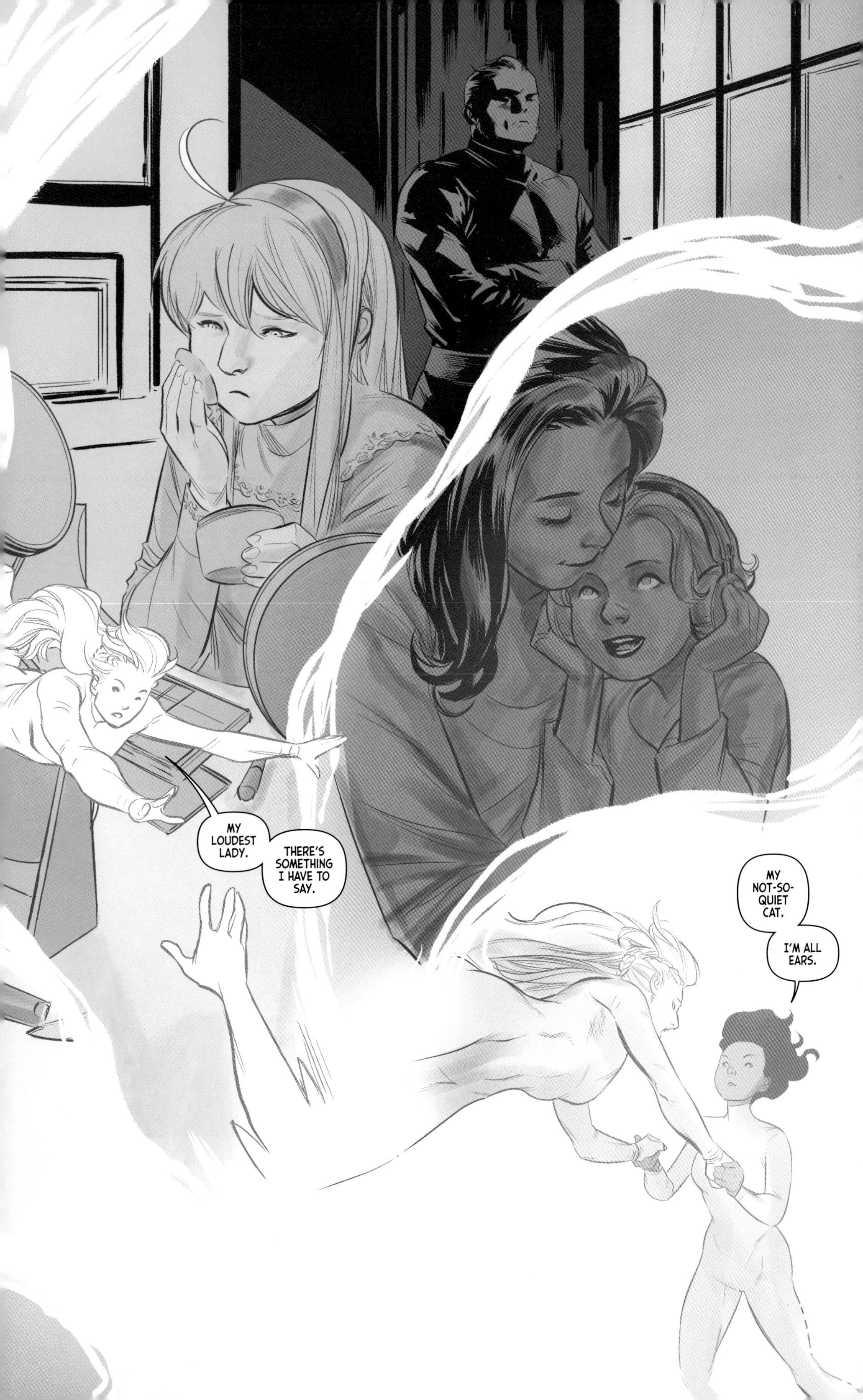
MY LOUDEST LADY.
THERE'S SOMETHING I HAVE TO SAY.
MY NOT-SO-QUIET CAT.
I'M ALL EARS.

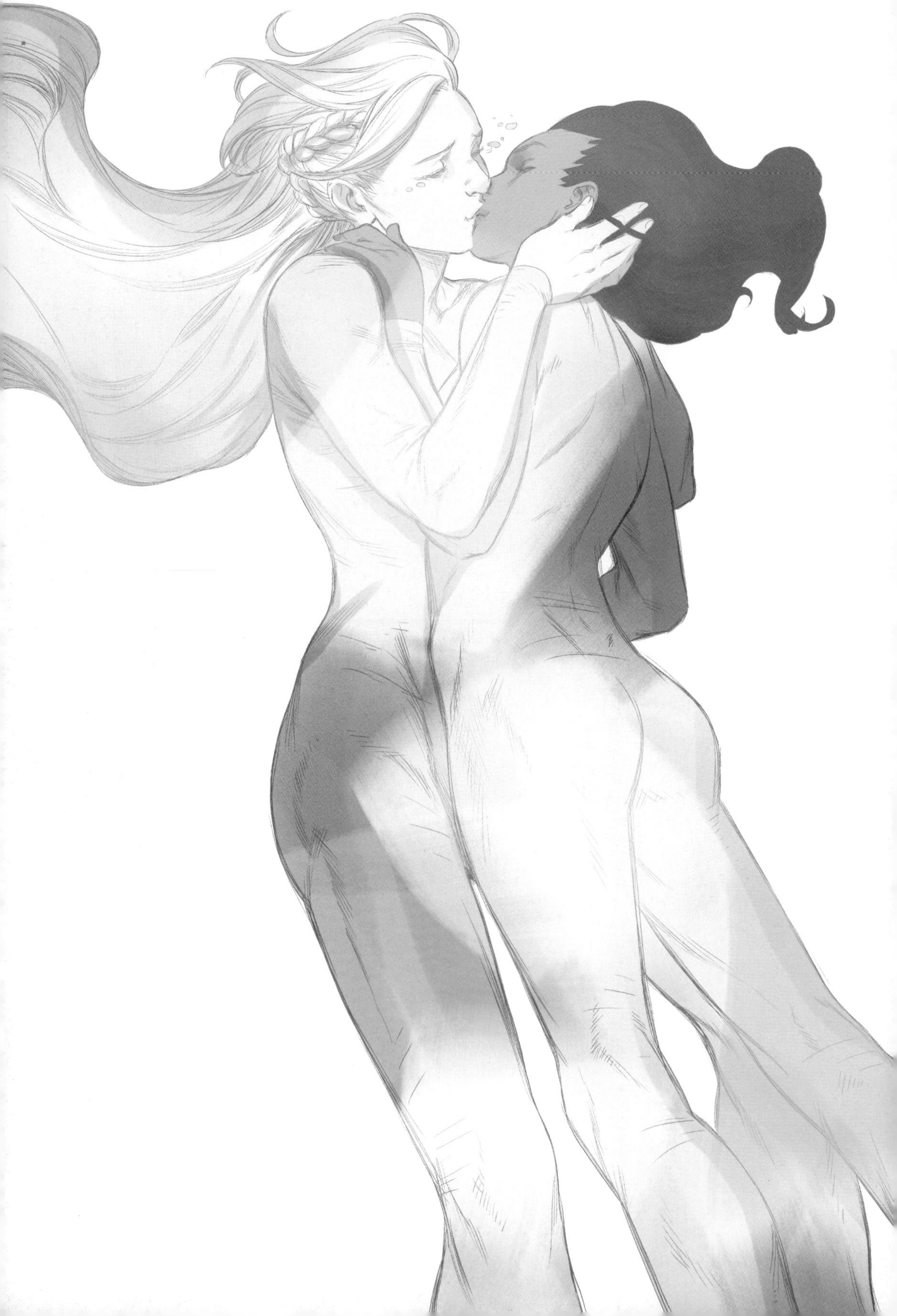

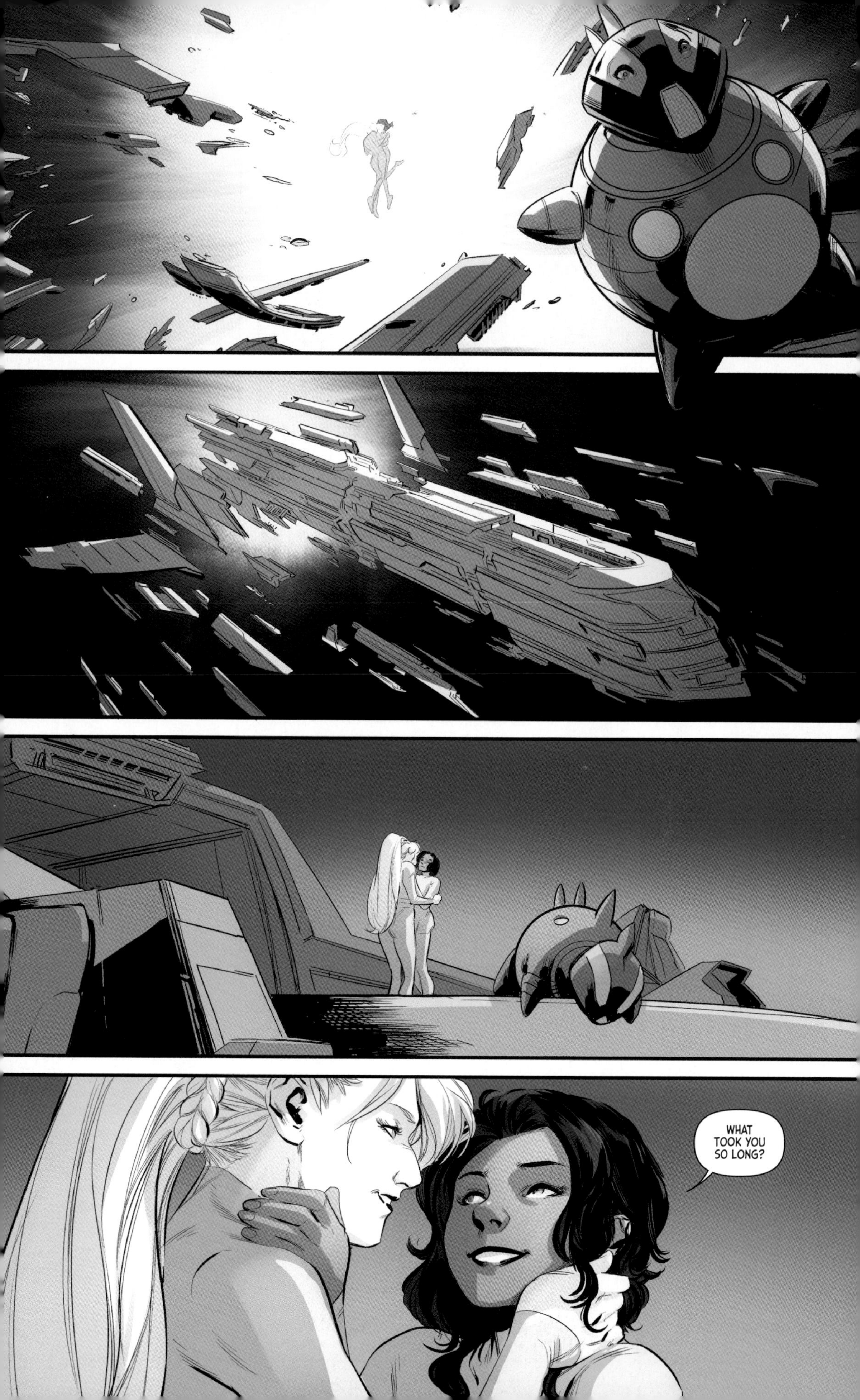
WHAT TOOK YOU SO LONG?

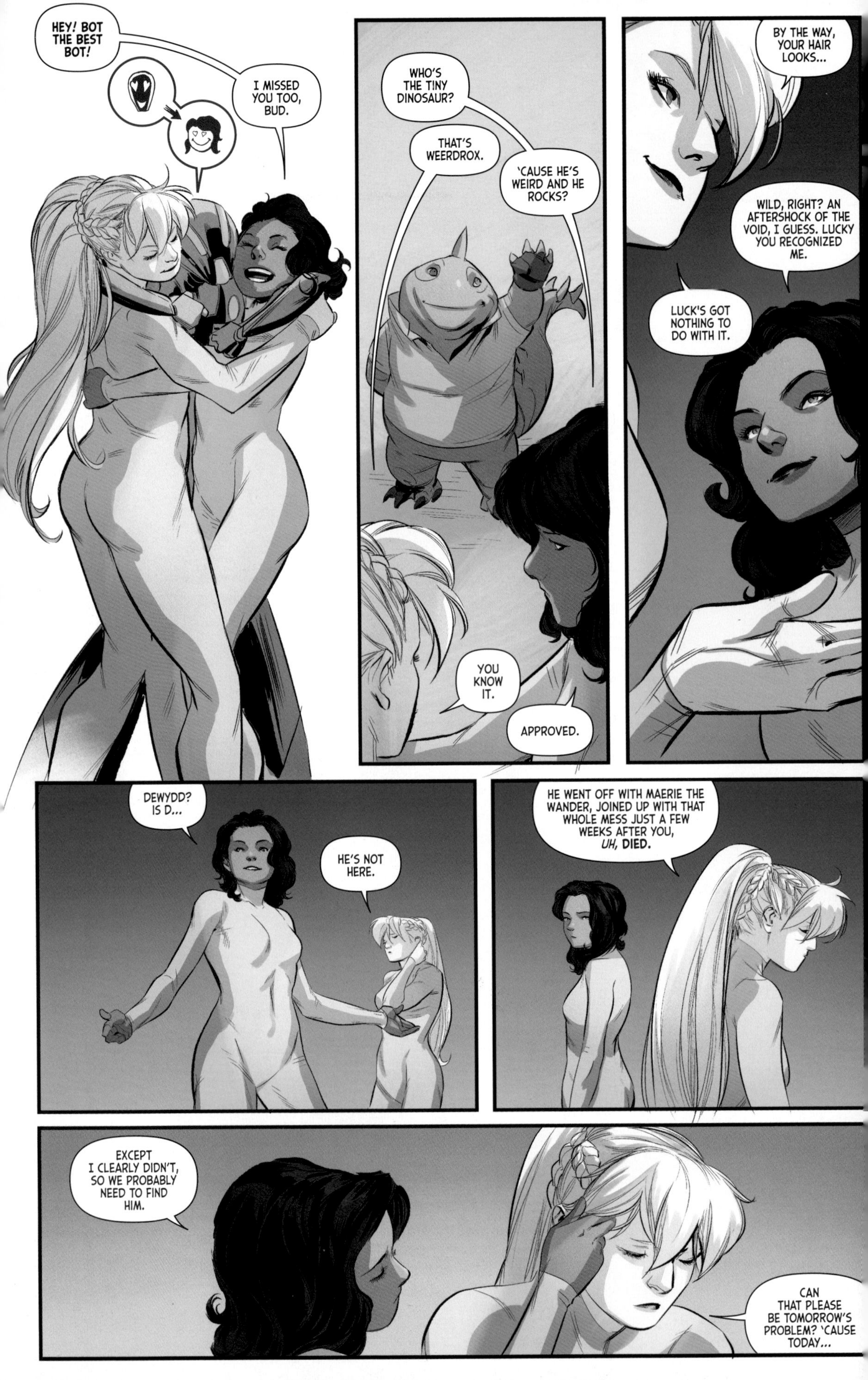
HEY! BOT THE BEST BOT!
I MISSED YOU TOO, BUD.
WHO'S THE T!NY DINOSAUR?
THAT'S WEERDROX.
'CAUSE HE'S WEIRD AND HE ROCKS?
YOU KNOW IT.
APPROVED.
BY THE WAY, YOUR HAIR LOOKS...
WILD, RIGHT? AN AFTERSHOCK OF THE VOID, I GUESS. LUCKY YOU RECOGNIZED ME.
LUCK'S GOT NOTHING TO DO WITH IT.
DEWYDD? IS D...
HE'S NOT HERE.
HE WENT OFF WITH MAERIE THE WANDER, JOINED UP WITH THAT WHOLE MESS JUST A FEW WEEKS AFTER YOU, UH, DIED.
EXCEPT I CLEARLY DIDN'T, SO WE PROBABLY NEED TO FIND HIM.
CAN THAT PLEASE BE TOMORROW'S PROBLEM? 'CAUSE TODAY...

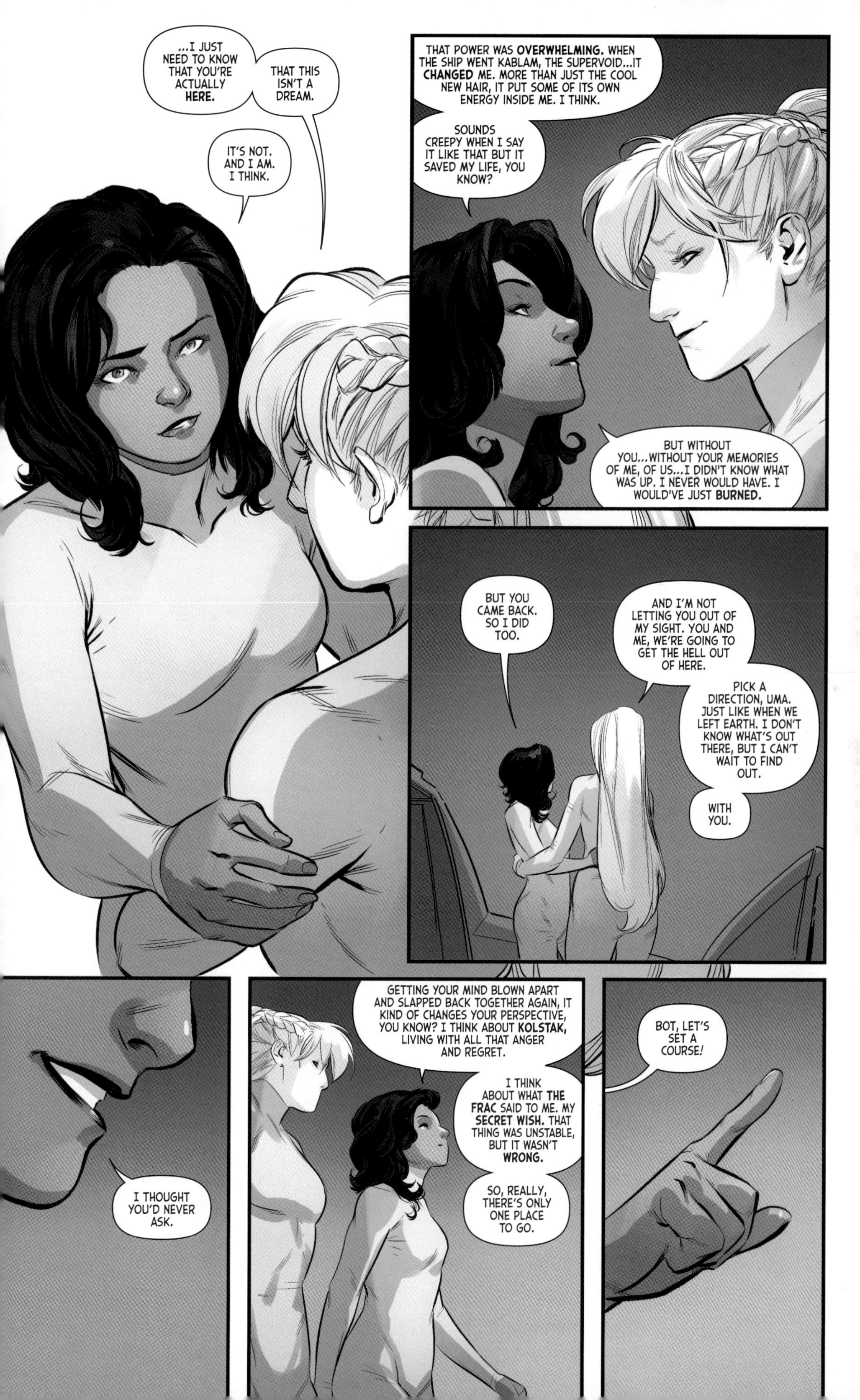
...I JUST NEED TO KNOW THAT YOU'RE ACTUALLY **HERE.**
THAT THIS ISN'T A DREAM.
IT'S NOT. AND I AM. I THINK.
THAT POWER WAS **OVERWHELMING.** WHEN THE SHIP WENT KABLAM, THE SUPERVOID...IT **CHANGED** ME. MORE THAN JUST THE COOL NEW HAIR, IT PUT SOME OF ITS OWN ENERGY INSIDE ME. I THINK.
SOUNDS CREEPY WHEN I SAY IT LIKE THAT BUT IT SAVED MY LIFE, YOU KNOW?
BUT WITHOUT YOU...WITHOUT YOUR MEMORIES OF ME, OF US...I DIDN'T KNOW WHAT WAS UP. I NEVER WOULD HAVE. I WOULD'VE JUST **BURNED.**
BUT YOU CAME BACK. SO I DID TOO.
AND I'M NOT LETTING YOU OUT OF MY SIGHT. YOU AND ME, WE'RE GOING TO GET THE HELL OUT OF HERE.
PICK A DIRECTION, UMA. JUST LIKE WHEN WE LEFT EARTH. I DON'T KNOW WHAT'S OUT THERE, BUT I CAN'T WAIT TO FIND OUT.
WITH YOU.
I THOUGHT YOU'D NEVER ASK.
GETTING YOUR MIND BLOWN APART AND SLAPPED BACK TOGETHER AGAIN, IT KIND OF CHANGES YOUR PERSPECTIVE, YOU KNOW? I THINK ABOUT **KOLSTAK,** LIVING WITH ALL THAT ANGER AND REGRET.
I THINK ABOUT WHAT **THE FRAC** SAID TO ME. MY **SECRET WISH.** THAT THING WAS UNSTABLE, BUT IT WASN'T **WRONG.**
SO, REALLY, THERE'S ONLY ONE PLACE TO GO.
BOT, LET'S SET A COURSE!

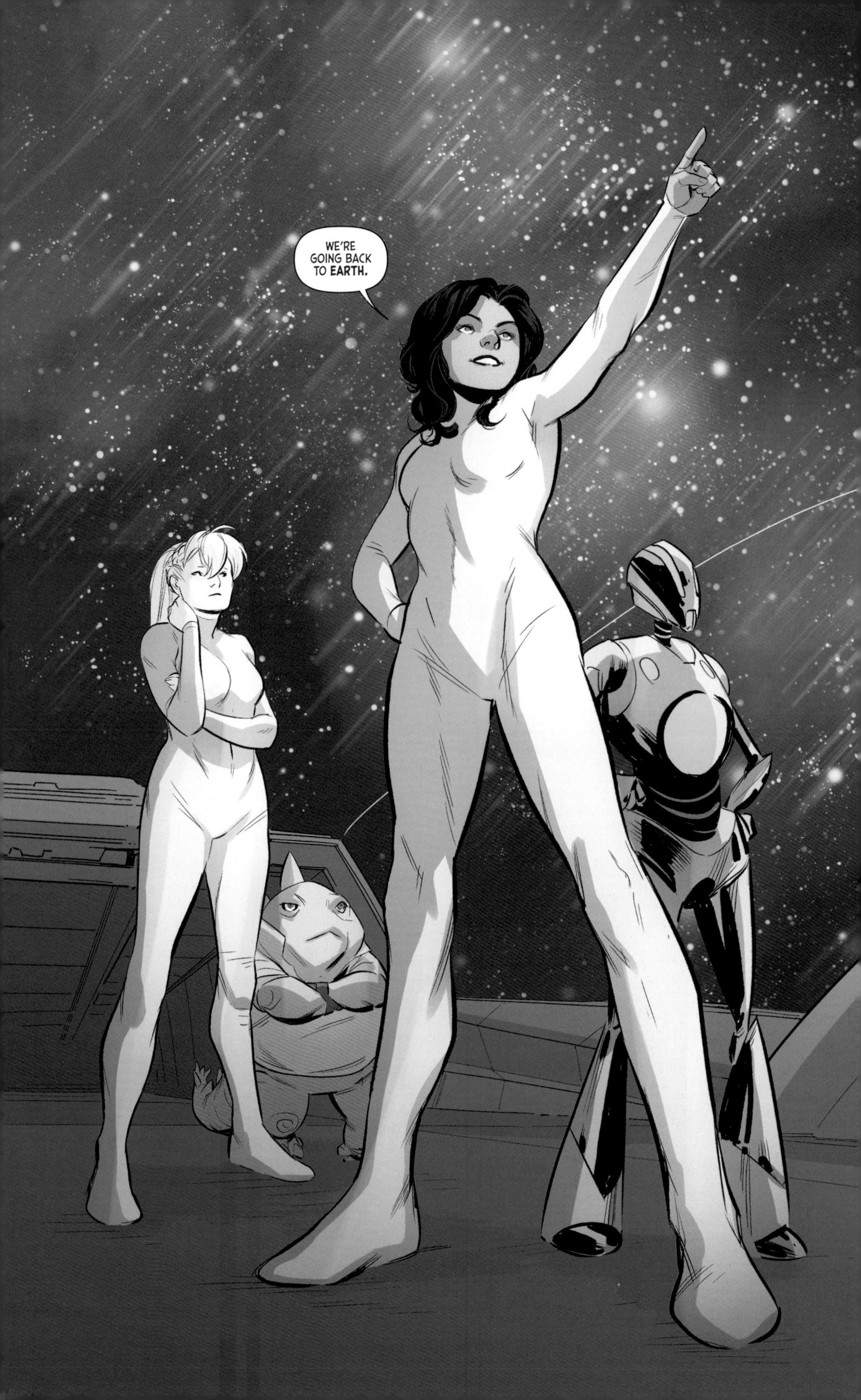
WE'RE GOING BACK TO EARTH.

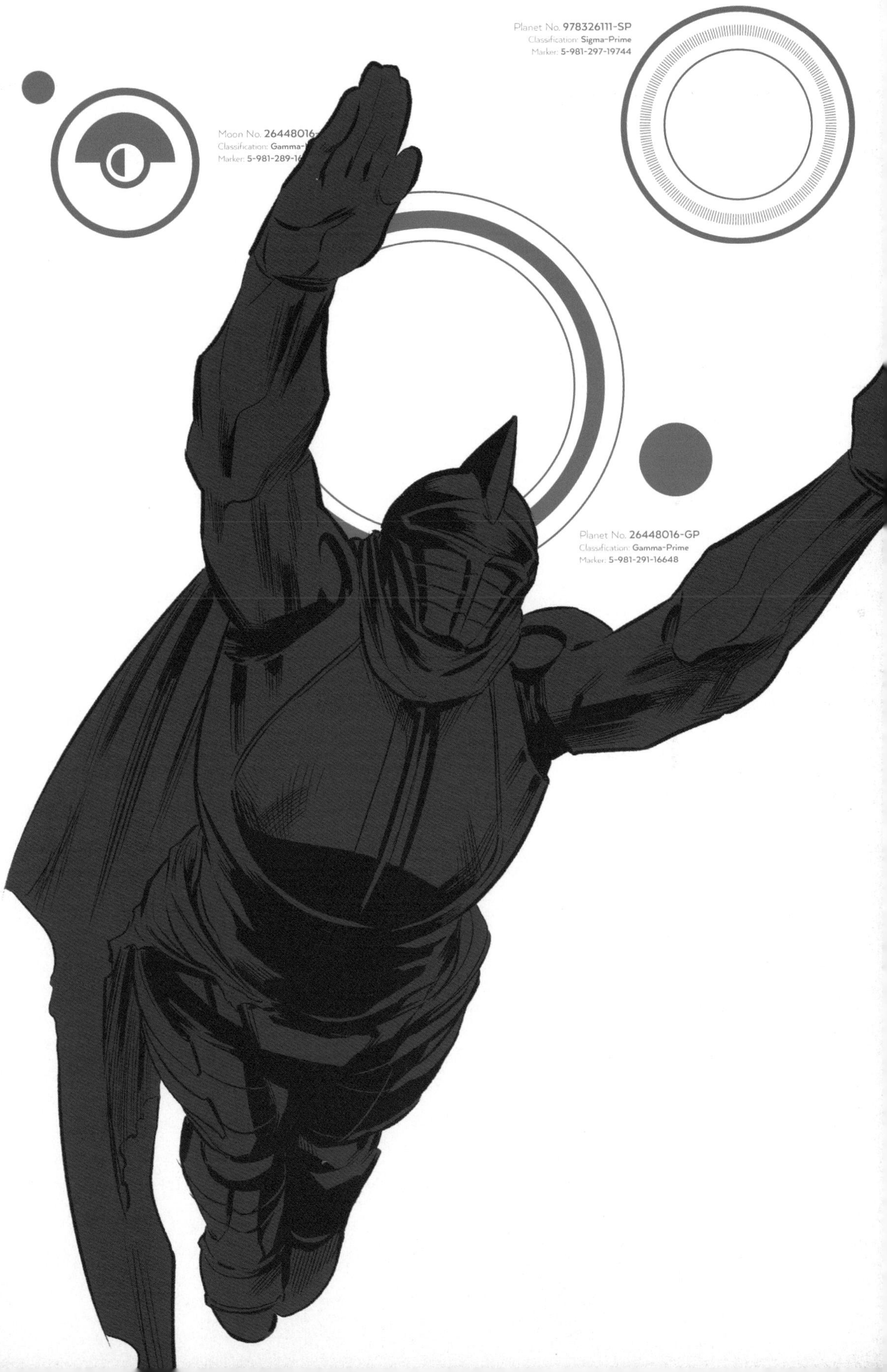

Planet No. 978326111-SP
Classification: Sigma-Prime
Marker: 5-981-297-19744
Moon No. 26448016-
Classification: Gamma-
Marker: 5-981-289-16
Planet No. 26448016-GP
Classification: Gamma-Prime
Marker: 5-981-291-16648

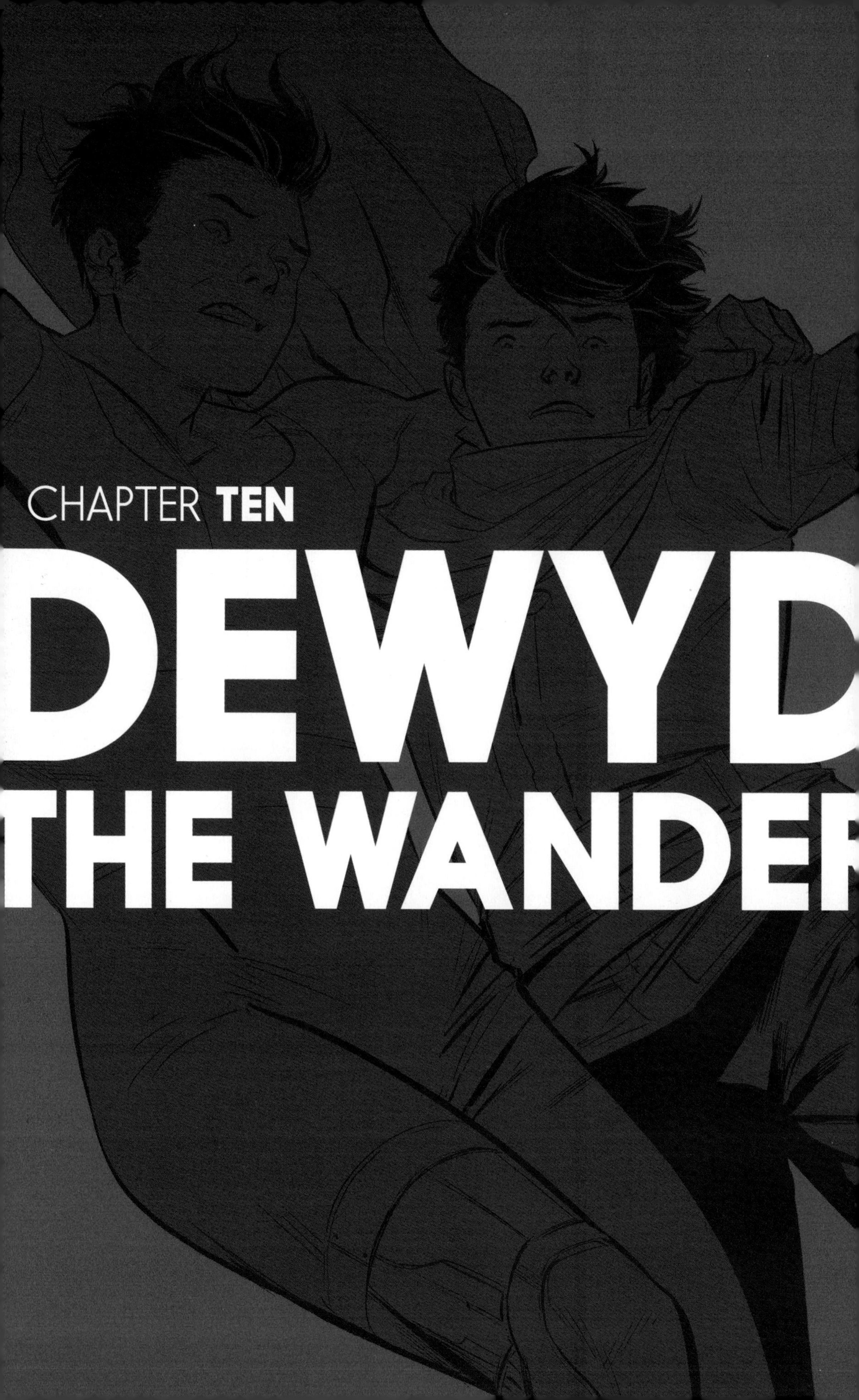
CHAPTER TEN
DEWYD
THE WANDER

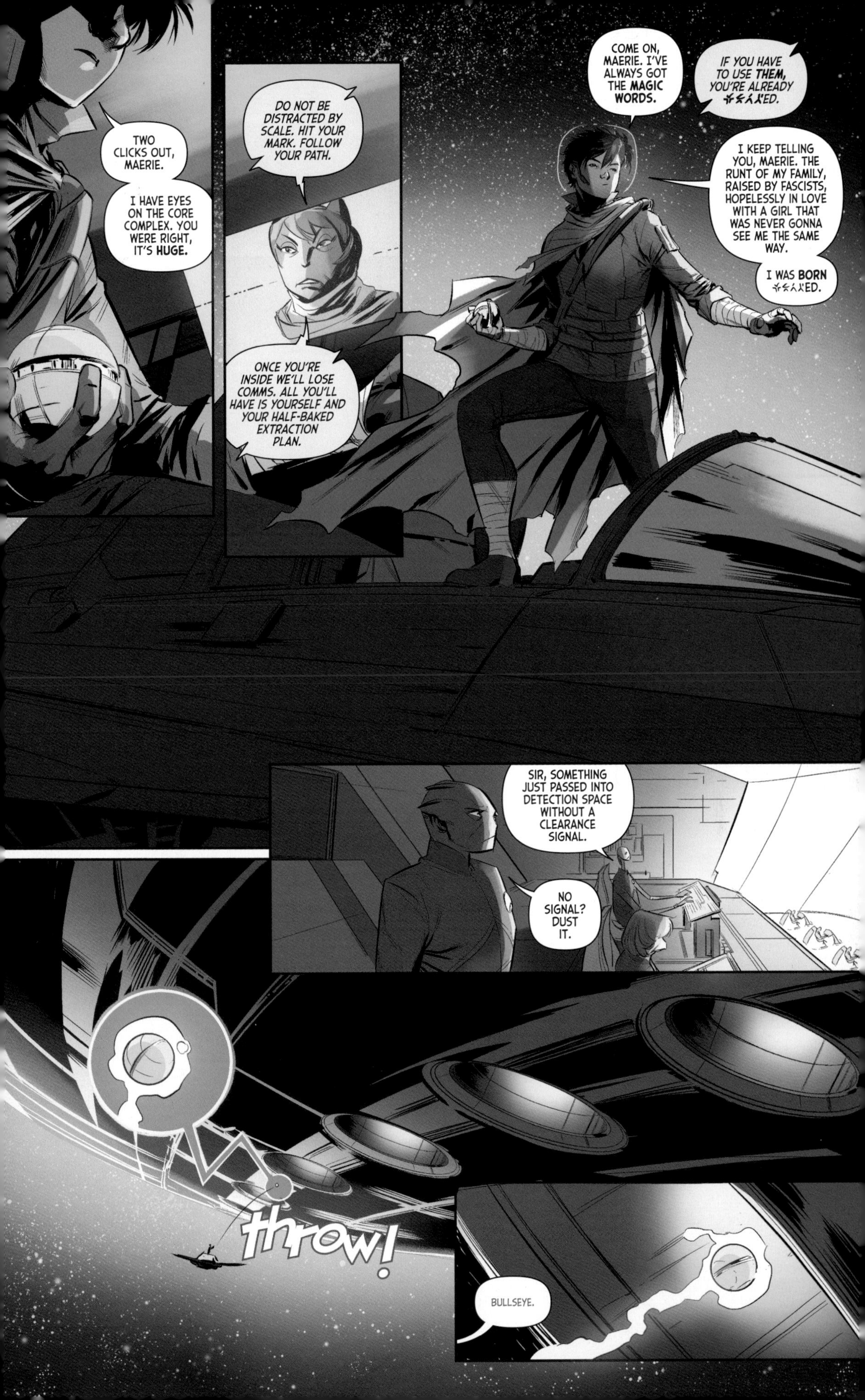

TWO CLICKS OUT, MAERIE.
I HAVE EYES ON THE CORE COMPLEX. YOU WERE RIGHT, IT'S HUGE.
DO NOT BE DISTRACTED BY SCALE. HIT YOUR MARK. FOLLOW YOUR PATH.
ONCE YOU'RE INSIDE WE'LL LOSE COMMS. ALL YOU'LL HAVE IS YOURSELF AND YOUR HALF-BAKED EXTRACTION PLAN.
COME ON, MAERIE. I'VE ALWAYS GOT THE MAGIC WORDS.
IF YOU HAVE TO USE THEM, YOU'RE ALREADY ED.
I KEEP TELLING YOU, MAERIE. THE RUNT OF MY FAMILY, RAISED BY FASCISTS, HOPELESSLY IN LOVE WITH A GIRL THAT WAS NEVER GONNA SEE ME THE SAME WAY.
I WAS BORN ED.
SIR, SOMETHING JUST PASSED INTO DETECTION SPACE WITHOUT A CLEARANCE SIGNAL.
NO SIGNAL? DUST IT.
throw!
BULLSEYE.

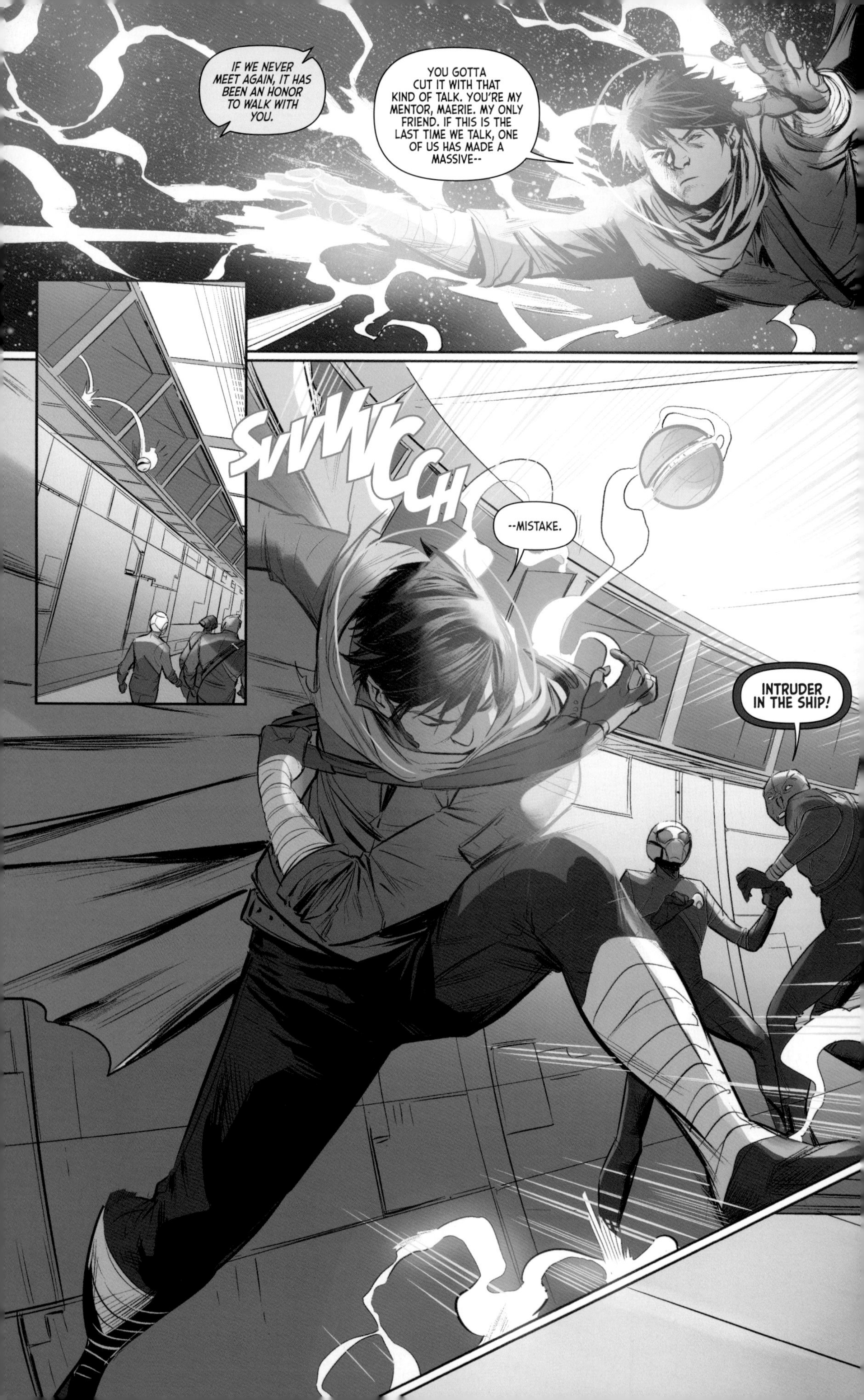
IF WE NEVER MEET AGAIN, IT HAS BEEN AN HONOR TO WALK WITH YOU.
YOU GOTTA CUT IT WITH THAT KIND OF TALK. YOU'RE MY MENTOR, MAERIE. MY ONLY FRIEND. IF THIS IS THE LAST TIME WE TALK, ONE OF US HAS MADE A MASSIVE--
SVVVVCCH
--MISTAKE.
INTRUDER IN THE SHIP!

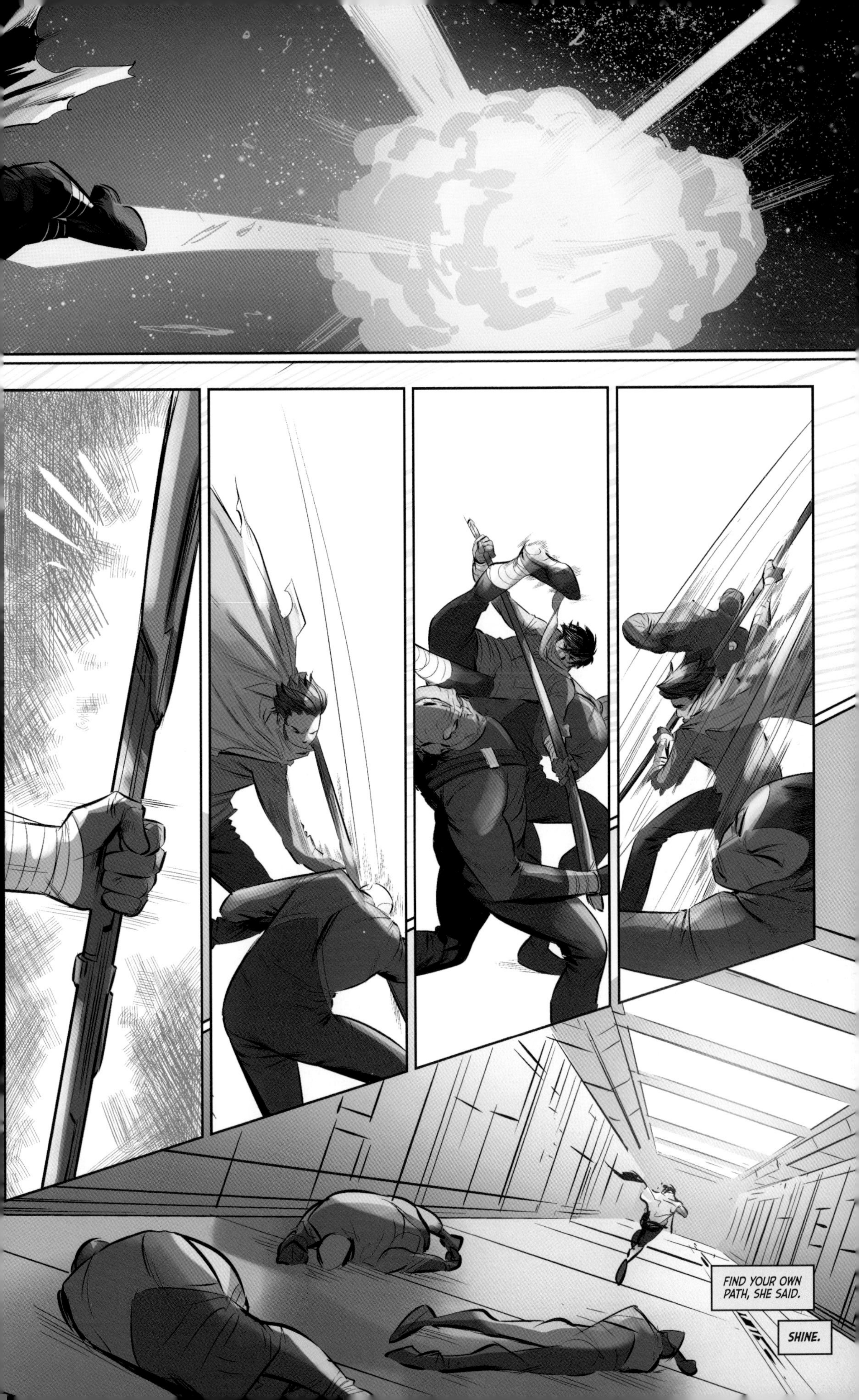
FIND YOUR OWN PATH, SHE SAID.
SHINE.

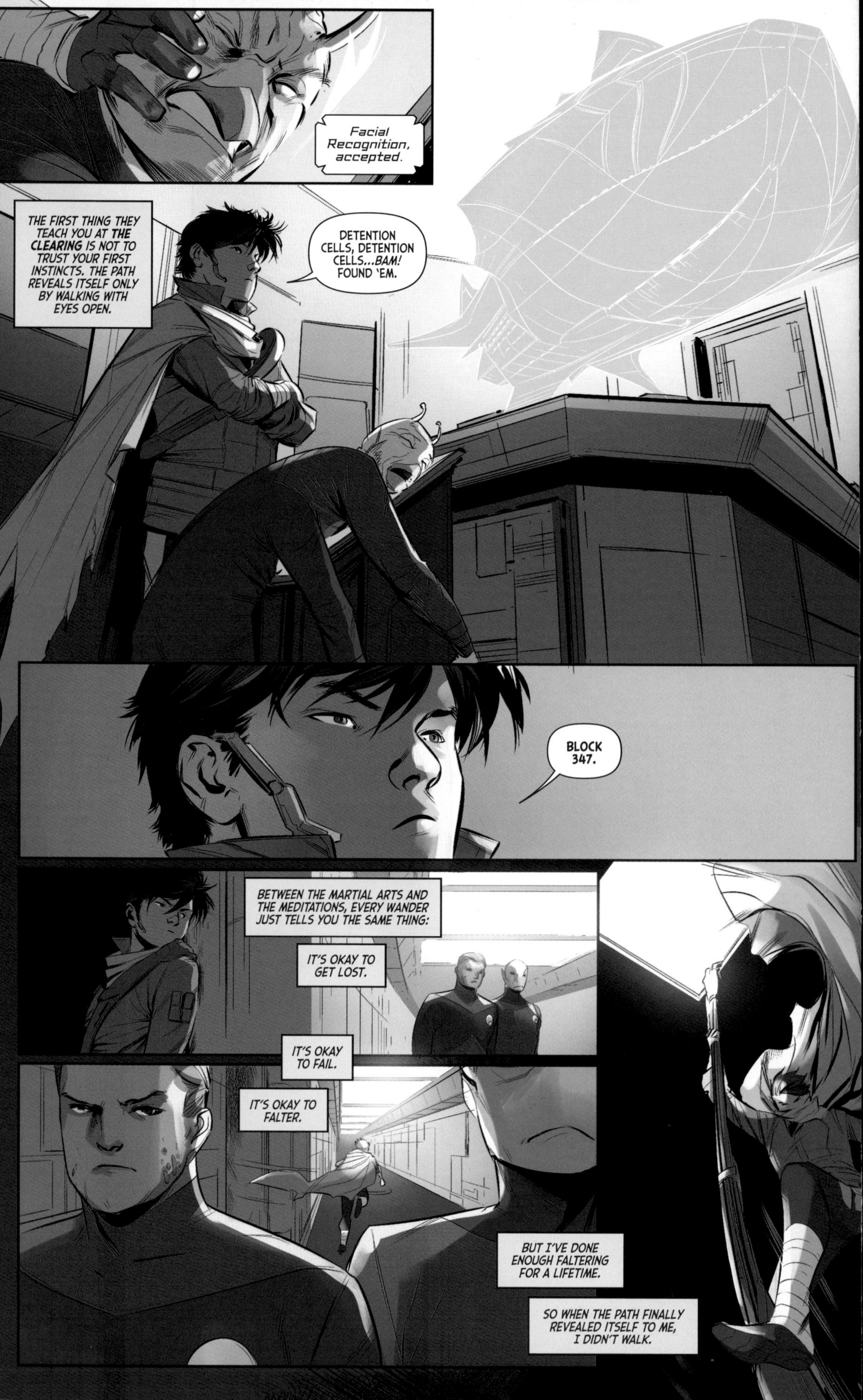

Facial Recognition, accepted.
THE FIRST THING THEY TEACH YOU AT THE CLEARING IS NOT TO TRUST YOUR FIRST INSTINCTS. THE PATH REVEALS ITSELF ONLY BY WALKING WITH EYES OPEN.
DETENTION CELLS, DETENTION CELLS...BAM! FOUND 'EM.
BLOCK 347.
BETWEEN THE MARTIAL ARTS AND THE MEDITATIONS, EVERY WANDER JUST TELLS YOU THE SAME THING:
IT'S OKAY TO GET LOST.
IT'S OKAY TO FAIL.
IT'S OKAY TO FALTER.
BUT I'VE DONE ENOUGH FALTERING FOR A LIFETIME.
SO WHEN THE PATH FINALLY REVEALED ITSELF TO ME, I DIDN'T WALK.

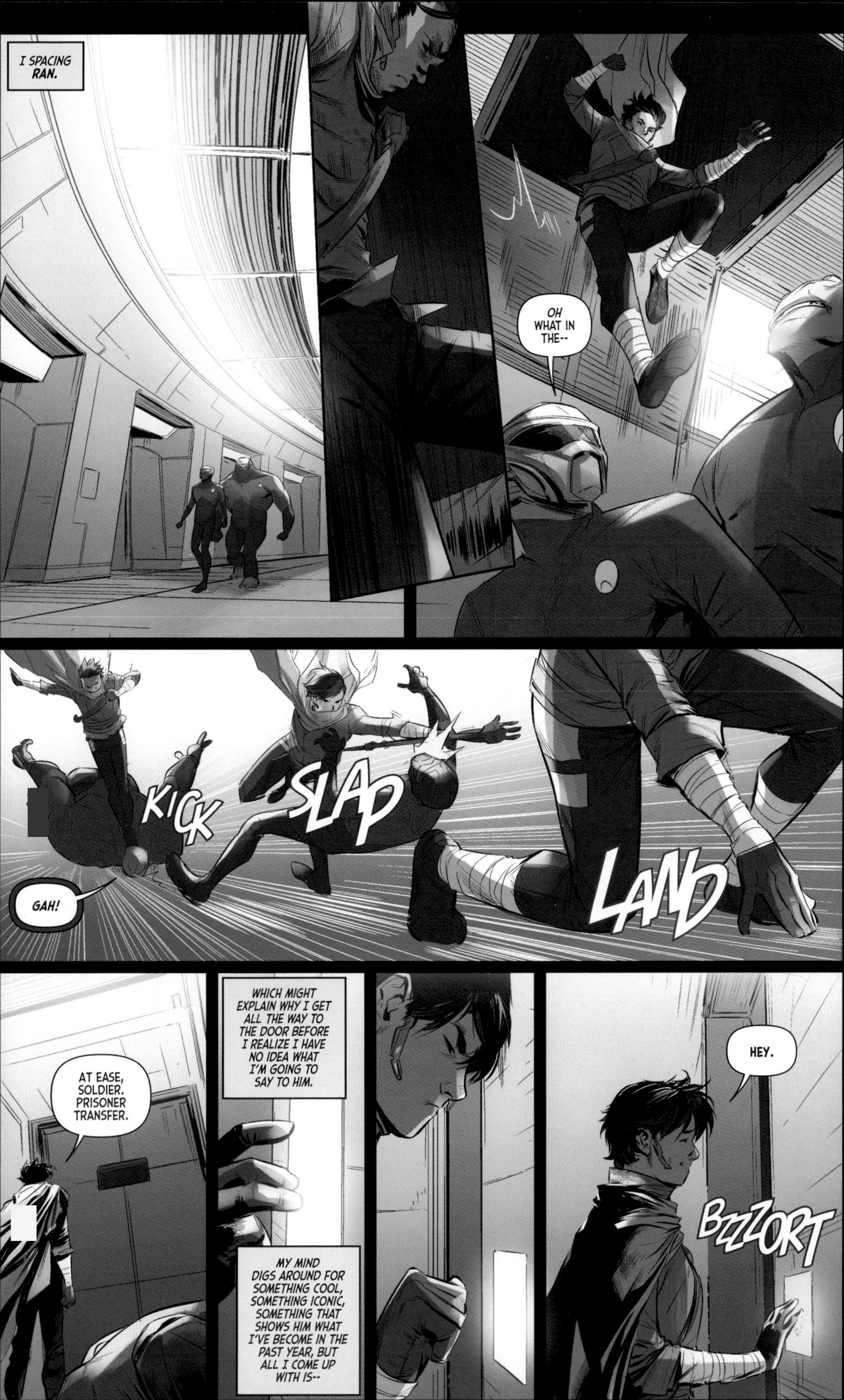
I SPACING RAN.
OH WHAT IN THE--
KICK
SLAP
GAH!
LAND
AT EASE, SOLDIER. PRISONER TRANSFER.
WHICH MIGHT EXPLAIN WHY I GET ALL THE WAY TO THE DOOR BEFORE I REALIZE I HAVE NO IDEA WHAT I'M GOING TO SAY TO HIM.
MY MIND DIGS AROUND FOR SOMETHING COOL, SOMETHING ICONIC, SOMETHING THAT SHOWS HIM WHAT I'VE BECOME IN THE PAST YEAR, BUT ALL I COME UP WITH IS--
HEY.
BZZZORT

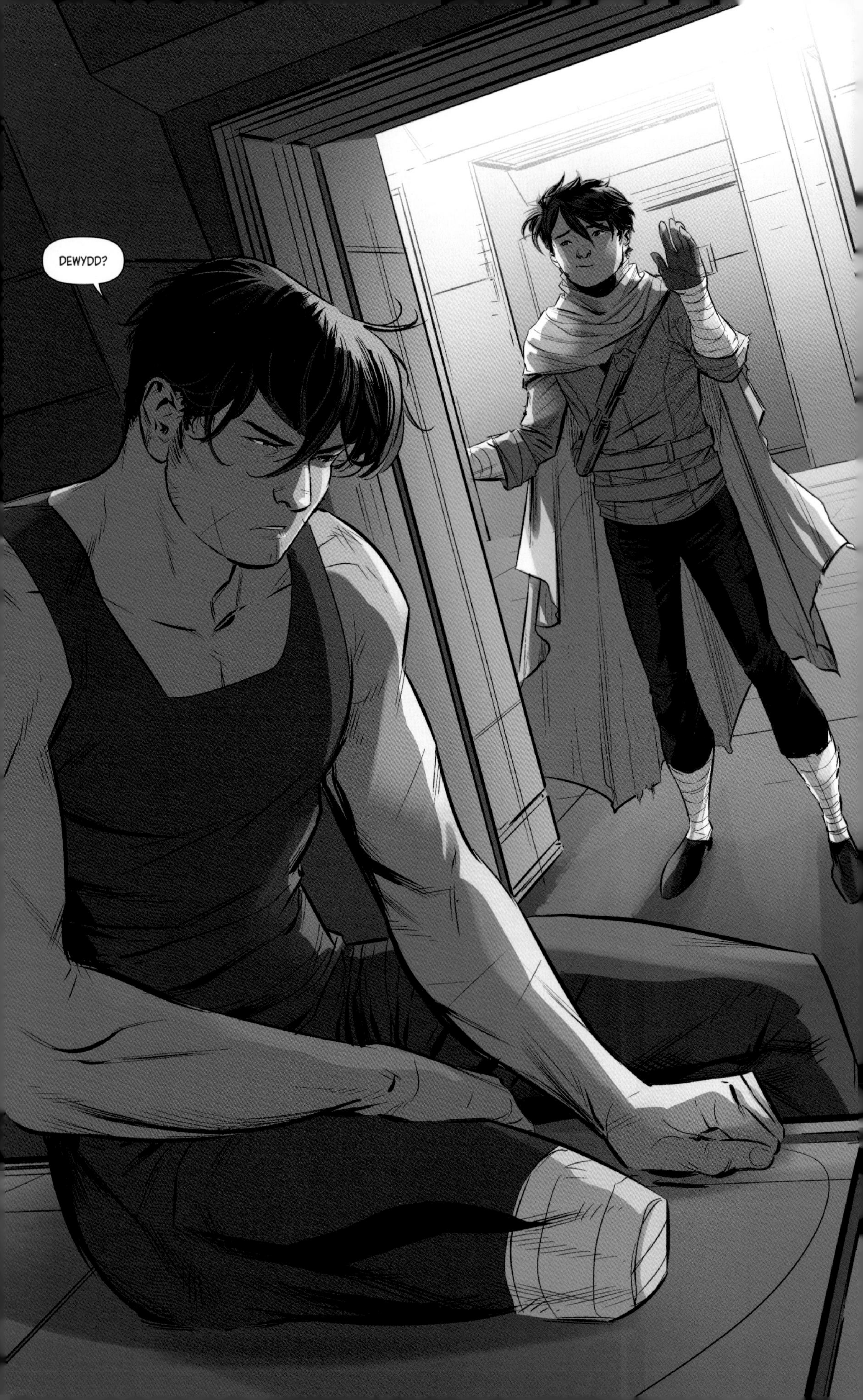
DEWYDD?

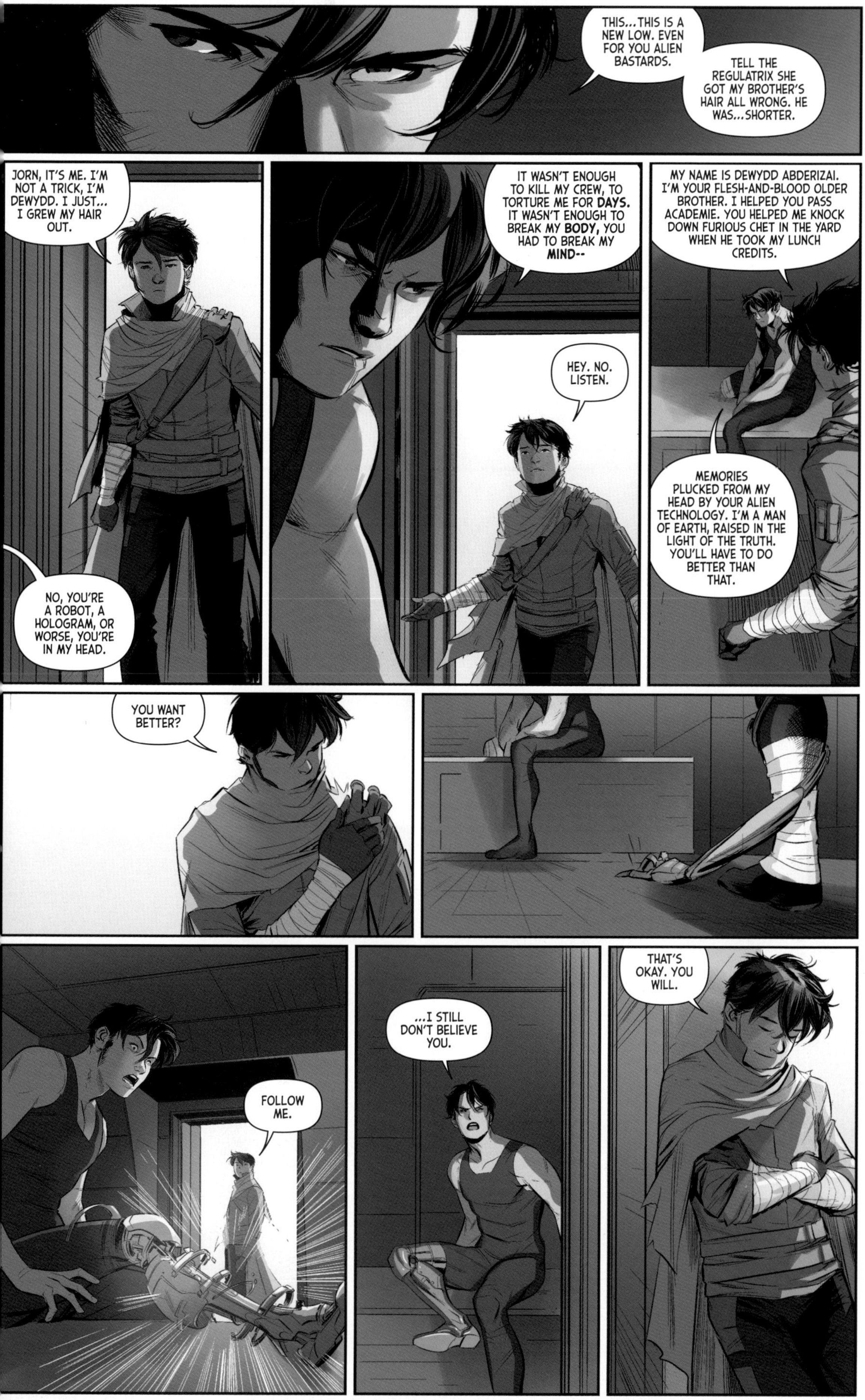
THIS...THIS IS A NEW LOW. EVEN FOR YOU ALIEN BASTARDS.
TELL THE REGULATRIX SHE GOT MY BROTHER'S HAIR ALL WRONG. HE WAS...SHORTER.
JORN, IT'S ME. I'M NOT A TRICK, I'M DEWYDD. I JUST... I GREW MY HAIR OUT.
NO, YOU'RE A ROBOT, A HOLOGRAM, OR WORSE, YOU'RE IN MY HEAD.
IT WASN'T ENOUGH TO KILL MY CREW, TO TORTURE ME FOR DAYS. IT WASN'T ENOUGH TO BREAK MY BODY, YOU HAD TO BREAK MY MIND--
HEY. NO. LISTEN.
MY NAME IS DEWYDD ABDERIZAI. I'M YOUR FLESH-AND-BLOOD OLDER BROTHER. I HELPED YOU PASS ACADEMIE. YOU HELPED ME KNOCK DOWN FURIOUS CHET IN THE YARD WHEN HE TOOK MY LUNCH CREDITS.
MEMORIES PLUCKED FROM MY HEAD BY YOUR ALIEN TECHNOLOGY. I'M A MAN OF EARTH, RAISED IN THE LIGHT OF THE TRUTH. YOU'LL HAVE TO DO BETTER THAN THAT.
YOU WANT BETTER?
FOLLOW ME.
...I STILL DON'T BELIEVE YOU.
THAT'S OKAY. YOU WILL.

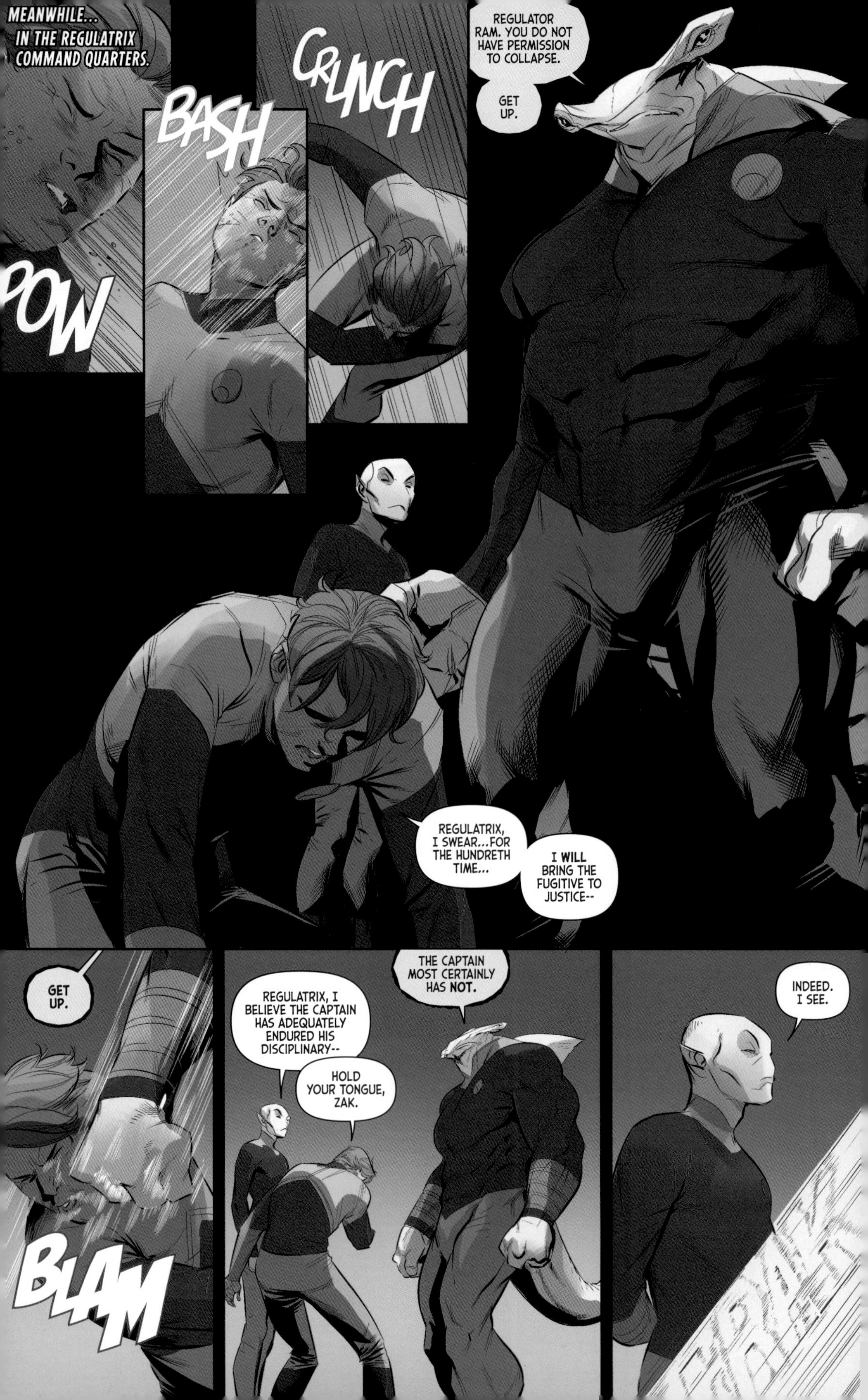
MEANWHILE... IN THE REGULATRIX COMMAND QUARTERS.
POW
BASH
CRUNCH
REGULATOR RAM. YOU DO NOT HAVE PERMISSION TO COLLAPSE.
GET UP.
REGULATRIX, I SWEAR...FOR THE HUNDRETH TIME...
I WILL BRING THE FUGITIVE TO JUSTICE--
GET UP.
BLAM
REGULATRIX, I BELIEVE THE CAPTAIN HAS ADEQUATELY ENDURED HIS DISCIPLINARY--
THE CAPTAIN MOST CERTAINLY HAS NOT.
HOLD YOUR TONGUE, ZAK.
INDEED. I SEE.

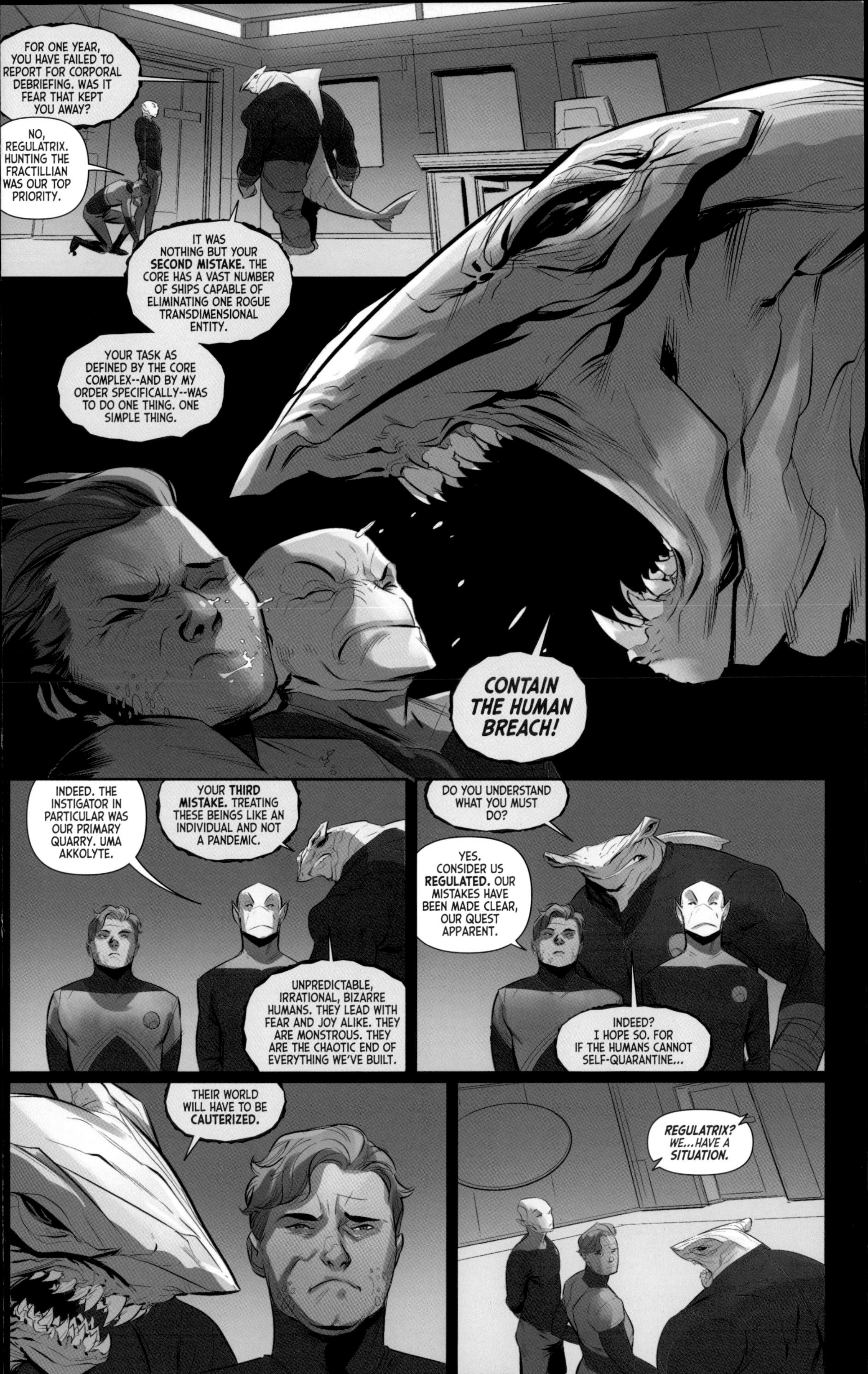
FOR ONE YEAR, YOU HAVE FAILED TO REPORT FOR CORPORAL DEBRIEFING. WAS IT FEAR THAT KEPT YOU AWAY?
NO, REGULATRIX. HUNTING THE FRACTILLIAN WAS OUR TOP PRIORITY.
IT WAS NOTHING BUT YOUR **SECOND MISTAKE.** THE CORE HAS A VAST NUMBER OF SHIPS CAPABLE OF ELIMINATING ONE ROGUE TRANSDIMENSIONAL ENTITY.
YOUR TASK AS DEFINED BY THE CORE COMPLEX--AND BY MY ORDER SPECIFICALLY--WAS TO DO ONE THING. ONE SIMPLE THING.
CONTAIN THE HUMAN BREACH!
INDEED. THE INSTIGATOR IN PARTICULAR WAS OUR PRIMARY QUARRY. UMA AKKOLYTE.
YOUR **THIRD MISTAKE.** TREATING THESE BEINGS LIKE AN INDIVIDUAL AND NOT A PANDEMIC.
UNPREDICTABLE, IRRATIONAL, BIZARRE HUMANS. THEY LEAD WITH FEAR AND JOY ALIKE. THEY ARE MONSTROUS. THEY ARE THE CHAOTIC END OF EVERYTHING WE'VE BUILT.
DO YOU UNDERSTAND WHAT YOU MUST DO?
YES. CONSIDER US **REGULATED.** OUR MISTAKES HAVE BEEN MADE CLEAR, OUR QUEST APPARENT.
INDEED? I HOPE SO. FOR IF THE HUMANS CANNOT SELF-QUARANTINE...
THEIR WORLD WILL HAVE TO BE **CAUTERIZED.**
REGULATRIX? WE...HAVE A ***SITUATION.***

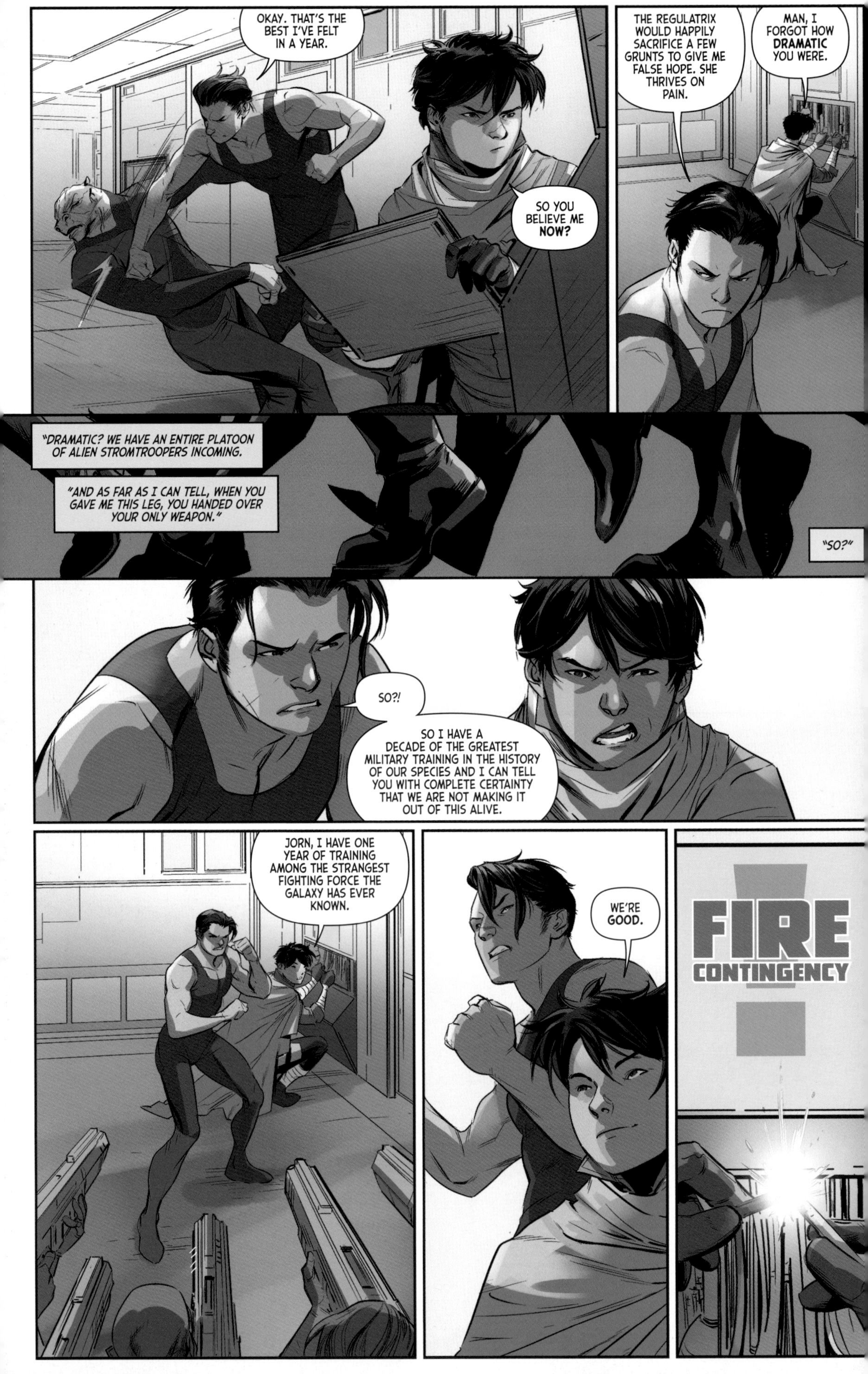
OKAY. THAT'S THE BEST I'VE FELT IN A YEAR.
SO YOU BELIEVE ME NOW?
THE REGULATRIX WOULD HAPPILY SACRIFICE A FEW GRUNTS TO GIVE ME FALSE HOPE. SHE THRIVES ON PAIN.
MAN, I FORGOT HOW DRAMATIC YOU WERE.
"DRAMATIC? WE HAVE AN ENTIRE PLATOON OF ALIEN STROMTROOPERS INCOMING.
"AND AS FAR AS I CAN TELL, WHEN YOU GAVE ME THIS LEG, YOU HANDED OVER YOUR ONLY WEAPON."
"SO?"
SO?!
SO I HAVE A DECADE OF THE GREATEST MILITARY TRAINING IN THE HISTORY OF OUR SPECIES AND I CAN TELL YOU WITH COMPLETE CERTAINTY THAT WE ARE NOT MAKING IT OUT OF THIS ALIVE.
JORN, I HAVE ONE YEAR OF TRAINING AMONG THE STRANGEST FIGHTING FORCE THE GALAXY HAS EVER KNOWN.
WE'RE GOOD.
FIRE
CONTINGENCY

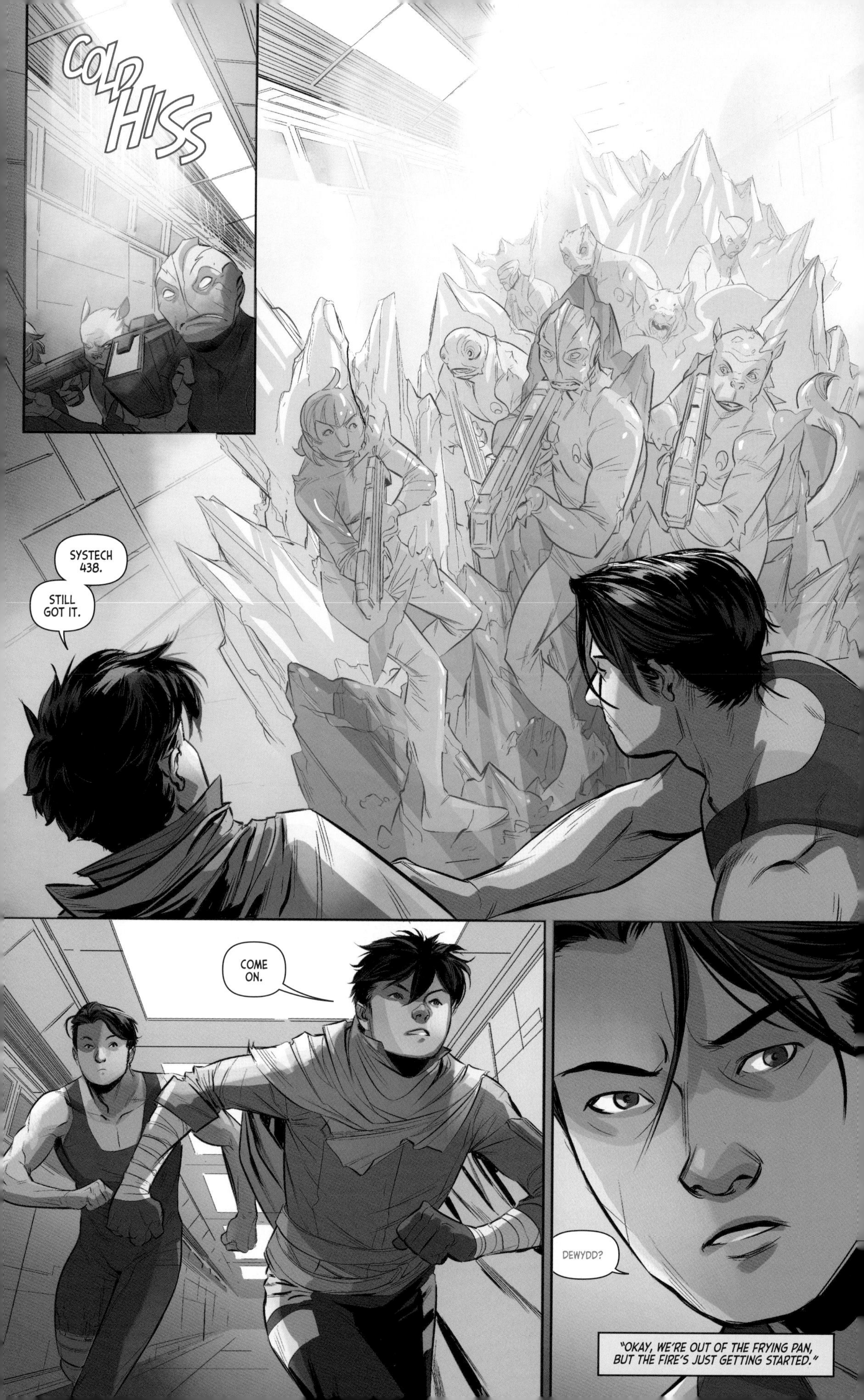
COLD HISS
SYSTECH 438.
STILL GOT IT.
COME ON.
DEWYDD?
"OKAY, WE'RE OUT OF THE FRYING PAN, BUT THE FIRE'S JUST GETTING STARTED."

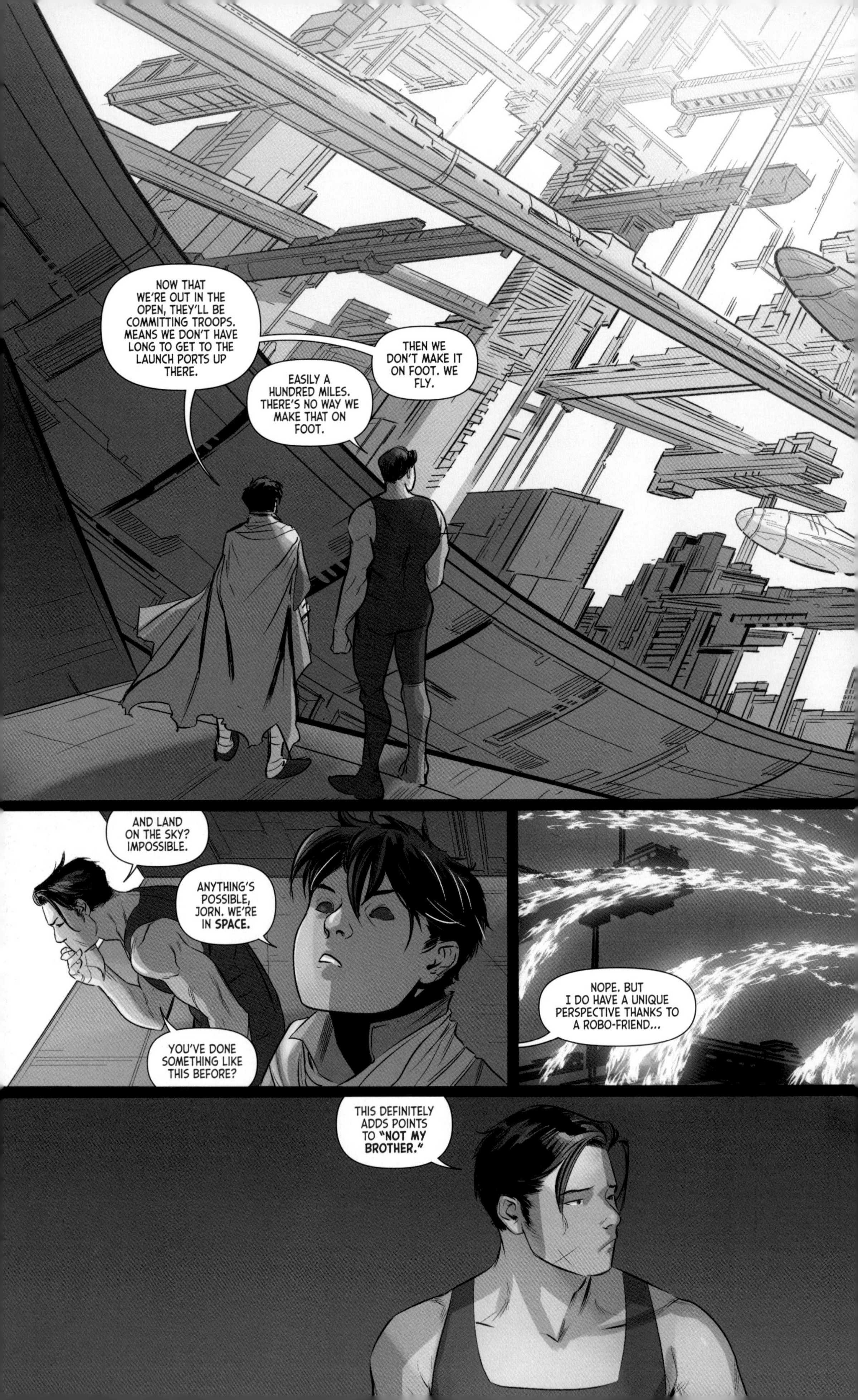
NOW THAT WE'RE OUT IN THE OPEN, THEY'LL BE COMMITTING TROOPS. MEANS WE DON'T HAVE LONG TO GET TO THE LAUNCH PORTS UP THERE.
EASILY A HUNDRED MILES. THERE'S NO WAY WE MAKE THAT ON FOOT.
THEN WE DON'T MAKE IT ON FOOT. WE FLY.
AND LAND ON THE SKY? IMPOSSIBLE.
ANYTHING'S POSSIBLE, JORN. WE'RE IN SPACE.
YOU'VE DONE SOMETHING LIKE THIS BEFORE?
NOPE. BUT I DO HAVE A UNIQUE PERSPECTIVE THANKS TO A ROBO-FRIEND...
THIS DEFINITELY ADDS POINTS TO "NOT MY BROTHER."

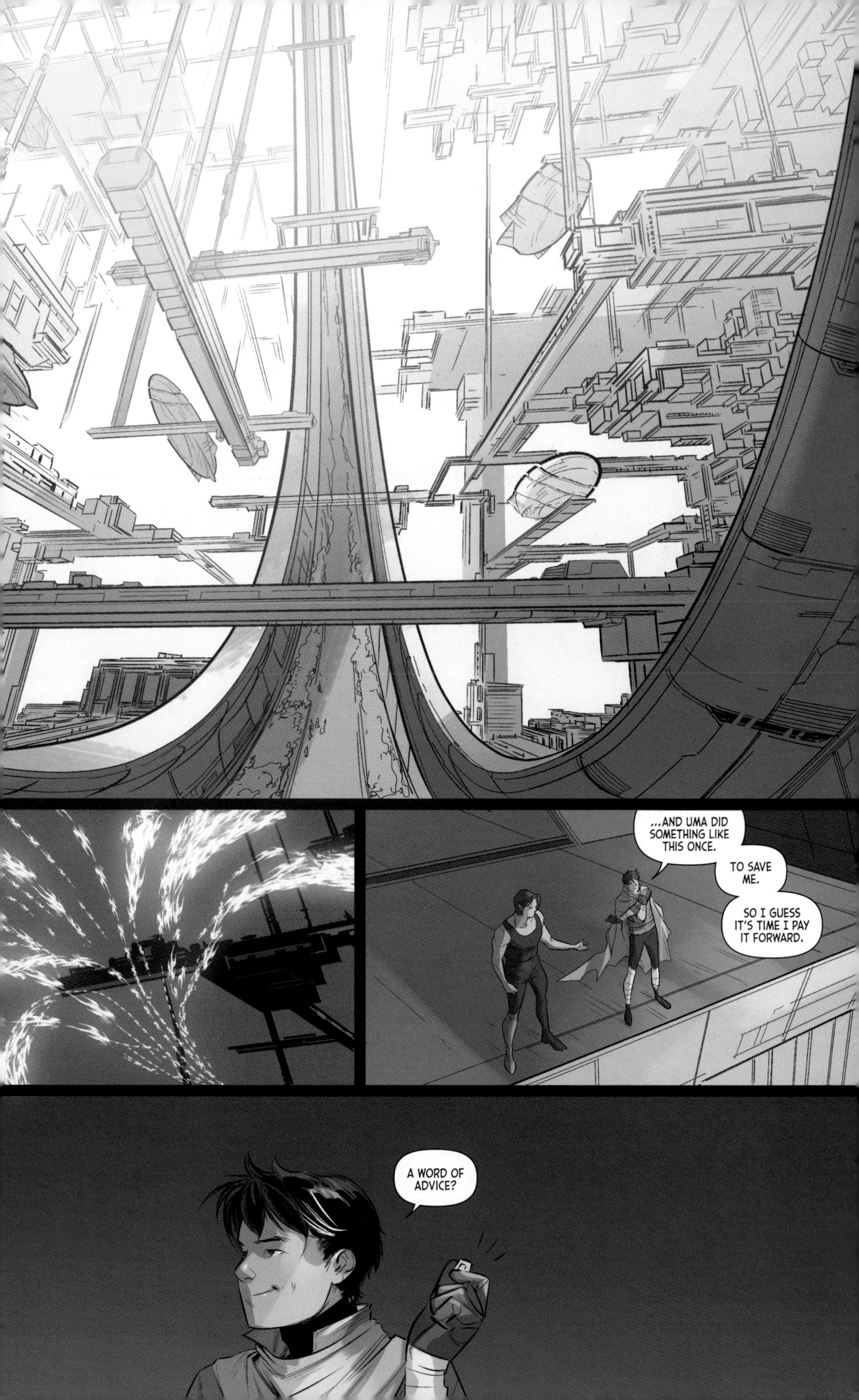
...AND UMA DID SOMETHING LIKE THIS ONCE.
TO SAVE ME.
SO I GUESS IT'S TIME I PAY IT FORWARD.
A WORD OF ADVICE?

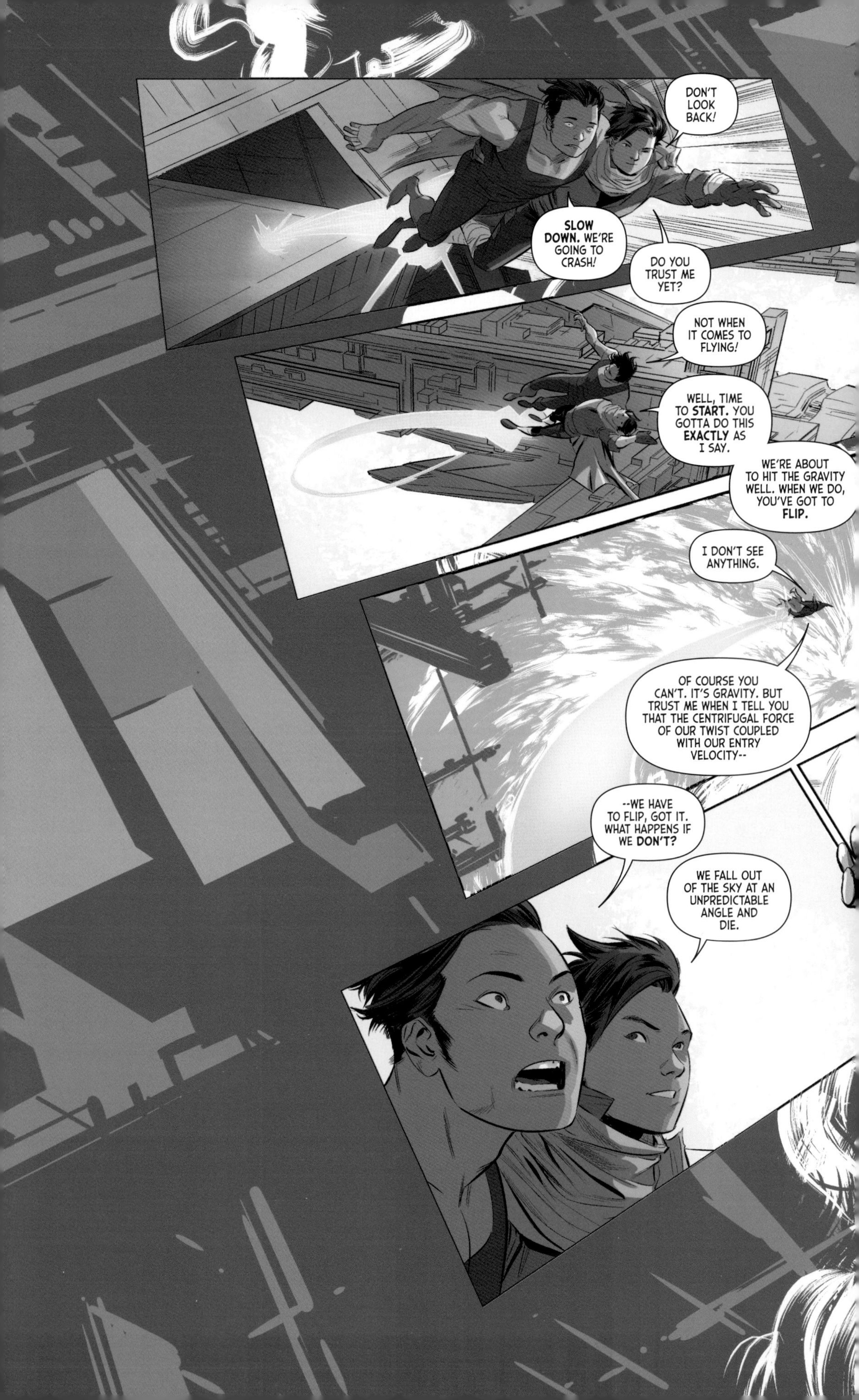
DON'T LOOK BACK!
SLOW DOWN. WE'RE GOING TO CRASH!
DO YOU TRUST ME YET?
NOT WHEN IT COMES TO FLYING!
WELL, TIME TO START. YOU GOTTA DO THIS EXACTLY AS I SAY.
WE'RE ABOUT TO HIT THE GRAVITY WELL. WHEN WE DO, YOU'VE GOT TO FLIP.
I DON'T SEE ANYTHING.
OF COURSE YOU CAN'T. IT'S GRAVITY. BUT TRUST ME WHEN I TELL YOU THAT THE CENTRIFUGAL FORCE OF OUR TWIST COUPLED WITH OUR ENTRY VELOCITY--
--WE HAVE TO FLIP, GOT IT. WHAT HAPPENS IF WE DON'T?
WE FALL OUT OF THE SKY AT AN UNPREDICTABLE ANGLE AND DIE.

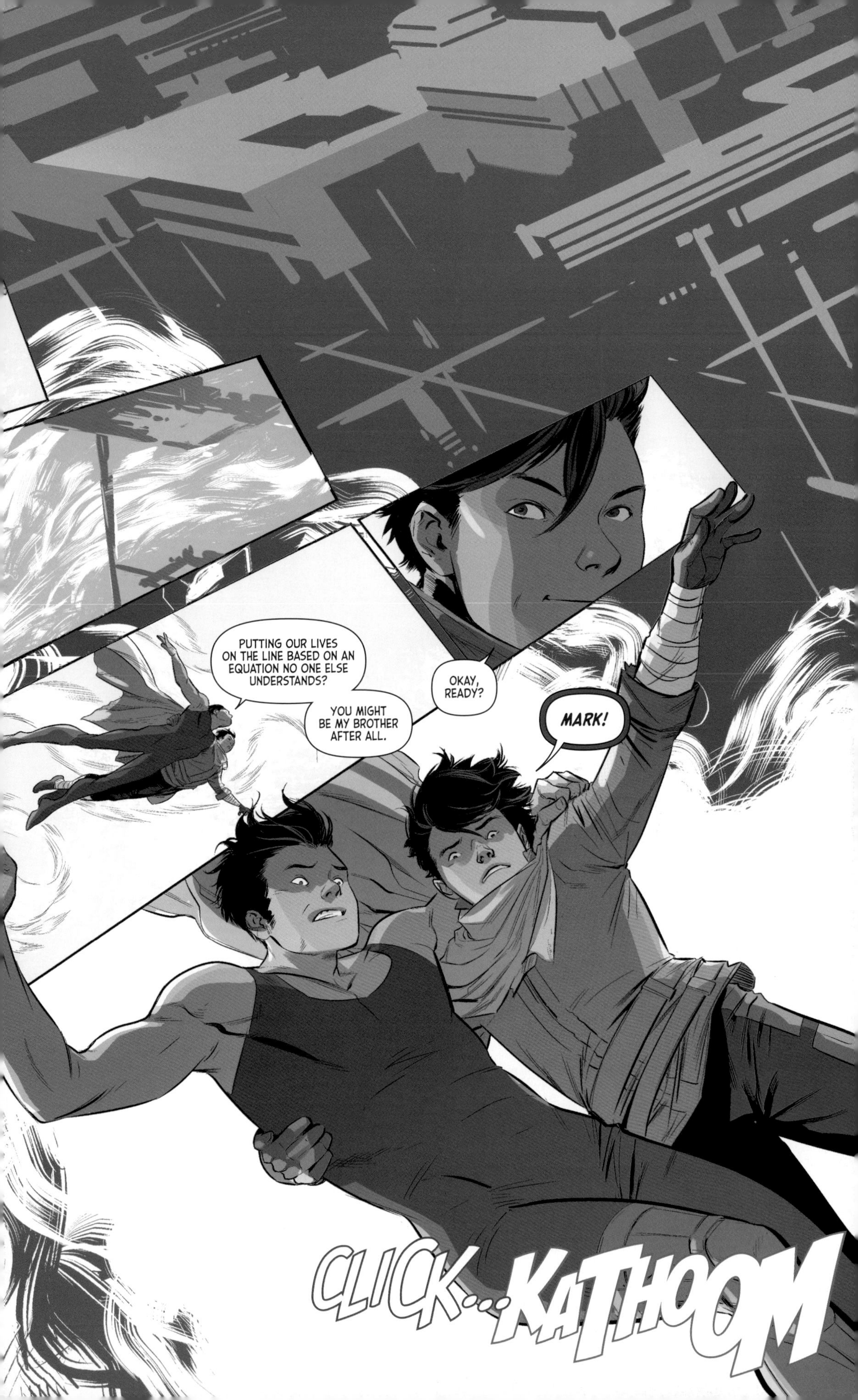
PUTTING OUR LIVES ON THE LINE BASED ON AN EQUATION NO ONE ELSE UNDERSTANDS?
YOU MIGHT BE MY BROTHER AFTER ALL.
OKAY, READY?
MARK!
CLICK...KATHOOM

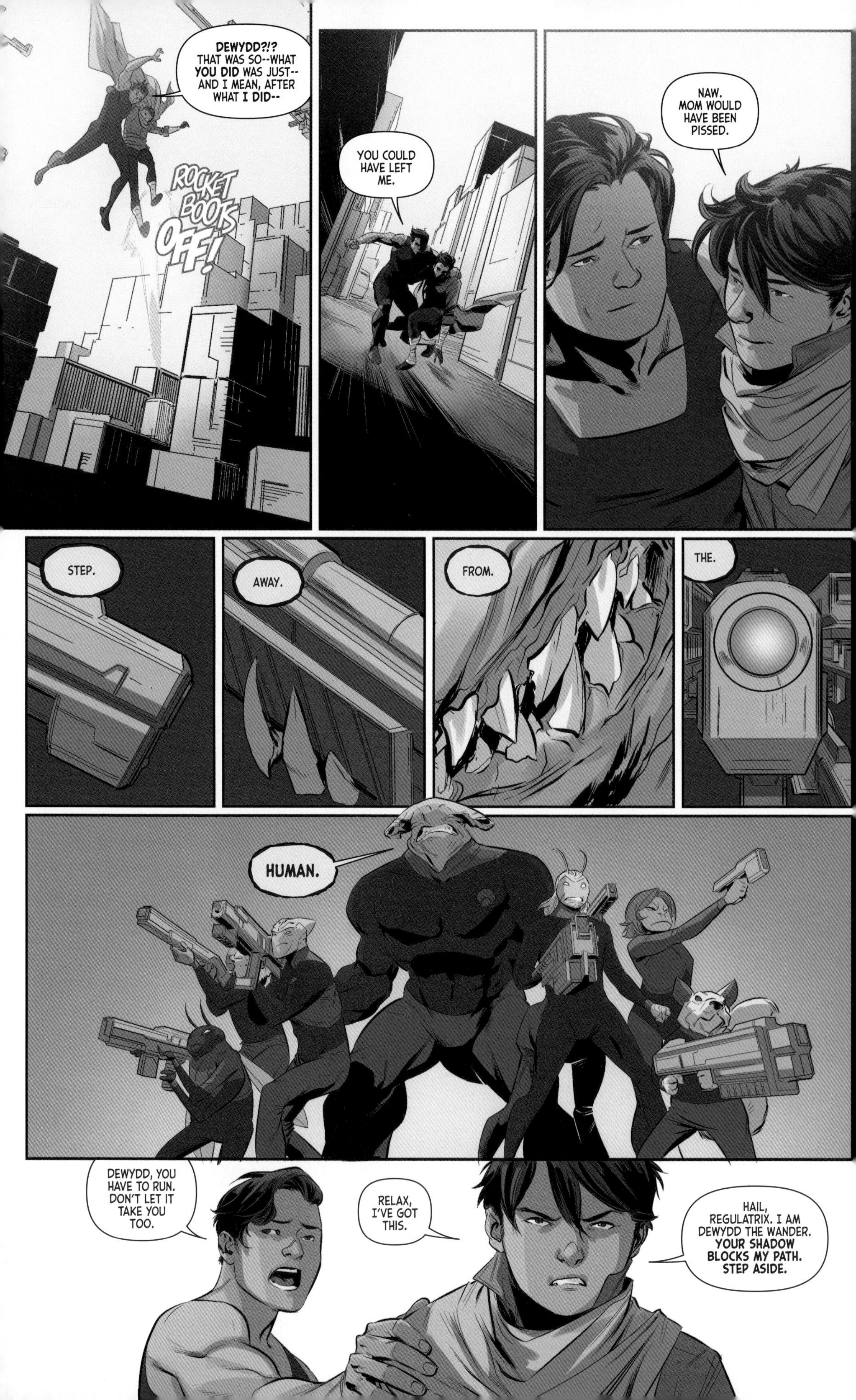
DEWYDD?!? THAT WAS SO--WHAT YOU DID WAS JUST-- AND I MEAN, AFTER WHAT I DID--
ROCKET BOOTS OFF!
YOU COULD HAVE LEFT ME.
NAW. MOM WOULD HAVE BEEN PISSED.
STEP.
AWAY.
FROM.
THE.
HUMAN.
DEWYDD, YOU HAVE TO RUN. DON'T LET IT TAKE YOU TOO.
RELAX, I'VE GOT THIS.
HAIL, REGULATRIX. I AM DEWYDD THE WANDER. YOUR SHADOW BLOCKS MY PATH. STEP ASIDE.

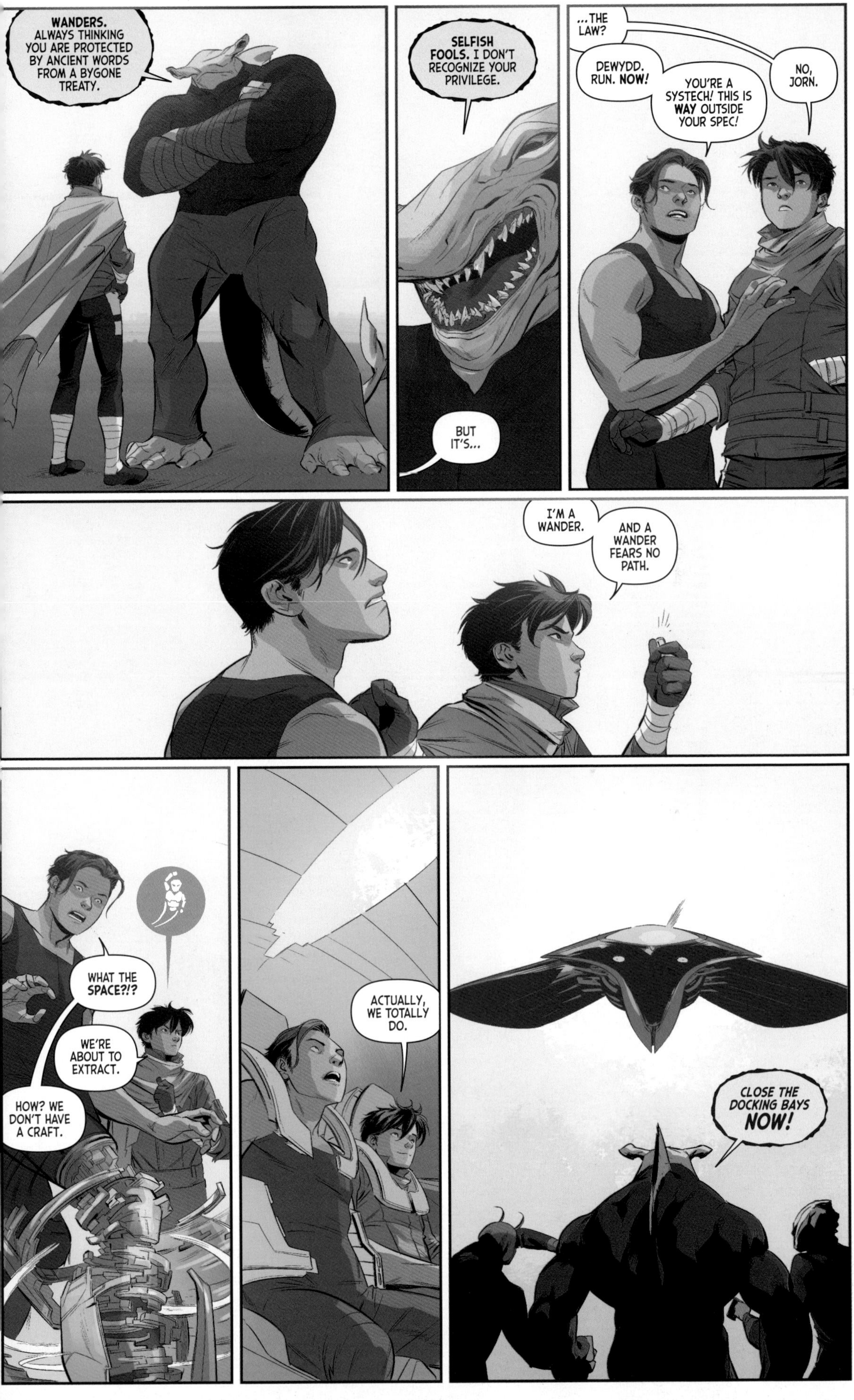
WANDERS. ALWAYS THINKING YOU ARE PROTECTED BY ANCIENT WORDS FROM A BYGONE TREATY.
SELFISH FOOLS. I DON'T RECOGNIZE YOUR PRIVILEGE.
BUT IT'S...
...THE LAW?
DEWYDD. RUN. NOW!
YOU'RE A SYSTECH! THIS IS WAY OUTSIDE YOUR SPEC!
NO, JORN.
I'M A WANDER.
AND A WANDER FEARS NO PATH.
WHAT THE SPACE?!?
WE'RE ABOUT TO EXTRACT.
HOW? WE DON'T HAVE A CRAFT.
ACTUALLY, WE TOTALLY DO.
CLOSE THE DOCKING BAYS NOW!

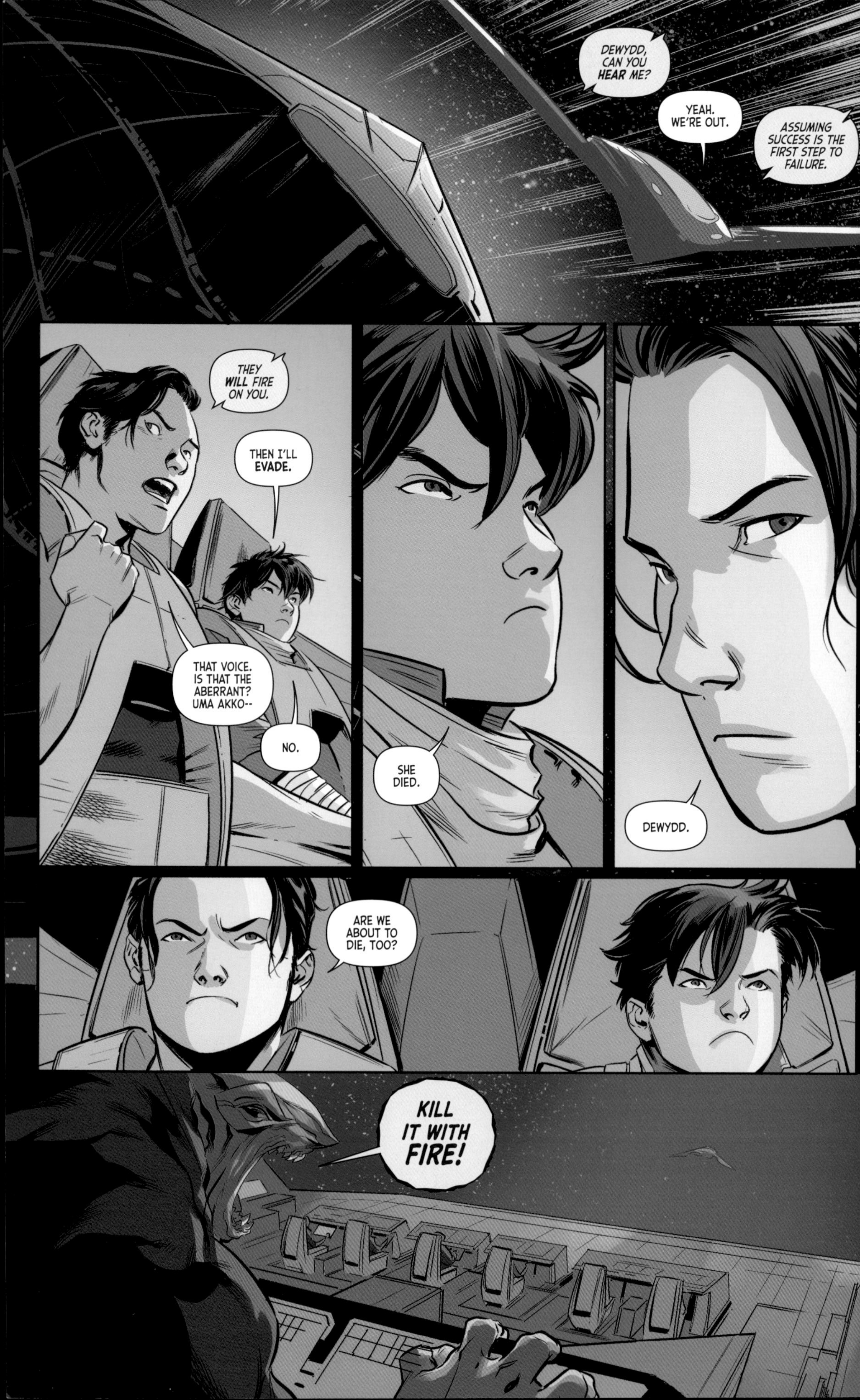
DEWYDD, CAN YOU HEAR ME?
YEAH. WE'RE OUT.
ASSUMING SUCCESS IS THE FIRST STEP TO FAILURE.
THEY WILL FIRE ON YOU.
THEN I'LL EVADE.
THAT VOICE. IS THAT THE ABERRANT? UMA AKKO--
NO.
SHE DIED.
DEWYDD.
ARE WE ABOUT TO DIE, TOO?
KILL IT WITH FIRE!

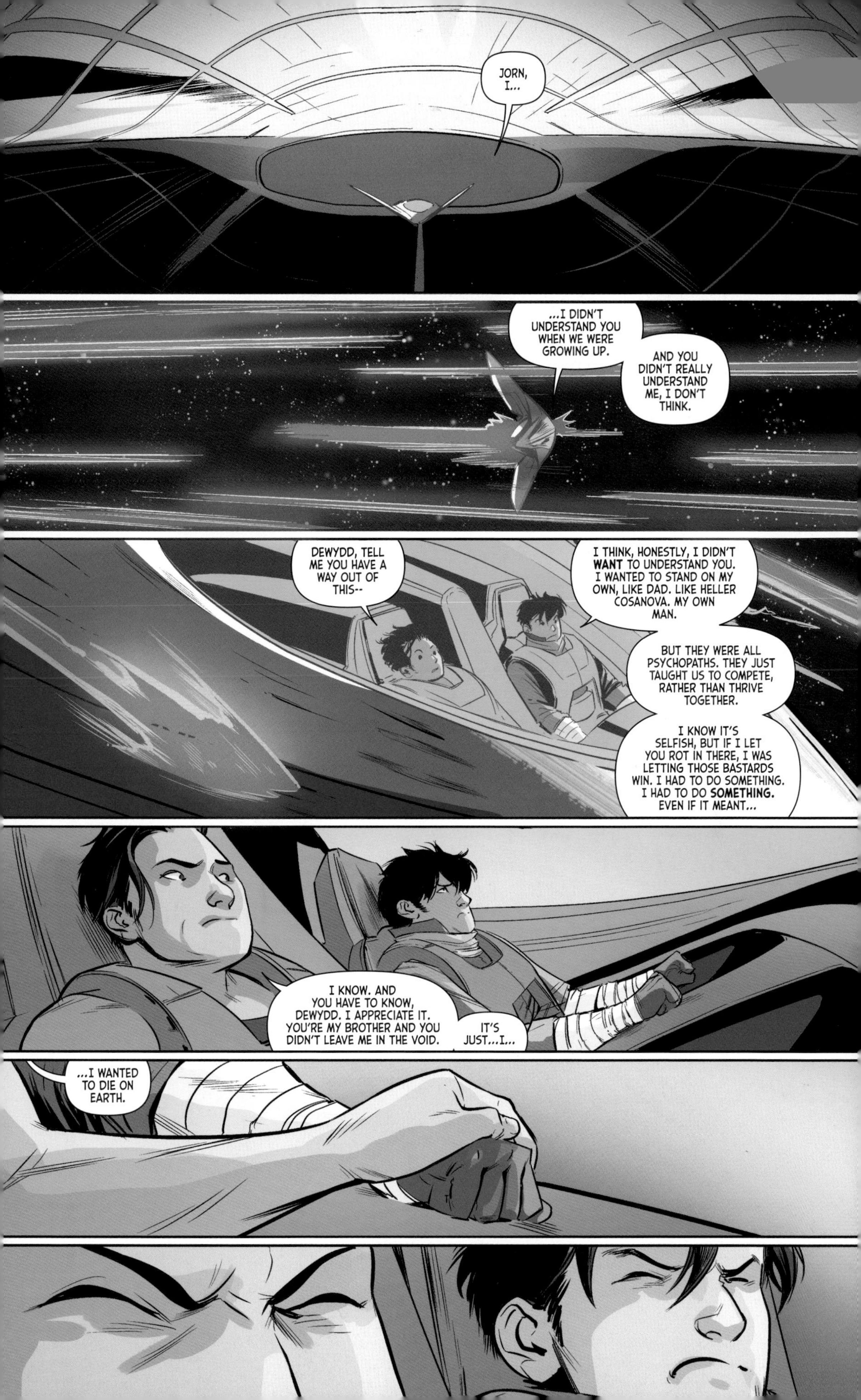
JORN, I...
...I DIDN'T UNDERSTAND YOU WHEN WE WERE GROWING UP.
AND YOU DIDN'T REALLY UNDERSTAND ME, I DON'T THINK.
DEWYDD, TELL ME YOU HAVE A WAY OUT OF THIS--
I THINK, HONESTLY, I DIDN'T **WANT** TO UNDERSTAND YOU. I WANTED TO STAND ON MY OWN, LIKE DAD. LIKE HELLER COSANOVA. MY OWN MAN.
BUT THEY WERE ALL PSYCHOPATHS. THEY JUST TAUGHT US TO COMPETE, RATHER THAN THRIVE TOGETHER.
I KNOW IT'S SELFISH, BUT IF I LET YOU ROT IN THERE, I WAS LETTING THOSE BASTARDS WIN. I HAD TO DO SOMETHING. I HAD TO DO **SOMETHING.** EVEN IF IT MEANT...
I KNOW. AND YOU HAVE TO KNOW, DEWYDD. I APPRECIATE IT. YOU'RE MY BROTHER AND YOU DIDN'T LEAVE ME IN THE VOID.
IT'S JUST...I...
...I WANTED TO DIE ON EARTH.

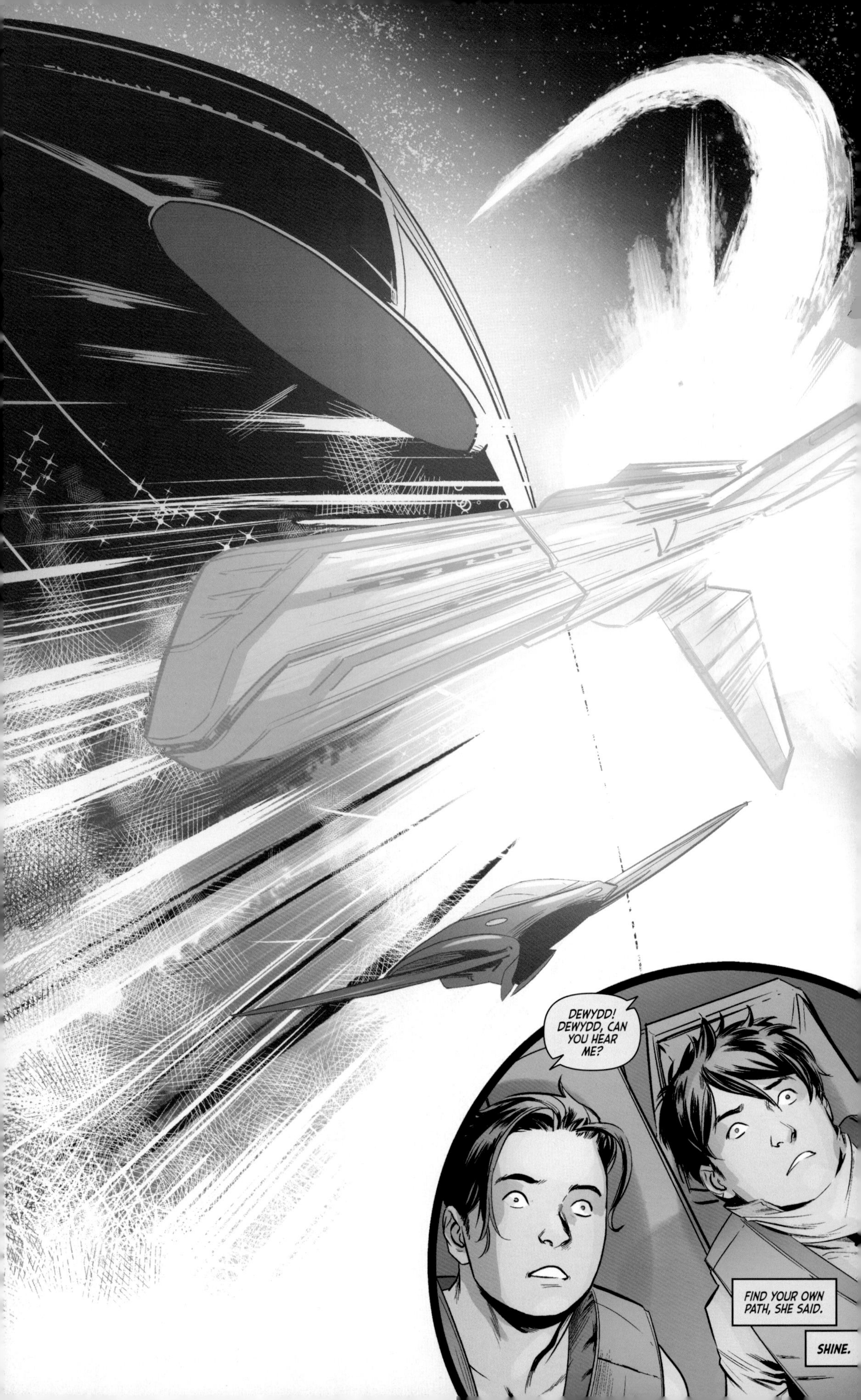
DEWYDD! DEWYDD, CAN YOU HEAR ME?
FIND YOUR OWN PATH, SHE SAID.
SHINE.

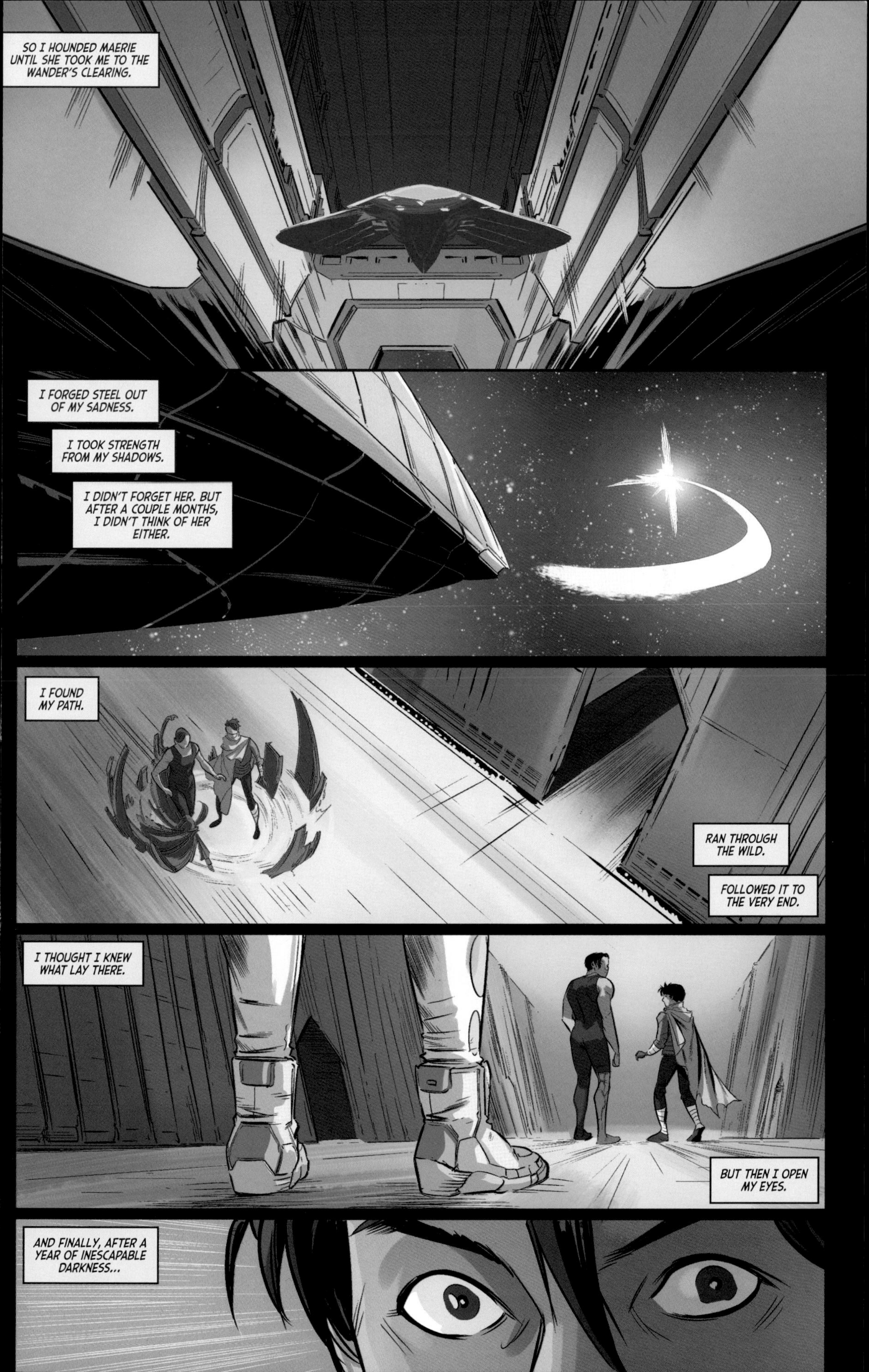
SO I HOUNDED MAERIE UNTIL SHE TOOK ME TO THE WANDER'S CLEARING.
I FORGED STEEL OUT OF MY SADNESS.
I TOOK STRENGTH FROM MY SHADOWS.
I DIDN'T FORGET HER. BUT AFTER A COUPLE MONTHS, I DIDN'T THINK OF HER EITHER.
I FOUND MY PATH.
RAN THROUGH THE WILD.
FOLLOWED IT TO THE VERY END.
I THOUGHT I KNEW WHAT LAY THERE.
BUT THEN I OPEN MY EYES.
AND FINALLY, AFTER A YEAR OF INESCAPABLE DARKNESS...

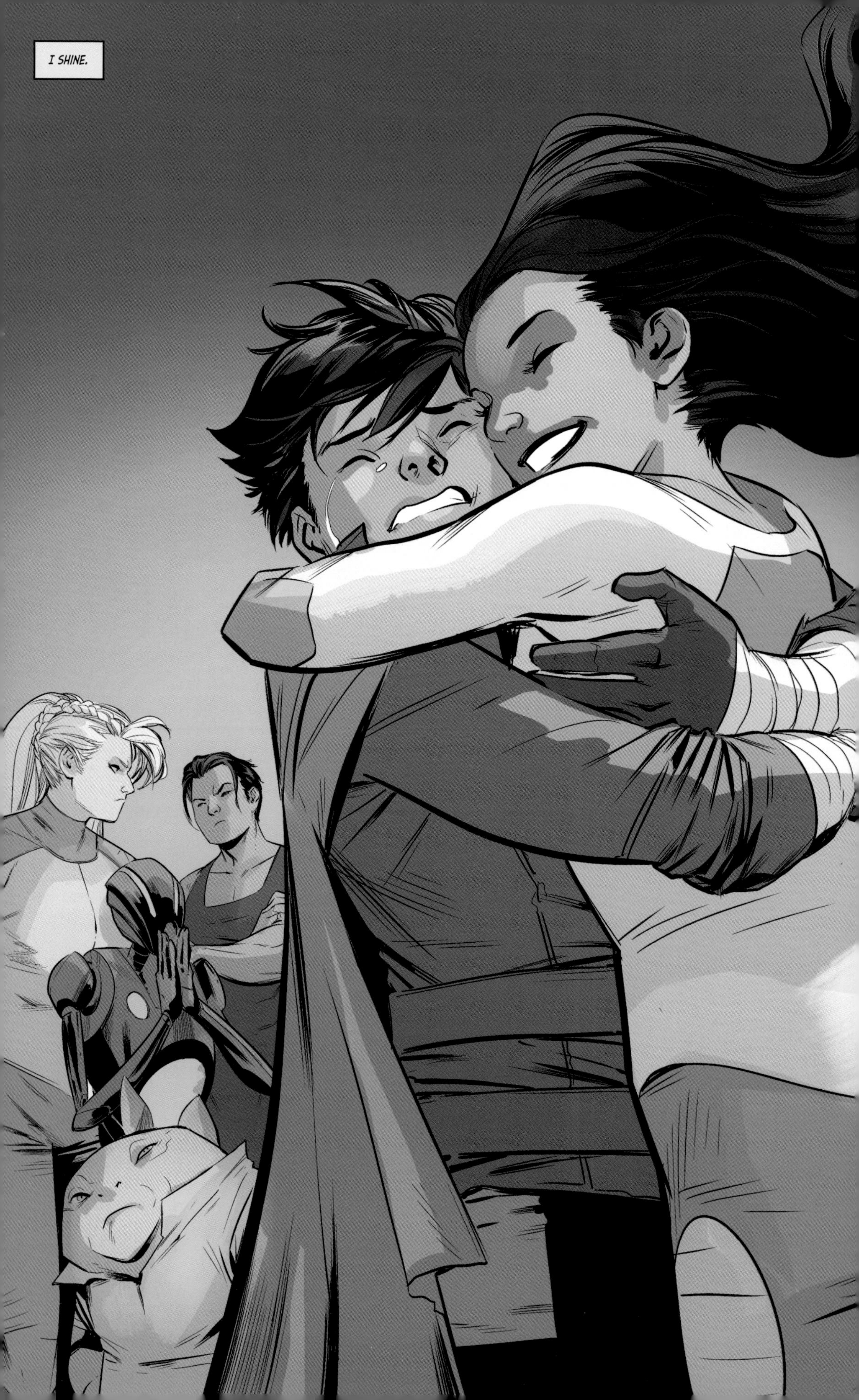
I SHINE.

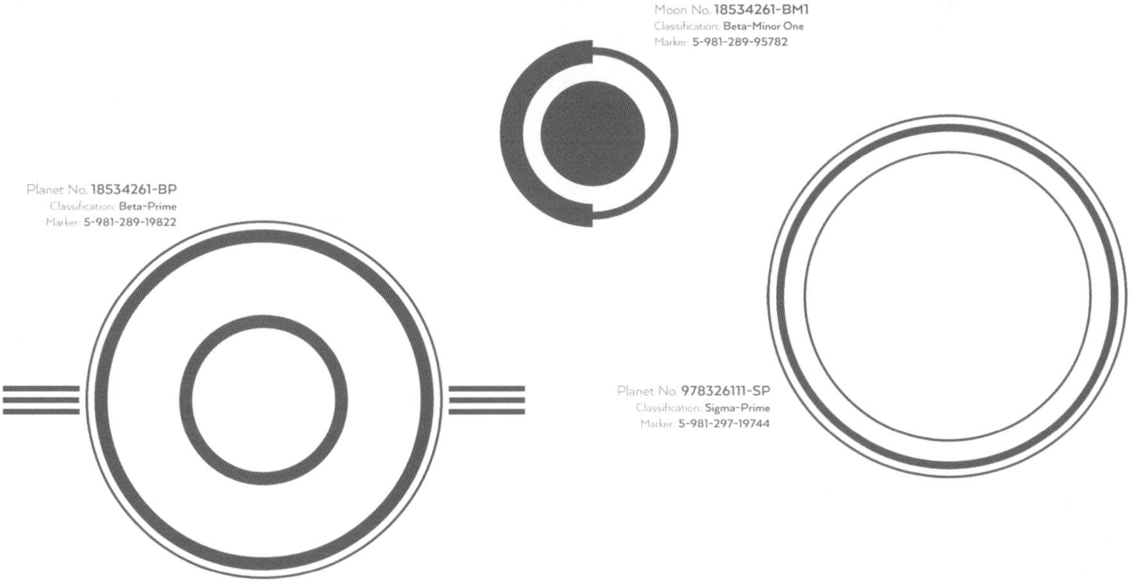
Moon No. 18534261-BM1
Classification: Beta-Minor One
Marker: 5-981-289-95782
Planet No. 18534261-BP
Classification: Beta-Prime
Marker: 5-981-289-19822
Planet No. 978326111-SP
Classification: Sigma-Prime
Marker: 5-981-297-19744

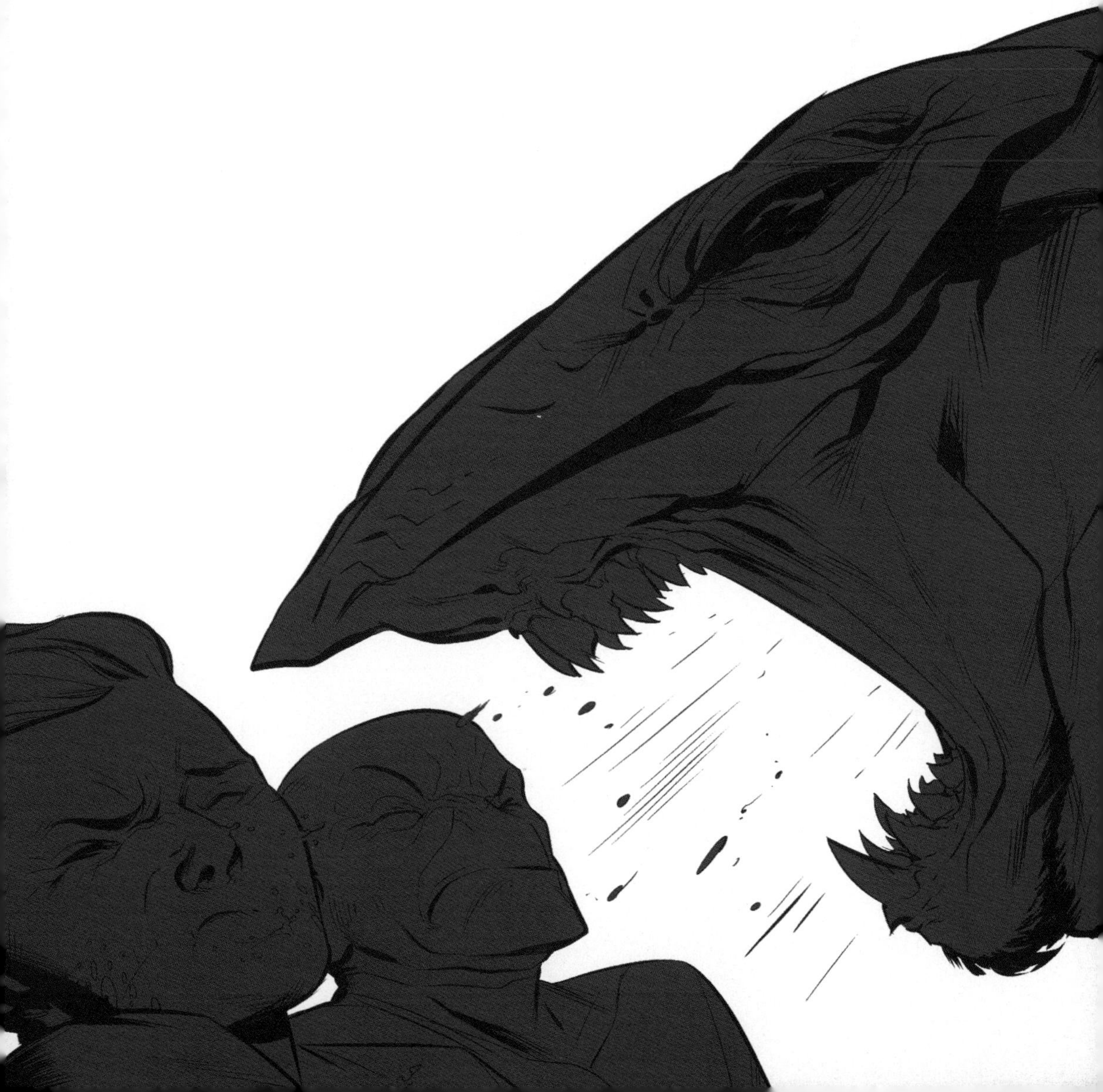

CHAPTER **ELEVEN**
TOUCH THE SKY

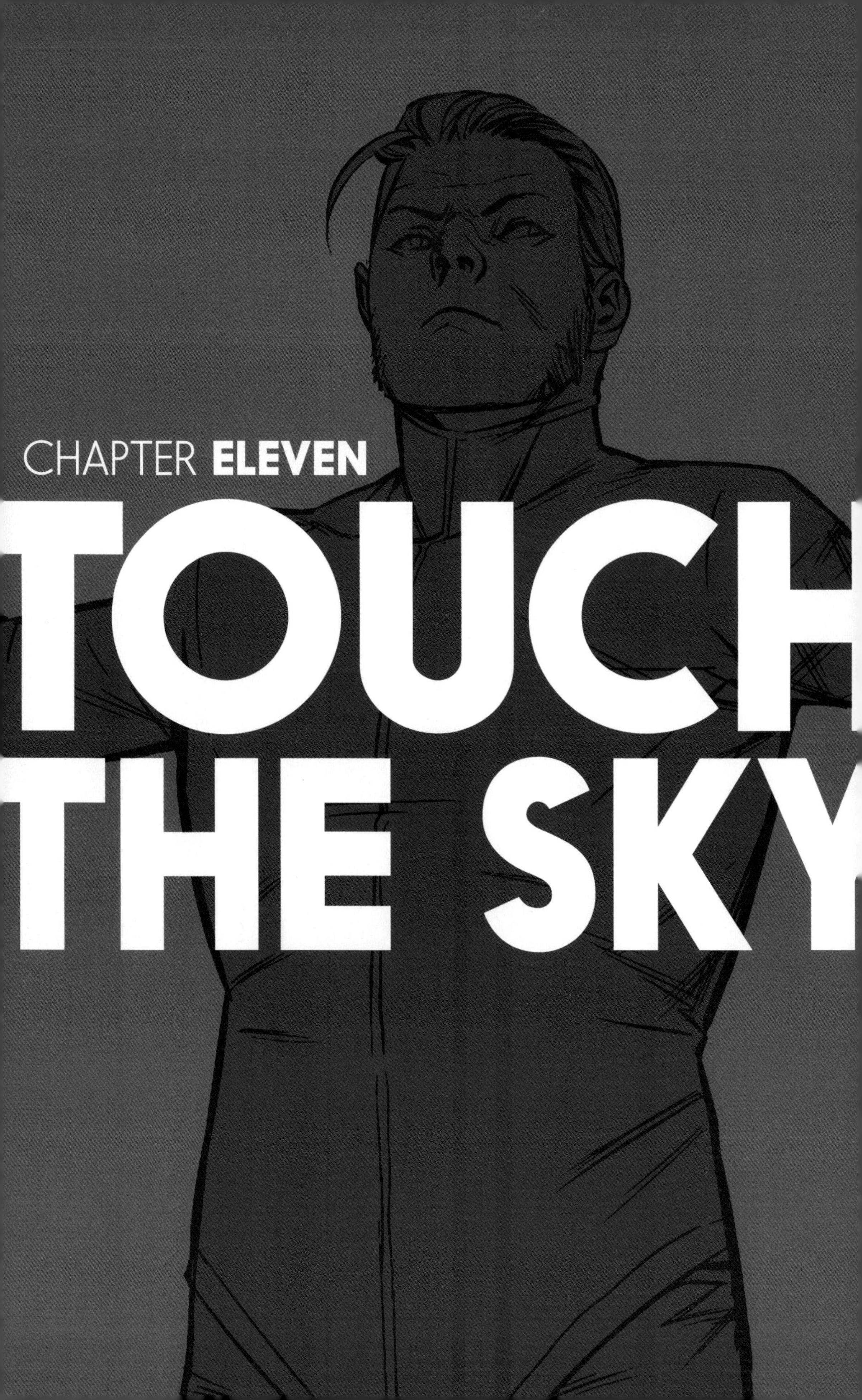

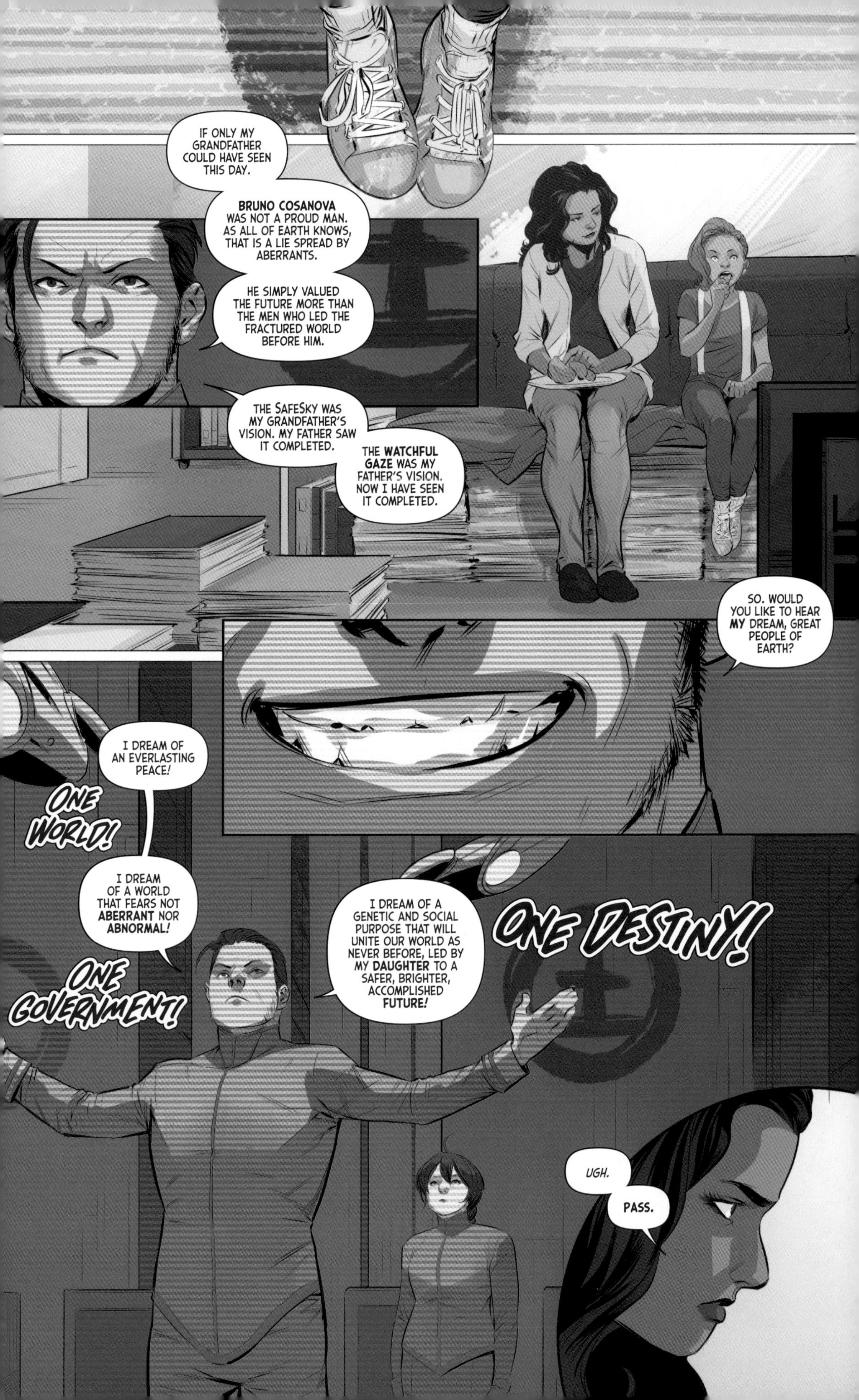

IF ONLY MY GRANDFATHER COULD HAVE SEEN THIS DAY.
BRUNO COSANOVA WAS NOT A PROUD MAN. AS ALL OF EARTH KNOWS, THAT IS A LIE SPREAD BY ABERRANTS.
HE SIMPLY VALUED THE FUTURE MORE THAN THE MEN WHO LED THE FRACTURED WORLD BEFORE HIM.
THE SAFESKY WAS MY GRANDFATHER'S VISION. MY FATHER SAW IT COMPLETED.
THE WATCHFUL GAZE WAS MY FATHER'S VISION. NOW I HAVE SEEN IT COMPLETED.
SO. WOULD YOU LIKE TO HEAR MY DREAM, GREAT PEOPLE OF EARTH?
I DREAM OF AN EVERLASTING PEACE!
ONE WORLD!
I DREAM OF A WORLD THAT FEARS NOT ABERRANT NOR ABNORMAL!
ONE GOVERNMENT!
I DREAM OF A GENETIC AND SOCIAL PURPOSE THAT WILL UNITE OUR WORLD AS NEVER BEFORE, LED BY MY DAUGHTER TO A SAFER, BRIGHTER, ACCOMPLISHED FUTURE!
ONE DESTINY!
UGH.
PASS.

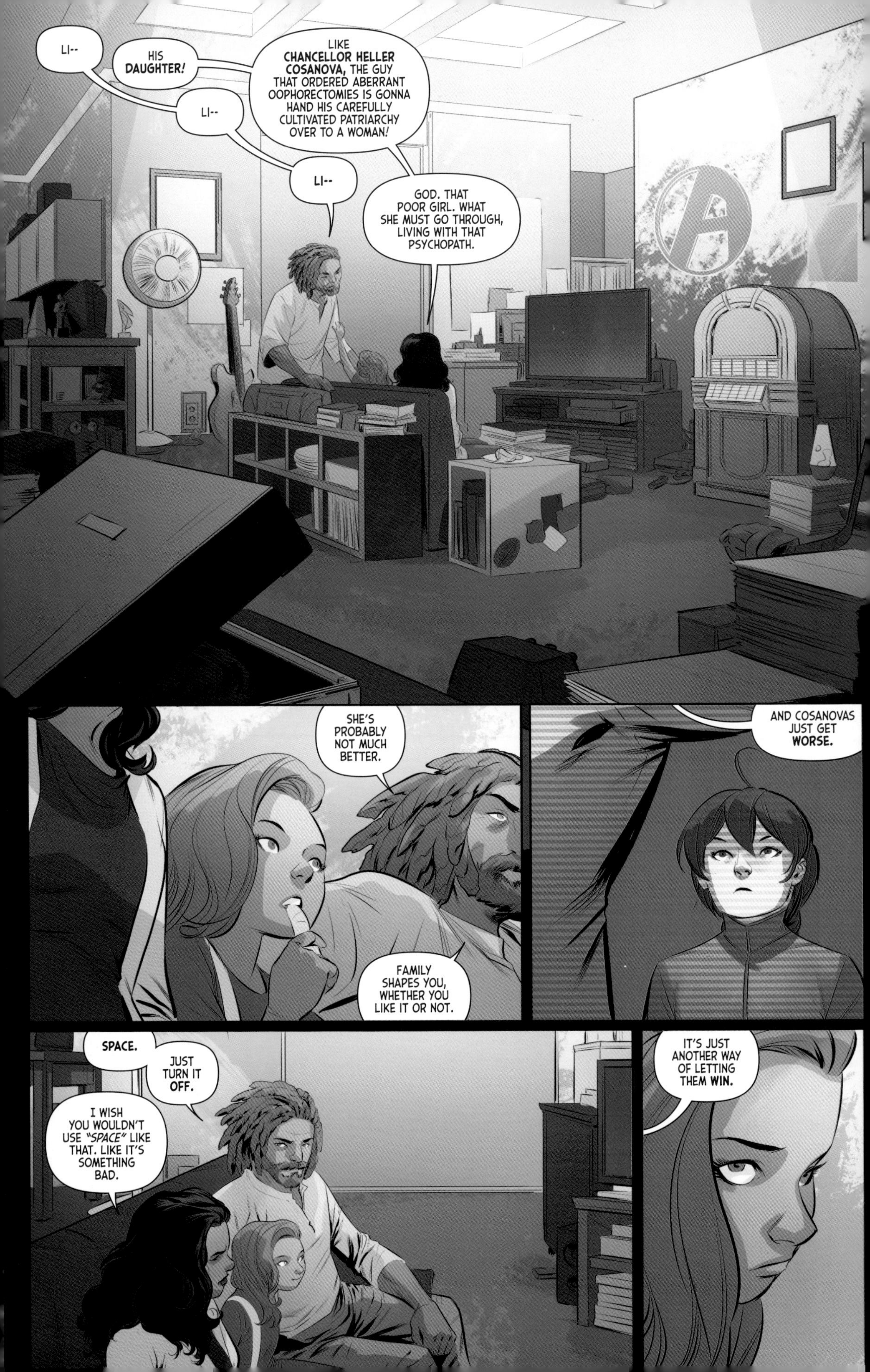

LI--
HIS DAUGHTER!
LIKE CHANCELLOR HELLER COSANOVA, THE GUY THAT ORDERED ABERRANT OOPHORECTOMIES IS GONNA HAND HIS CAREFULLY CULTIVATED PATRIARCHY OVER TO A WOMAN!
LI--
LI--
GOD. THAT POOR GIRL. WHAT SHE MUST GO THROUGH, LIVING WITH THAT PSYCHOPATH.
SHE'S PROBABLY NOT MUCH BETTER.
FAMILY SHAPES YOU, WHETHER YOU LIKE IT OR NOT.
AND COSANOVAS JUST GET WORSE.
SPACE.
JUST TURN IT OFF.
I WISH YOU WOULDN'T USE "SPACE" LIKE THAT. LIKE IT'S SOMETHING BAD.
IT'S JUST ANOTHER WAY OF LETTING THEM WIN.

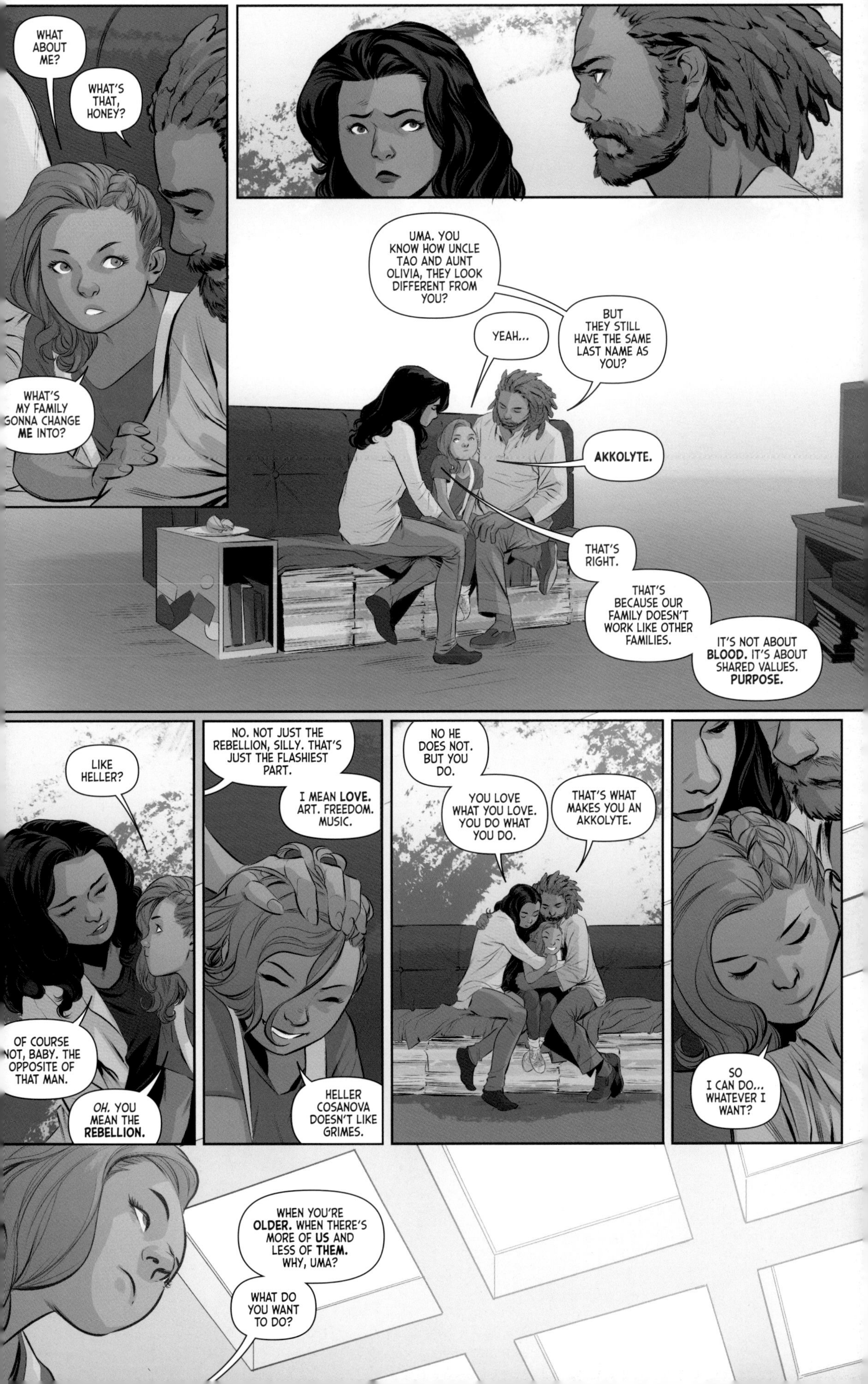

WHAT ABOUT ME?
WHAT'S THAT, HONEY?
WHAT'S MY FAMILY GONNA CHANGE **ME** INTO?
UMA. YOU KNOW HOW UNCLE TAO AND AUNT OLIVIA, THEY LOOK DIFFERENT FROM YOU?
YEAH...
BUT THEY STILL HAVE THE SAME LAST NAME AS YOU?
AKKOLYTE.
THAT'S RIGHT.
THAT'S BECAUSE OUR FAMILY DOESN'T WORK LIKE OTHER FAMILIES.
IT'S NOT ABOUT **BLOOD.** IT'S ABOUT SHARED VALUES. **PURPOSE.**
LIKE HELLER?
OF COURSE NOT, BABY. THE OPPOSITE OF THAT MAN.
OH. YOU MEAN THE **REBELLION.**
NO. NOT JUST THE REBELLION, SILLY. THAT'S JUST THE FLASHIEST PART.
I MEAN **LOVE.** ART. FREEDOM. MUSIC.
HELLER COSANOVA DOESN'T LIKE GRIMES.
NO HE DOES NOT. BUT YOU DO.
YOU LOVE WHAT YOU LOVE. YOU DO WHAT YOU DO.
THAT'S WHAT MAKES YOU AN AKKOLYTE.
SO I CAN DO... WHATEVER I WANT?
WHEN YOU'RE **OLDER.** WHEN THERE'S MORE OF **US** AND LESS OF **THEM.** WHY, UMA?
WHAT DO YOU WANT TO DO?

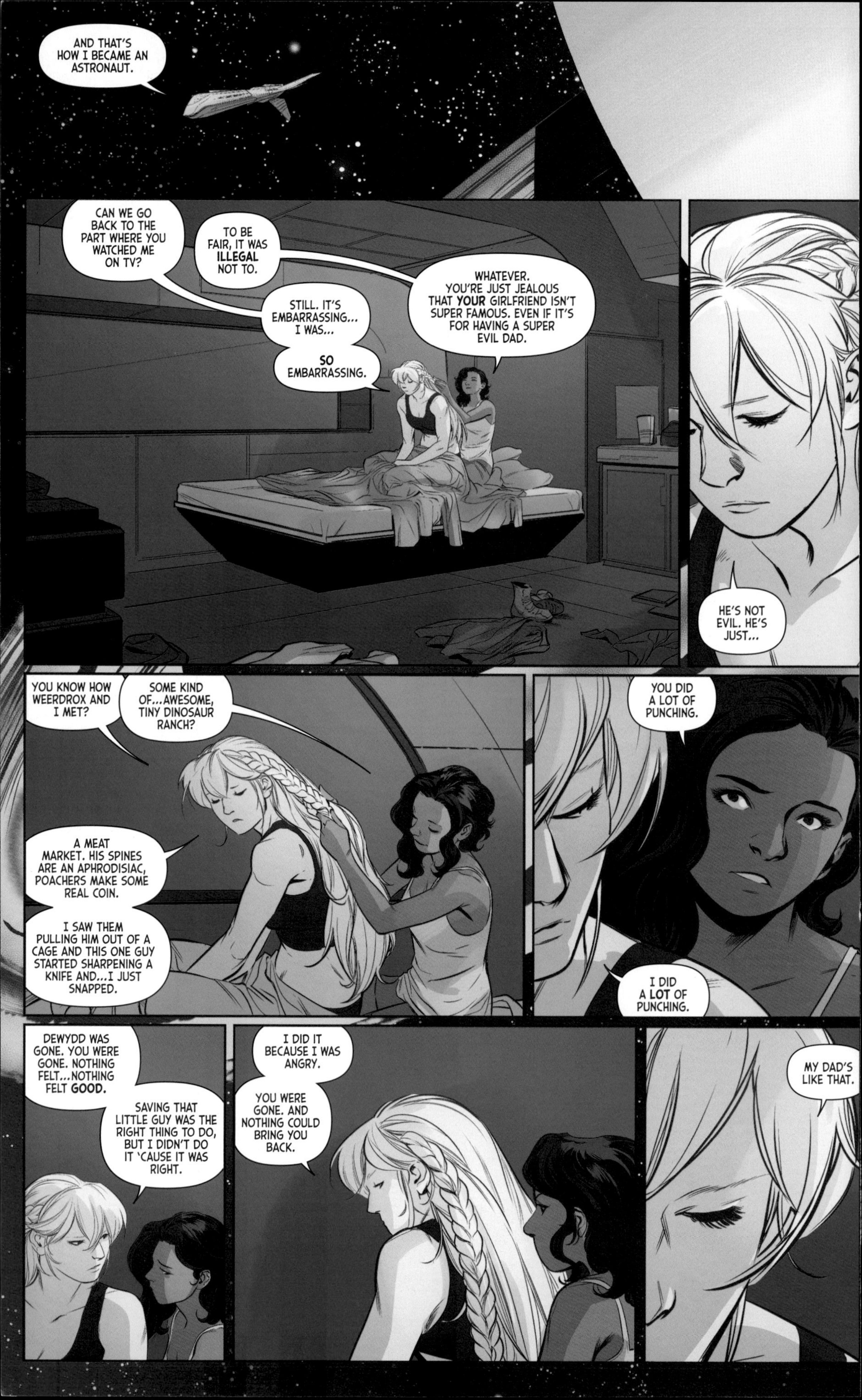
AND THAT'S HOW I BECAME AN ASTRONAUT.
CAN WE GO BACK TO THE PART WHERE YOU WATCHED ME ON TV?
TO BE FAIR, IT WAS **ILLEGAL** NOT TO.
STILL. IT'S EMBARRASSING... I WAS...
SO EMBARRASSING.
WHATEVER. YOU'RE JUST JEALOUS THAT **YOUR** GIRLFRIEND ISN'T SUPER FAMOUS. EVEN IF IT'S FOR HAVING A SUPER EVIL DAD.
HE'S NOT EVIL. HE'S JUST...
YOU KNOW HOW WEERDROX AND I MET?
SOME KIND OF...AWESOME, TINY DINOSAUR RANCH?
A MEAT MARKET. HIS SPINES ARE AN APHRODISIAC, POACHERS MAKE SOME REAL COIN.
I SAW THEM PULLING HIM OUT OF A CAGE AND THIS ONE GUY STARTED SHARPENING A KNIFE AND...I JUST SNAPPED.
YOU DID A LOT OF PUNCHING.
I DID A **LOT** OF PUNCHING.
DEWYDD WAS GONE. YOU WERE GONE. NOTHING FELT...NOTHING FELT **GOOD.**
SAVING THAT LITTLE GUY WAS THE RIGHT THING TO DO, BUT I DIDN'T DO IT 'CAUSE IT WAS RIGHT.
I DID IT BECAUSE I WAS ANGRY.
YOU WERE GONE. AND NOTHING COULD BRING YOU BACK.
MY DAD'S LIKE THAT.

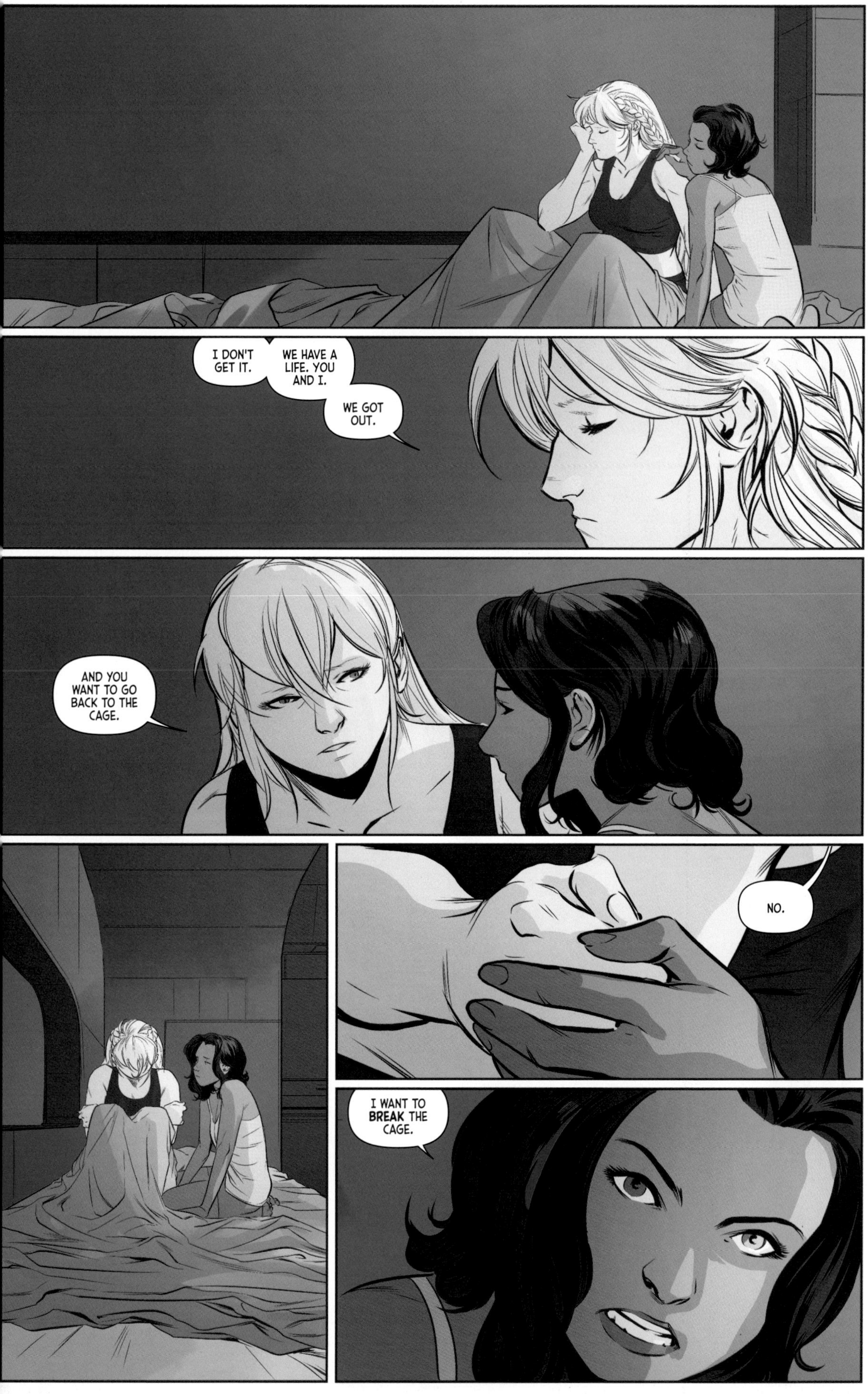
I DON'T GET IT.
WE HAVE A LIFE. YOU AND I.
WE GOT OUT.
AND YOU WANT TO GO BACK TO THE CAGE.
NO.
I WANT TO **BREAK** THE CAGE.

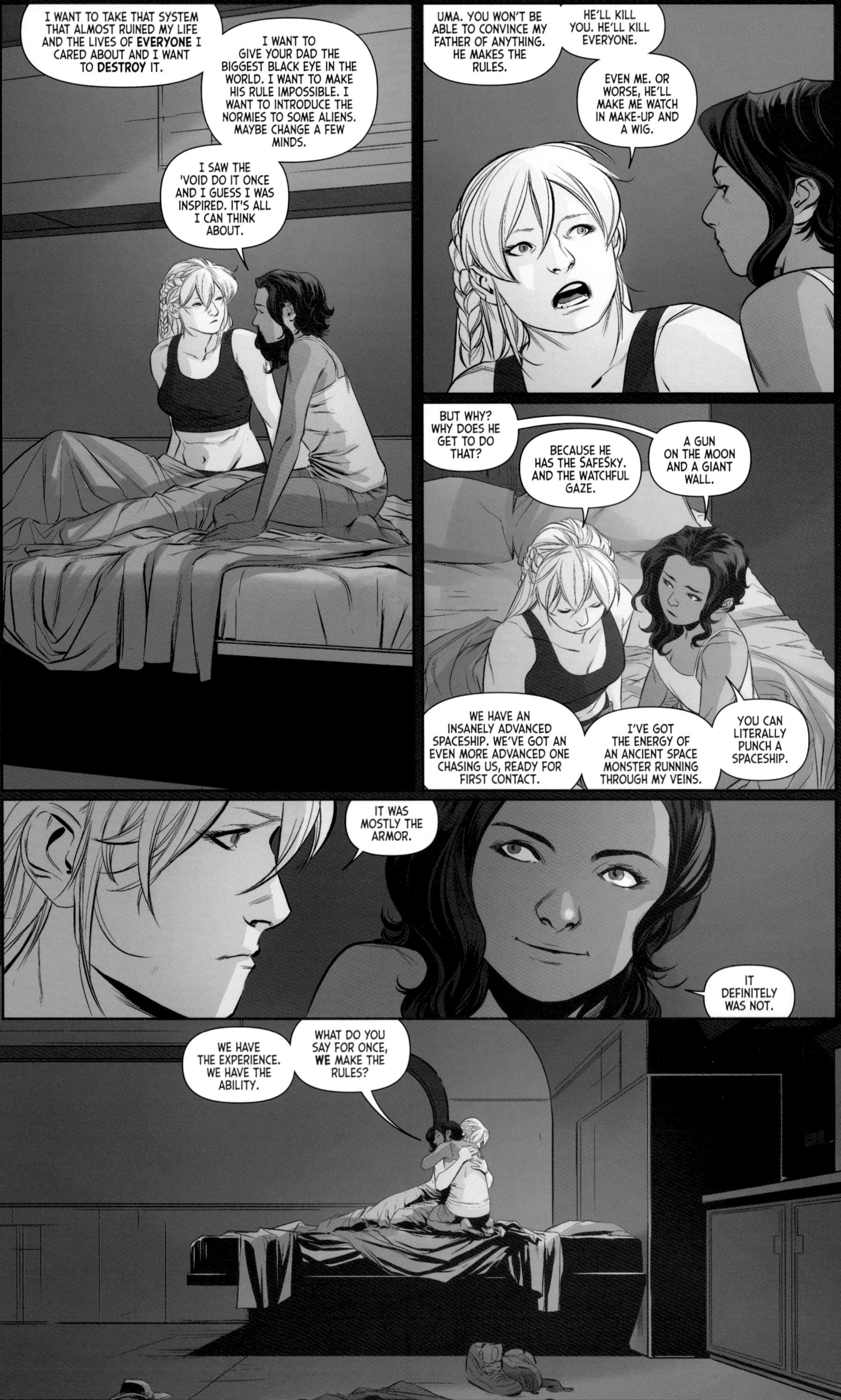
I WANT TO TAKE THAT SYSTEM THAT ALMOST RUINED MY LIFE AND THE LIVES OF **EVERYONE** I CARED ABOUT AND I WANT TO **DESTROY** IT.
I WANT TO GIVE YOUR DAD THE BIGGEST BLACK EYE IN THE WORLD. I WANT TO MAKE HIS RULE IMPOSSIBLE. I WANT TO INTRODUCE THE NORMIES TO SOME ALIENS. MAYBE CHANGE A FEW MINDS.
I SAW THE 'VOID DO IT ONCE AND I GUESS I WAS INSPIRED. IT'S ALL I CAN THINK ABOUT.
UMA. YOU WON'T BE ABLE TO CONVINCE MY FATHER OF ANYTHING. HE MAKES THE RULES.
HE'LL KILL YOU. HE'LL KILL EVERYONE.
EVEN ME. OR WORSE, HE'LL MAKE ME WATCH IN MAKE-UP AND A WIG.
BUT WHY? WHY DOES HE GET TO DO THAT?
BECAUSE HE HAS THE SAFESKY. AND THE WATCHFUL GAZE.
A GUN ON THE MOON AND A GIANT WALL.
WE HAVE AN INSANELY ADVANCED SPACESHIP. WE'VE GOT AN EVEN MORE ADVANCED ONE CHASING US, READY FOR FIRST CONTACT.
I'VE GOT THE ENERGY OF AN ANCIENT SPACE MONSTER RUNNING THROUGH MY VEINS.
YOU CAN LITERALLY PUNCH A SPACESHIP.
IT WAS MOSTLY THE ARMOR.
IT DEFINITELY WAS NOT.
WE HAVE THE EXPERIENCE. WE HAVE THE ABILITY.
WHAT DO YOU SAY FOR ONCE, **WE** MAKE THE RULES?

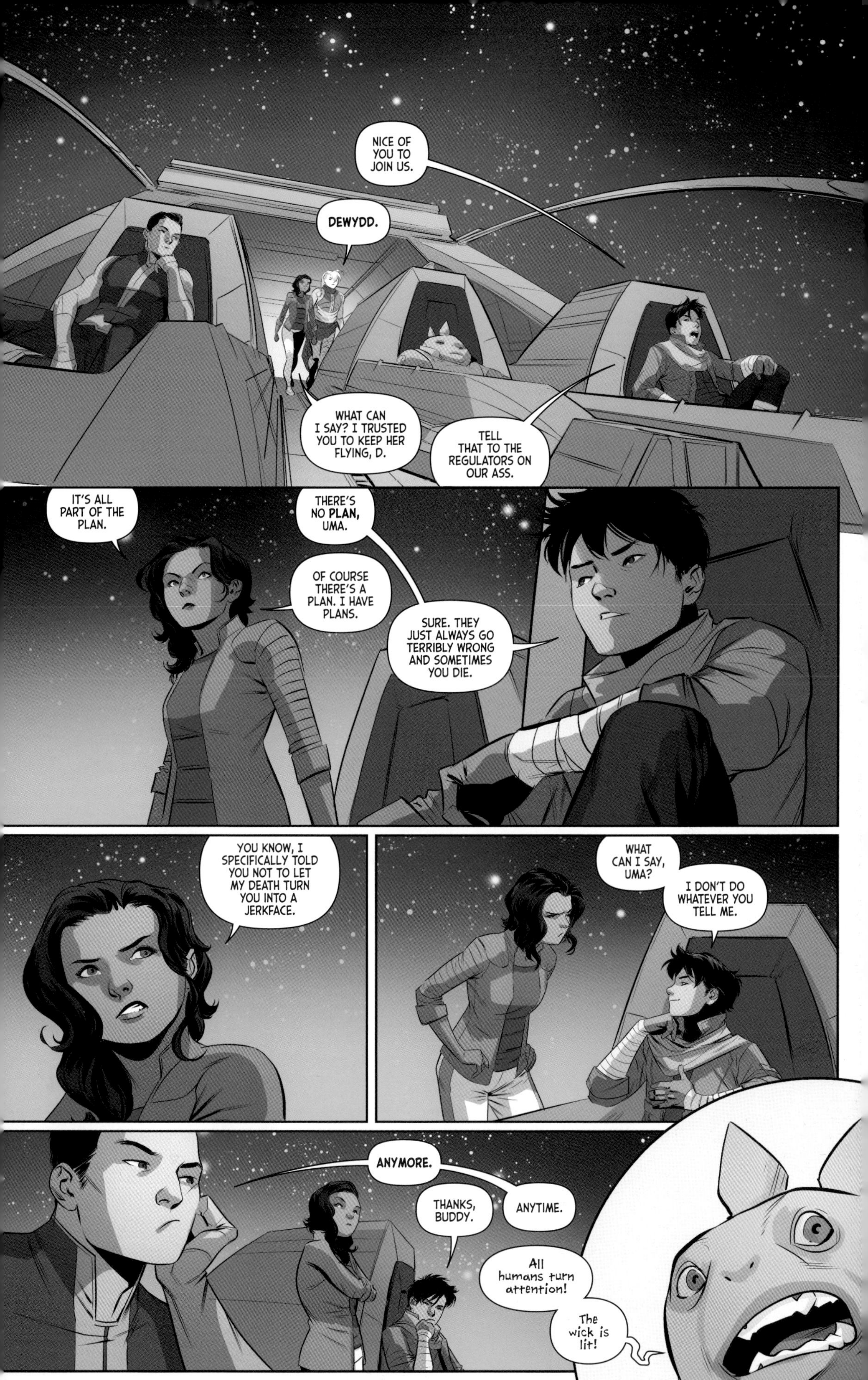
NICE OF YOU TO JOIN US.
DEWYDD.
WHAT CAN I SAY? I TRUSTED YOU TO KEEP HER FLYING, D.
TELL THAT TO THE REGULATORS ON OUR ASS.
IT'S ALL PART OF THE PLAN.
THERE'S NO PLAN, UMA.
OF COURSE THERE'S A PLAN. I HAVE PLANS.
SURE. THEY JUST ALWAYS GO TERRIBLY WRONG AND SOMETIMES YOU DIE.
YOU KNOW, I SPECIFICALLY TOLD YOU NOT TO LET MY DEATH TURN YOU INTO A JERKFACE.
WHAT CAN I SAY, UMA?
I DON'T DO WHATEVER YOU TELL ME.
ANYMORE.
THANKS, BUDDY.
ANYTIME.
All humans turn attention!
The wick is lit!

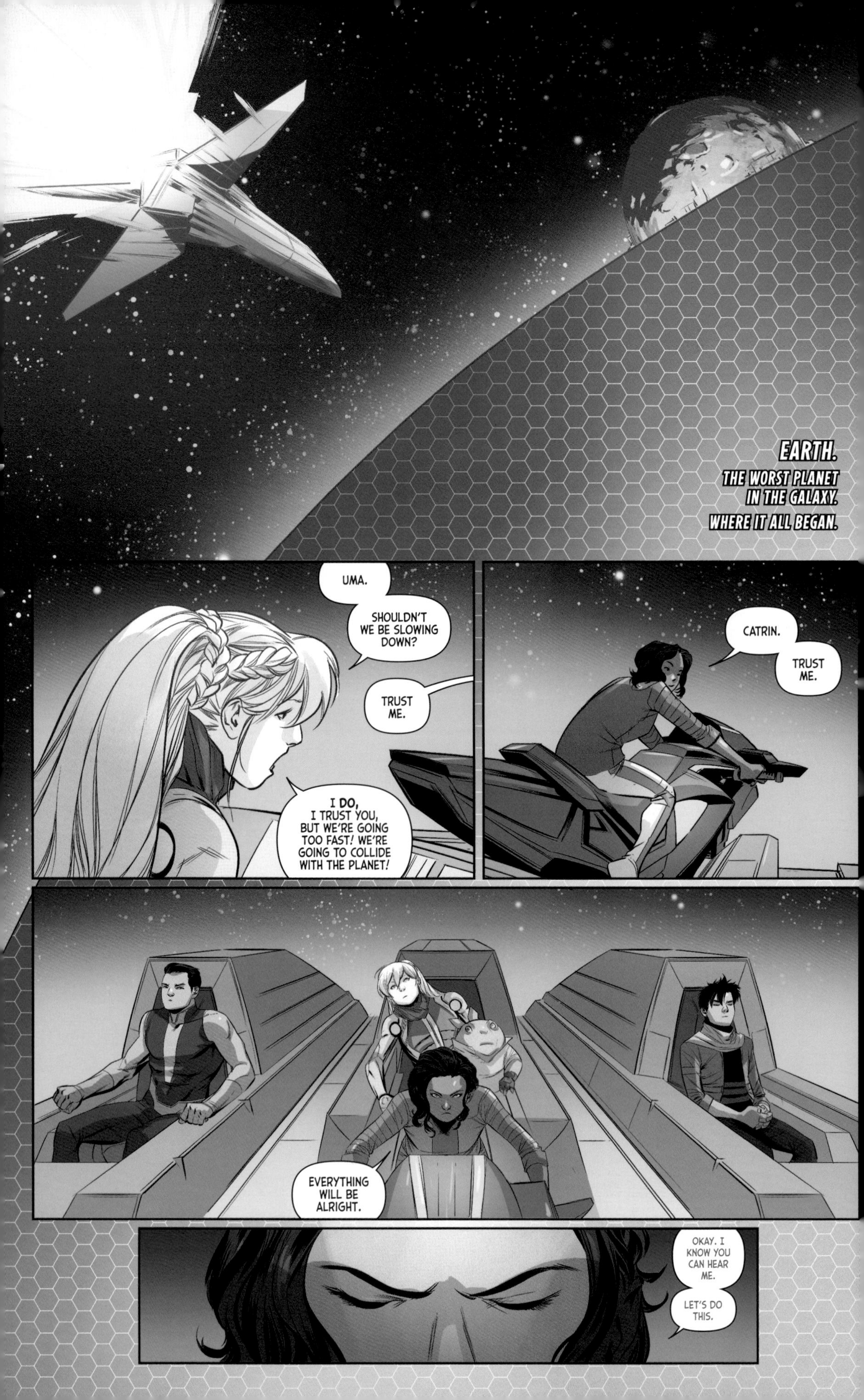
EARTH.
THE WORST PLANET IN THE GALAXY.
WHERE IT ALL BEGAN.
UMA.
SHOULDN'T WE BE SLOWING DOWN?
TRUST ME.
I DO, I TRUST YOU, BUT WE'RE GOING TOO FAST! WE'RE GOING TO COLLIDE WITH THE PLANET!
CATRIN.
TRUST ME.
EVERYTHING WILL BE ALRIGHT.
OKAY. I KNOW YOU CAN HEAR ME.
LET'S DO THIS.

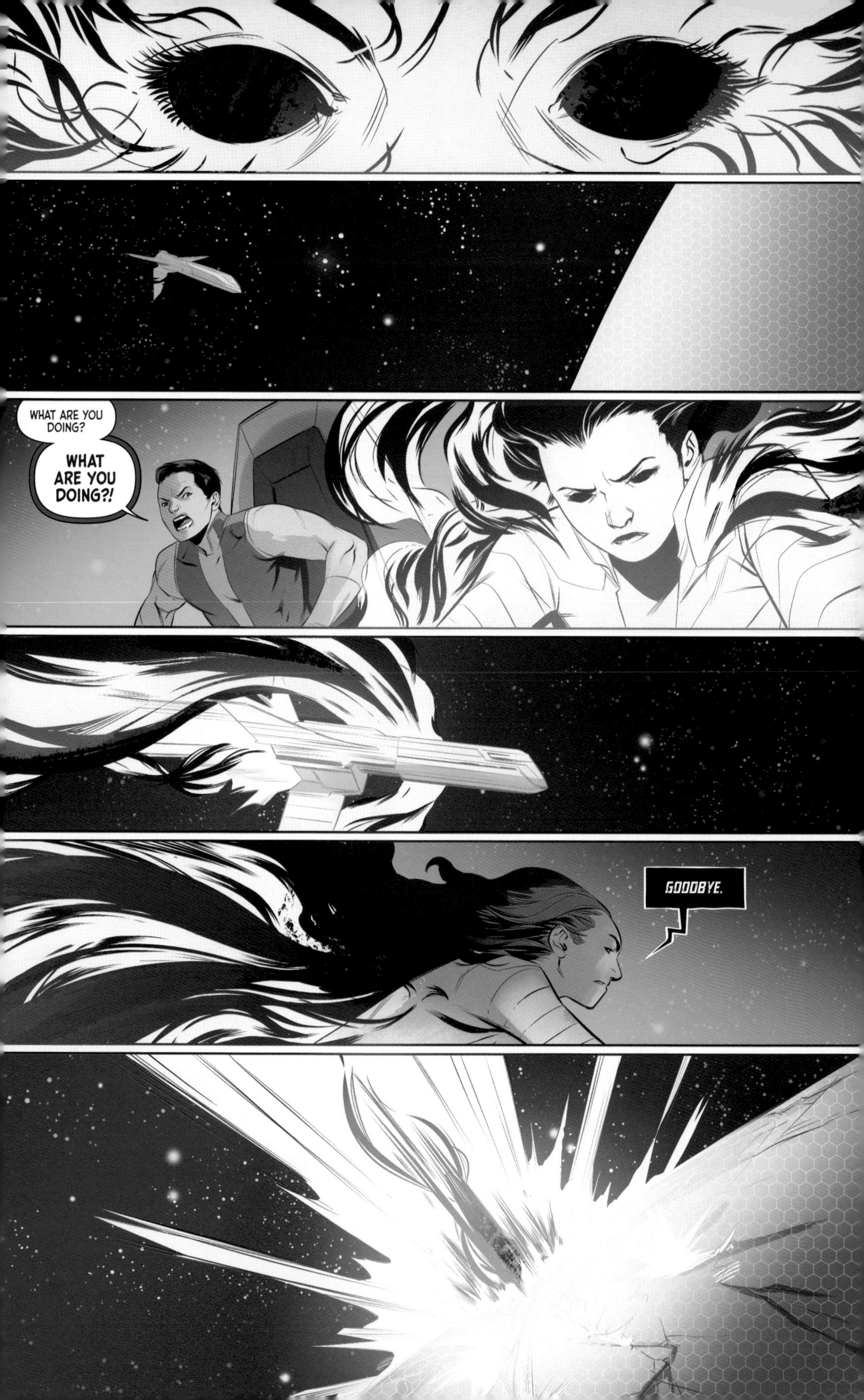
WHAT ARE YOU DOING?
WHAT ARE YOU DOING?!
GOODBYE.

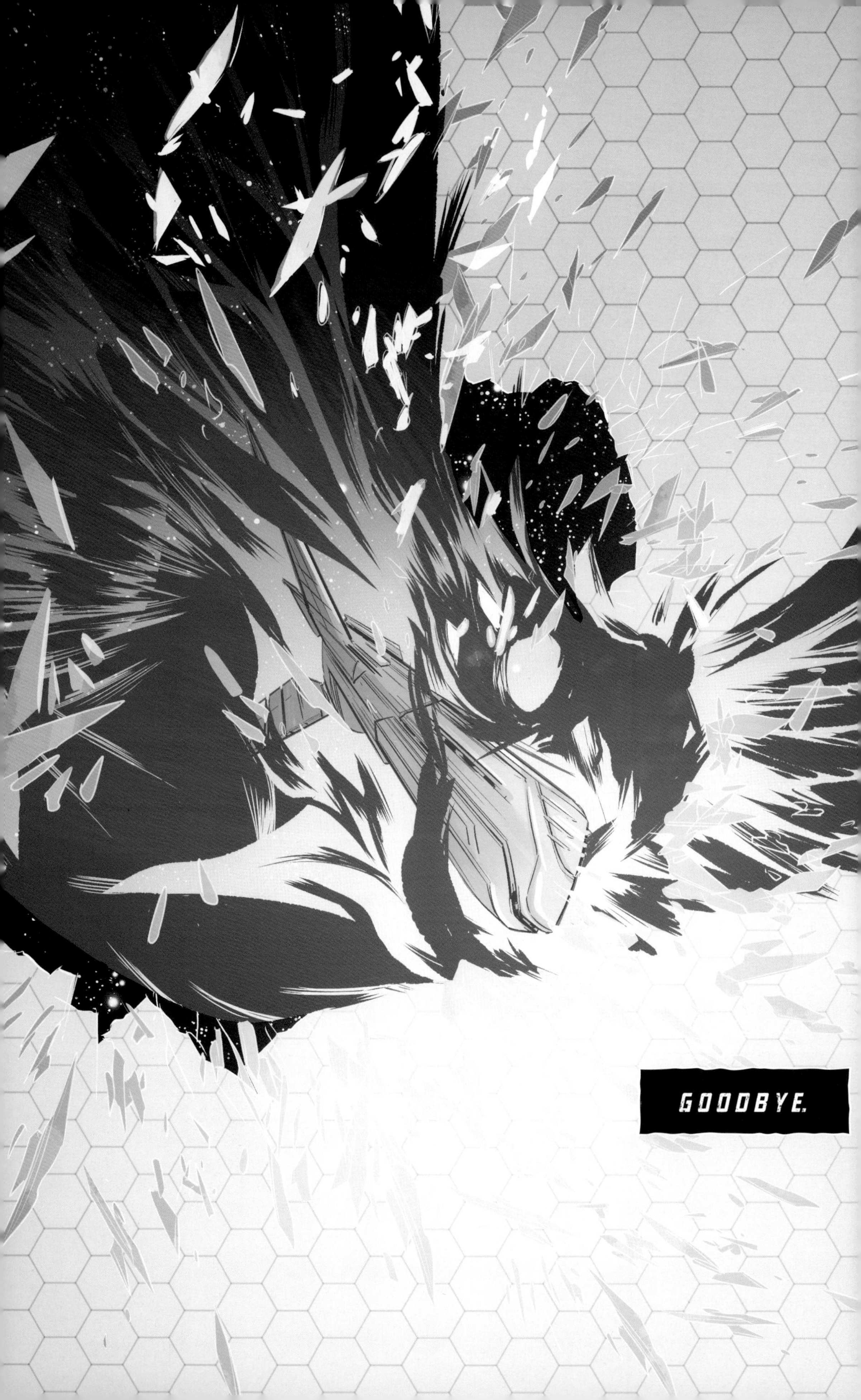
GOODBYE.

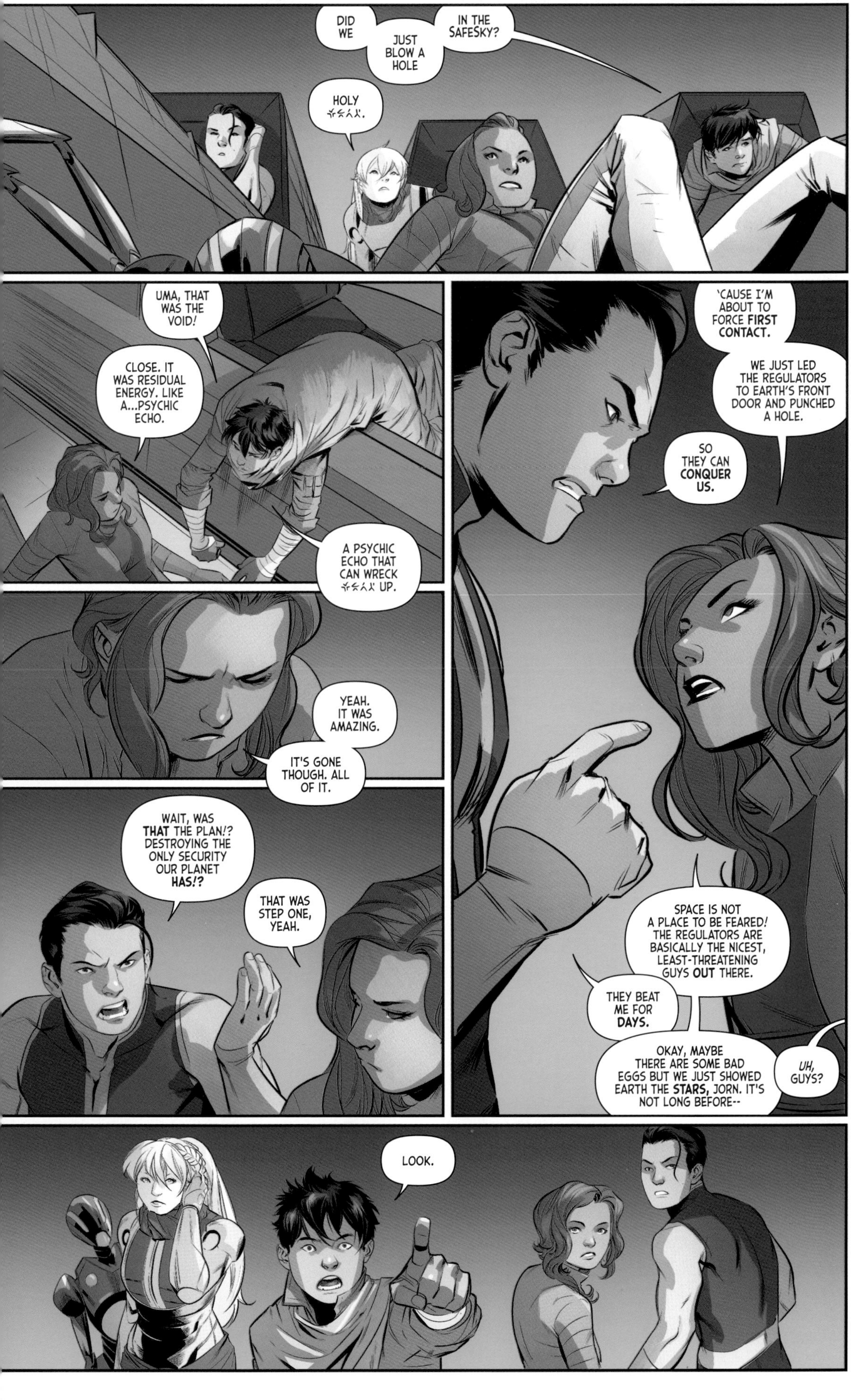
DID WE
JUST BLOW A HOLE
IN THE SAFESKY?
HOLY
UMA, THAT WAS THE VOID!
CLOSE. IT WAS RESIDUAL ENERGY. LIKE A...PSYCHIC ECHO.
A PSYCHIC ECHO THAT CAN WRECK UP.
YEAH. IT WAS AMAZING.
IT'S GONE THOUGH. ALL OF IT.
WAIT, WAS **THAT** THE PLAN!? DESTROYING THE ONLY SECURITY OUR PLANET **HAS!?**
THAT WAS STEP ONE, YEAH.
'CAUSE I'M ABOUT TO FORCE **FIRST CONTACT.**
WE JUST LED THE REGULATORS TO EARTH'S FRONT DOOR AND PUNCHED A HOLE.
SO THEY CAN **CONQUER US.**
SPACE IS NOT A PLACE TO BE FEARED! THE REGULATORS ARE BASICALLY THE NICEST, LEAST-THREATENING GUYS **OUT** THERE.
THEY BEAT ME FOR **DAYS.**
OKAY, MAYBE THERE ARE SOME BAD EGGS BUT WE JUST SHOWED EARTH THE **STARS,** JORN. IT'S NOT LONG BEFORE--
UH, GUYS?
LOOK.

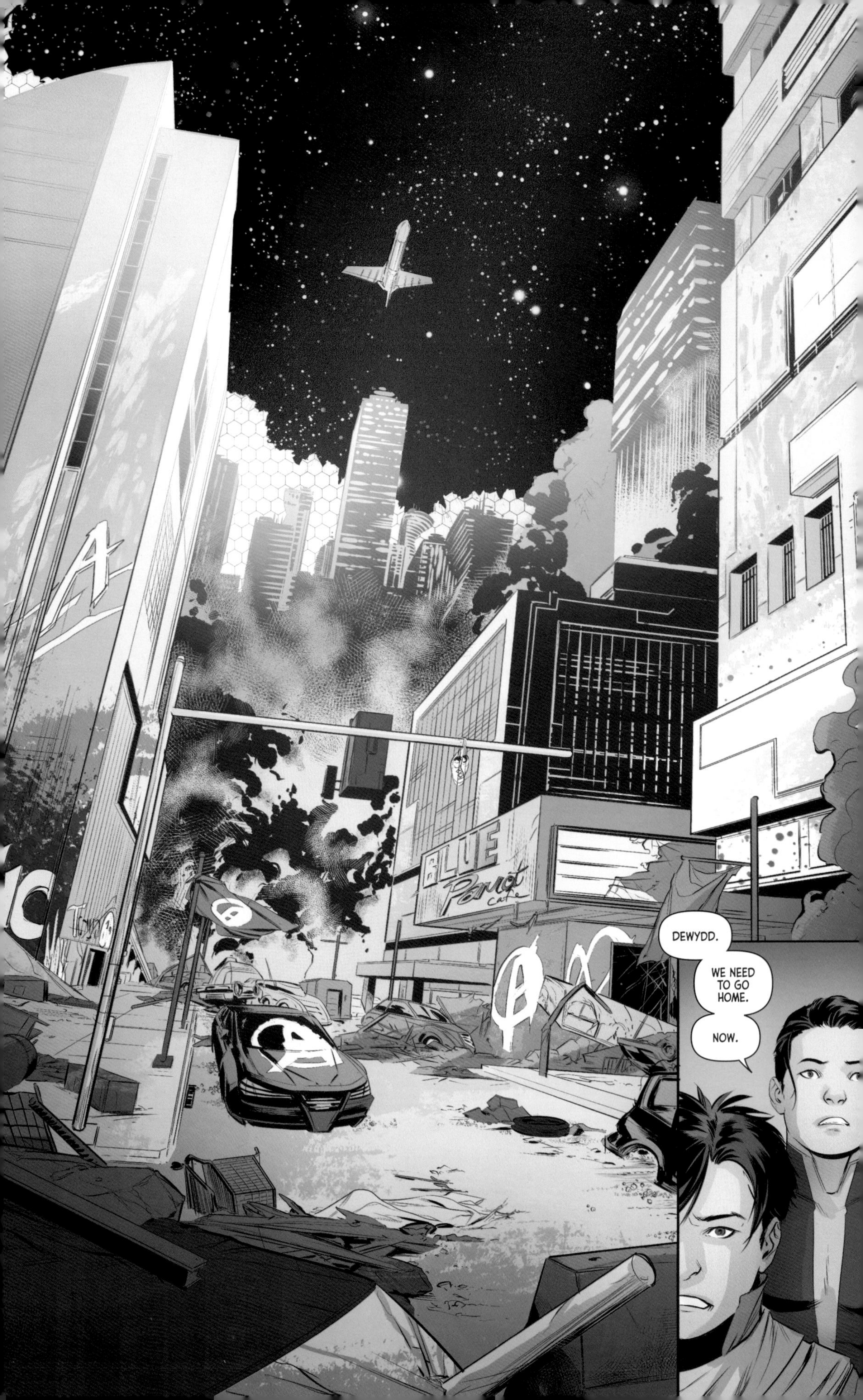

BLUE
Parrot
café
DEWYDD.
WE NEED TO GO HOME.
NOW.

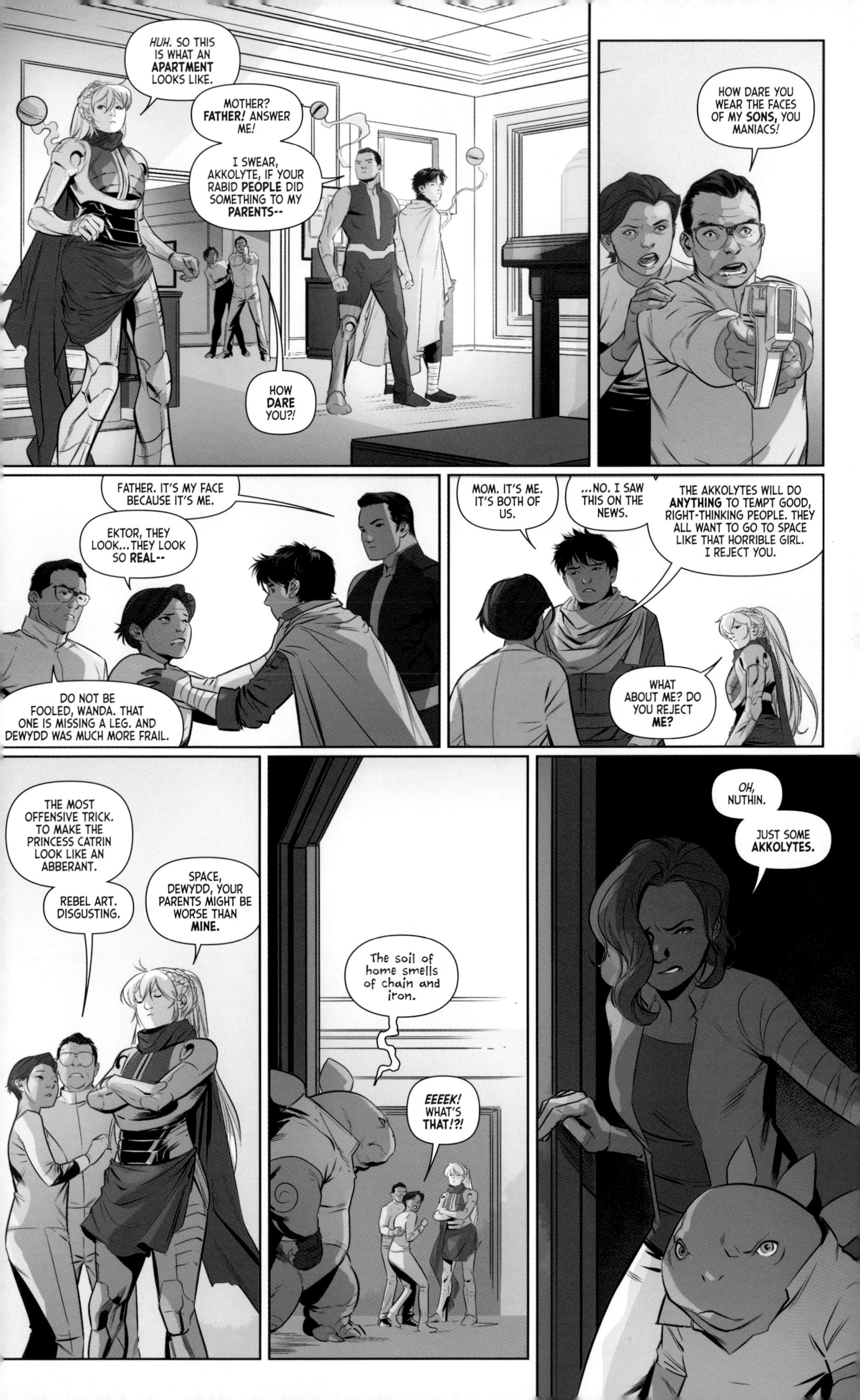
HUH. SO THIS IS WHAT AN APARTMENT LOOKS LIKE.
MOTHER? FATHER! ANSWER ME!
I SWEAR, AKKOLYTE, IF YOUR RABID PEOPLE DID SOMETHING TO MY PARENTS--
HOW DARE YOU?!
HOW DARE YOU WEAR THE FACES OF MY SONS, YOU MANIACS!
FATHER. IT'S MY FACE BECAUSE IT'S ME.
EKTOR, THEY LOOK...THEY LOOK SO REAL--
DO NOT BE FOOLED, WANDA. THAT ONE IS MISSING A LEG. AND DEWYDD WAS MUCH MORE FRAIL.
MOM. IT'S ME. IT'S BOTH OF US.
...NO. I SAW THIS ON THE NEWS.
THE AKKOLYTES WILL DO ANYTHING TO TEMPT GOOD, RIGHT-THINKING PEOPLE. THEY ALL WANT TO GO TO SPACE LIKE THAT HORRIBLE GIRL. I REJECT YOU.
WHAT ABOUT ME? DO YOU REJECT ME?
THE MOST OFFENSIVE TRICK. TO MAKE THE PRINCESS CATRIN LOOK LIKE AN ABBERANT.
REBEL ART. DISGUSTING.
SPACE, DEWYDD, YOUR PARENTS MIGHT BE WORSE THAN MINE.
The soil of home smells of chain and iron.
EEEEK! WHAT'S THAT!?!
OH, NUTHIN.
JUST SOME AKKOLYTES.

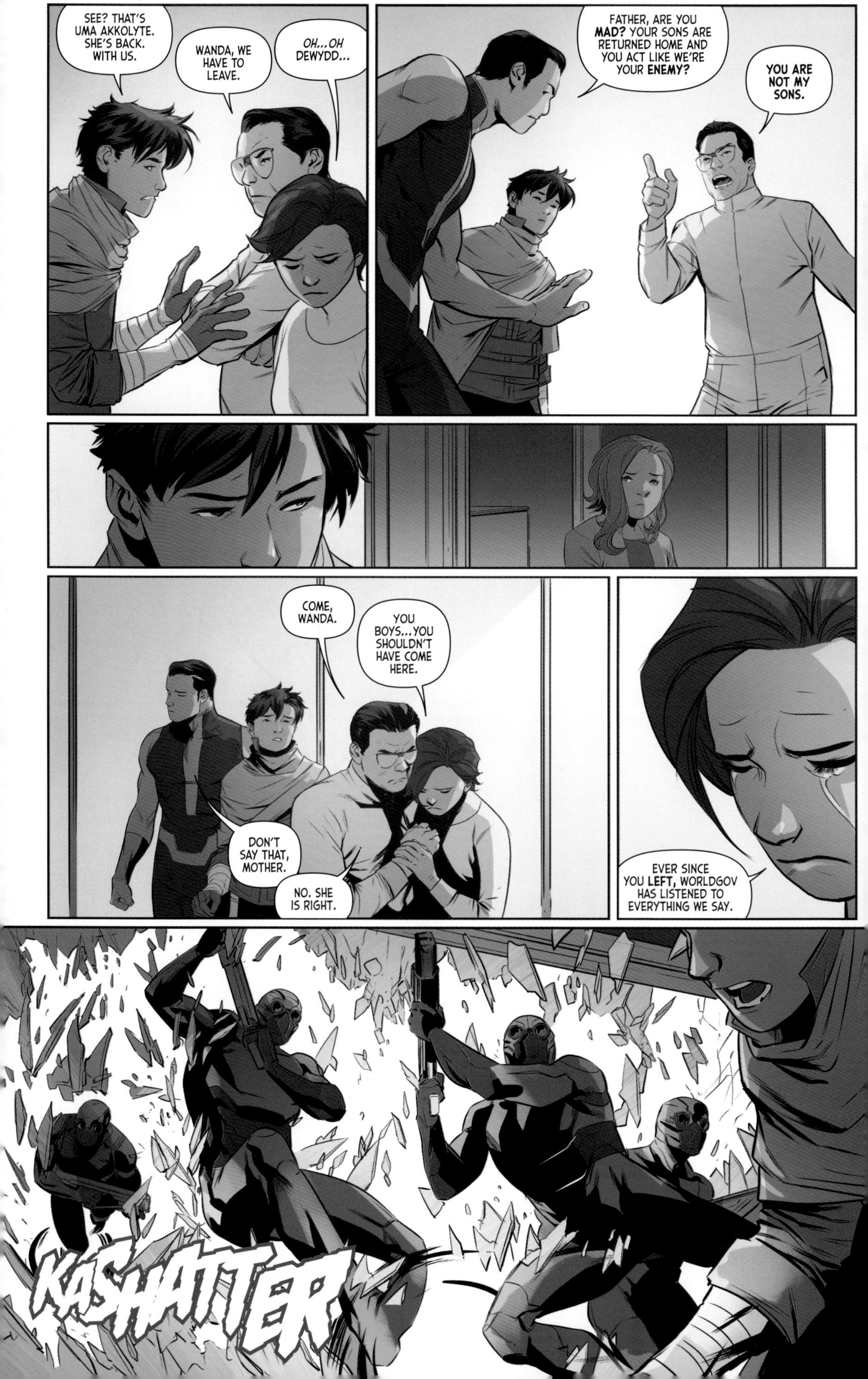
SEE? THAT'S UMA AKKOLYTE. SHE'S BACK. WITH US.
WANDA, WE HAVE TO LEAVE.
OH...OH DEWYDD...
FATHER, ARE YOU **MAD?** YOUR SONS ARE RETURNED HOME AND YOU ACT LIKE WE'RE YOUR **ENEMY?**
YOU ARE NOT MY SONS.
COME, WANDA.
YOU BOYS...YOU SHOULDN'T HAVE COME HERE.
DON'T SAY THAT, MOTHER.
NO. SHE IS RIGHT.
EVER SINCE YOU **LEFT,** WORLDGOV HAS LISTENED TO EVERYTHING WE SAY.
KASHATTER

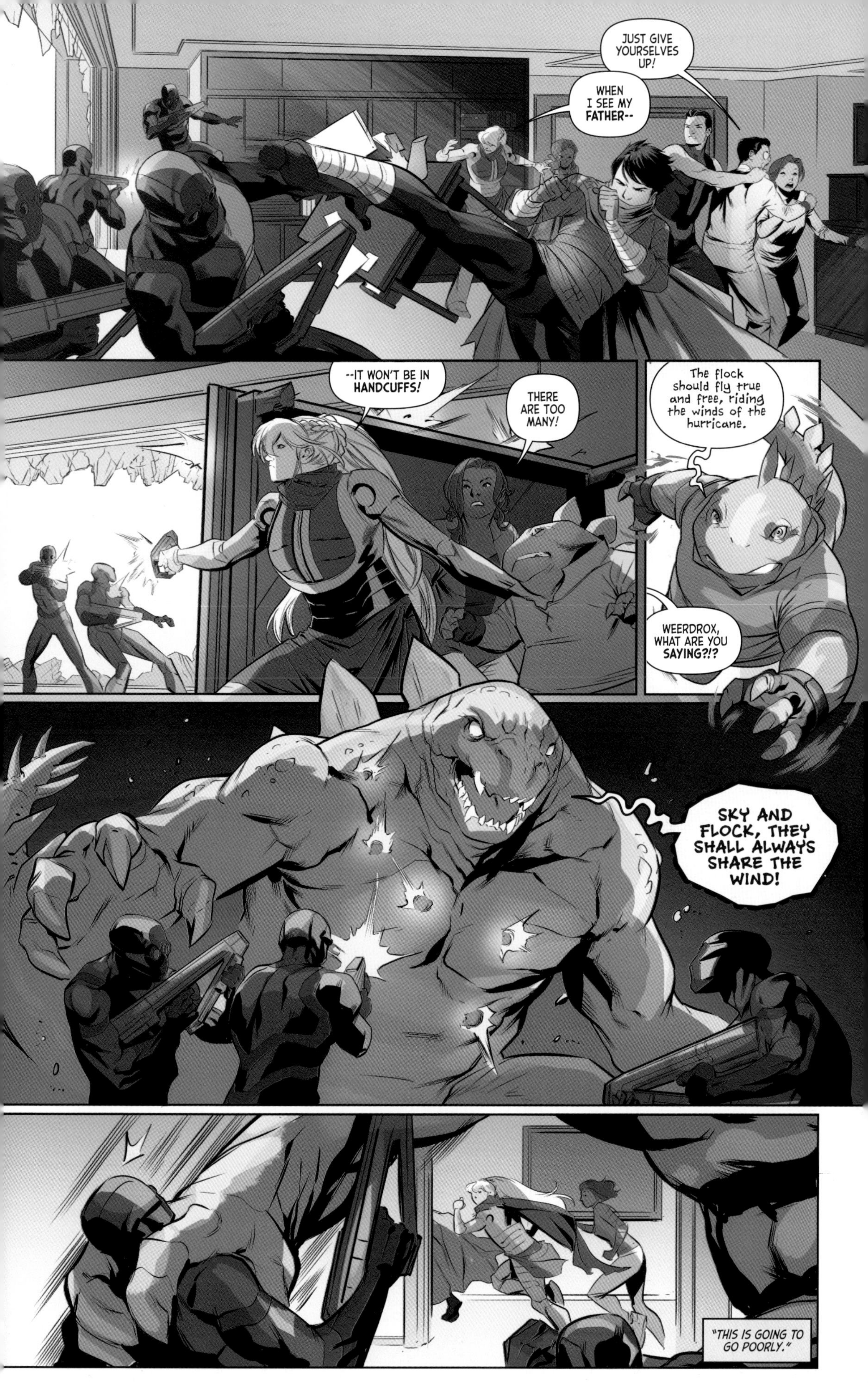
JUST GIVE YOURSELVES UP!
WHEN I SEE MY FATHER--
--IT WON'T BE IN HANDCUFFS!
THERE ARE TOO MANY!
The flock should fly true and free, riding the winds of the hurricane.
WEERDROX, WHAT ARE YOU SAYING?!?
SKY AND FLOCK, THEY SHALL ALWAYS SHARE THE WIND!
"THIS IS GOING TO GO POORLY."

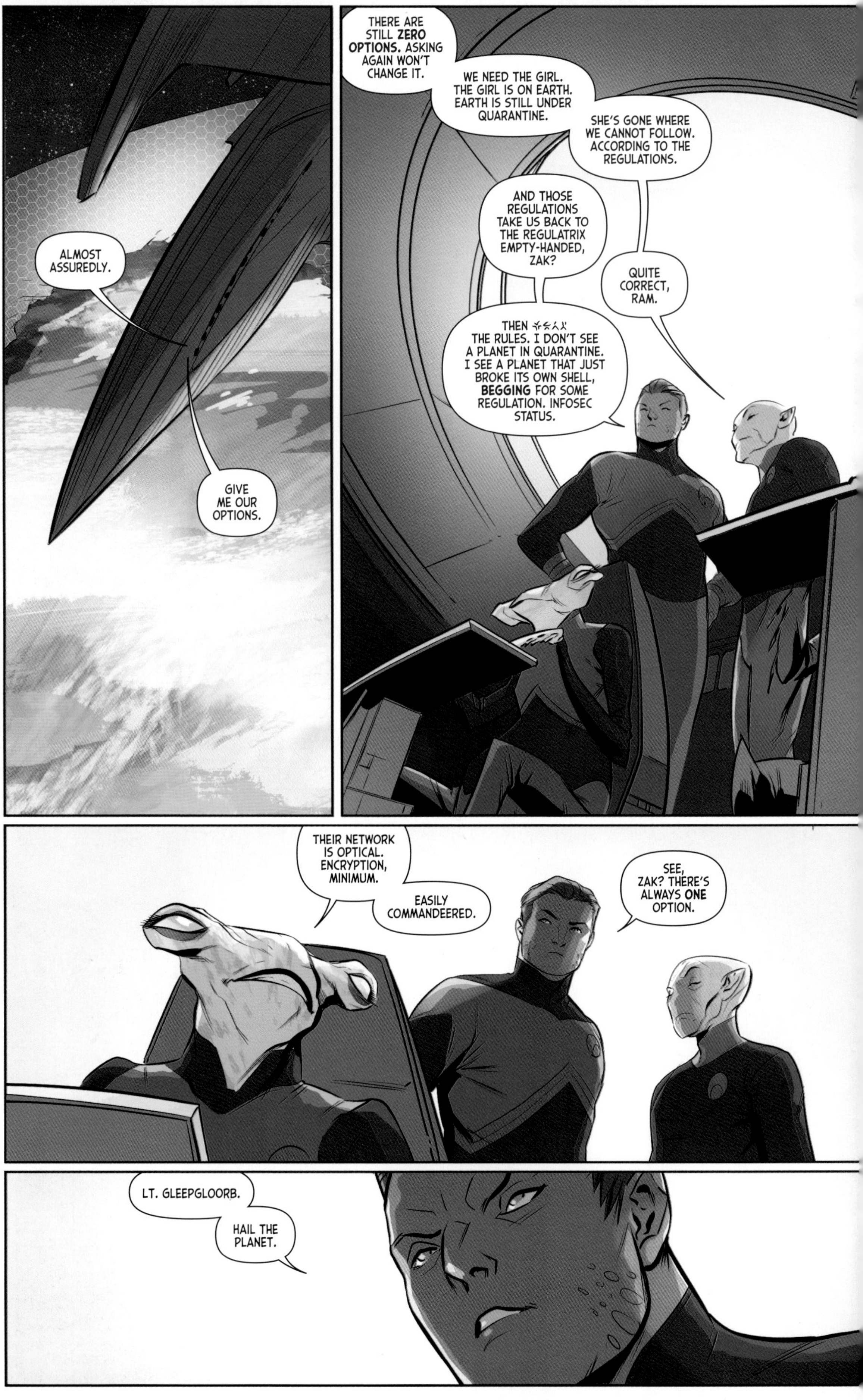
ALMOST ASSUREDLY.
GIVE ME OUR OPTIONS.
THERE ARE STILL **ZERO OPTIONS.** ASKING AGAIN WON'T CHANGE IT.
WE NEED THE GIRL. THE GIRL IS ON EARTH. EARTH IS STILL UNDER QUARANTINE.
SHE'S GONE WHERE WE CANNOT FOLLOW. ACCORDING TO THE REGULATIONS.
AND THOSE REGULATIONS TAKE US BACK TO THE REGULATRIX EMPTY-HANDED, ZAK?
QUITE CORRECT, RAM.
THEN THE RULES. I DON'T SEE A PLANET IN QUARANTINE. I SEE A PLANET THAT JUST BROKE ITS OWN SHELL, **BEGGING** FOR SOME REGULATION. INFOSEC STATUS.
THEIR NETWORK IS OPTICAL. ENCRYPTION, MINIMUM.
EASILY COMMANDEERED.
SEE, ZAK? THERE'S ALWAYS **ONE** OPTION.
LT. GLEEPGLOORB.
HAIL THE PLANET.

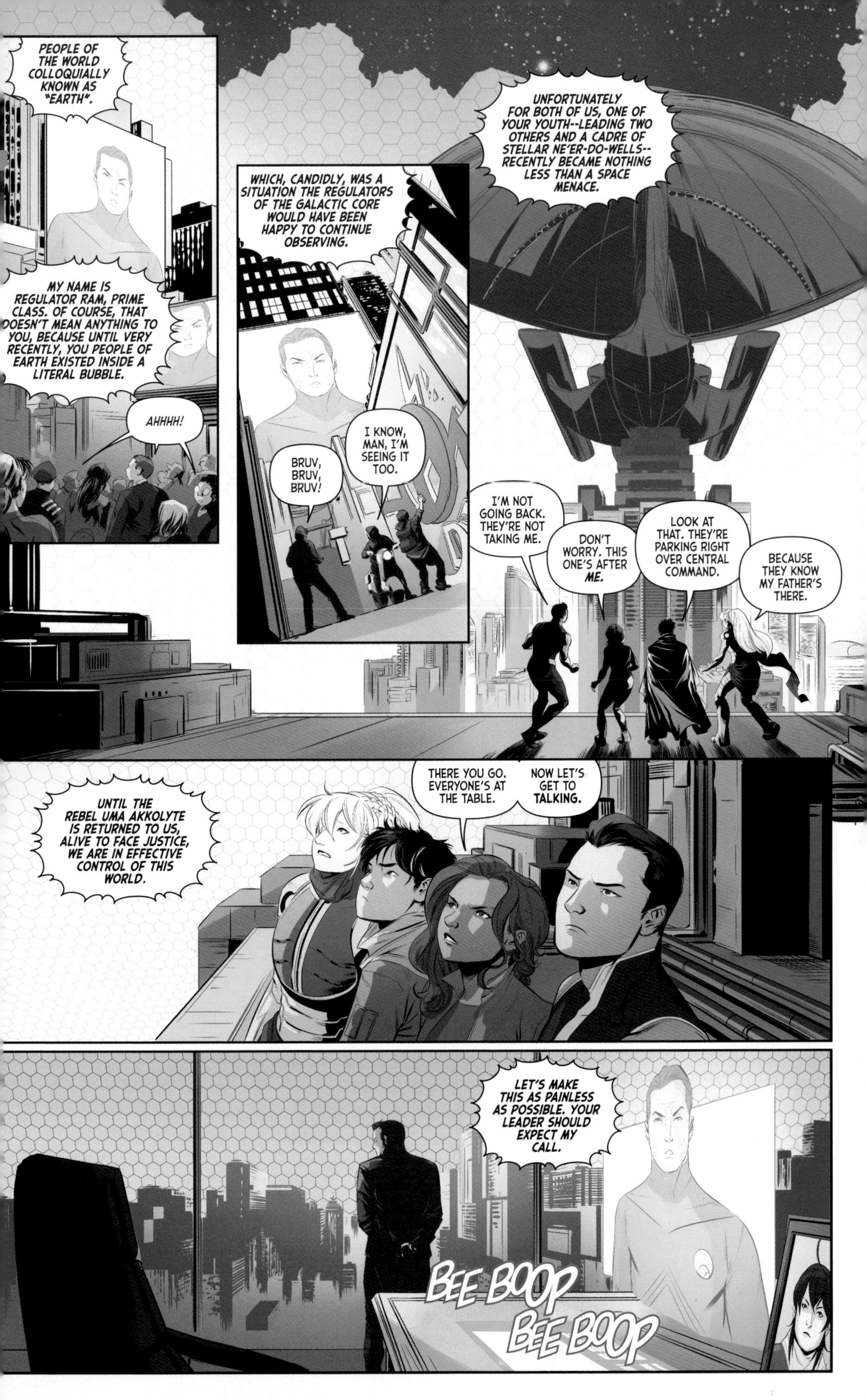
PEOPLE OF THE WORLD COLLOQUIALLY KNOWN AS "EARTH".
MY NAME IS REGULATOR RAM, PRIME CLASS. OF COURSE, THAT DOESN'T MEAN ANYTHING TO YOU, BECAUSE UNTIL VERY RECENTLY, YOU PEOPLE OF EARTH EXISTED INSIDE A LITERAL BUBBLE.
AHHHH!
WHICH, CANDIDLY, WAS A SITUATION THE REGULATORS OF THE GALACTIC CORE WOULD HAVE BEEN HAPPY TO CONTINUE OBSERVING.
BRUV, BRUV, BRUV!
I KNOW, MAN, I'M SEEING IT TOO.
UNFORTUNATELY FOR BOTH OF US, ONE OF YOUR YOUTH--LEADING TWO OTHERS AND A CADRE OF STELLAR NE'ER-DO-WELLS--RECENTLY BECAME NOTHING LESS THAN A SPACE MENACE.
I'M NOT GOING BACK. THEY'RE NOT TAKING ME.
DON'T WORRY. THIS ONE'S AFTER ME.
LOOK AT THAT. THEY'RE PARKING RIGHT OVER CENTRAL COMMAND.
BECAUSE THEY KNOW MY FATHER'S THERE.
UNTIL THE REBEL UMA AKKOLYTE IS RETURNED TO US, ALIVE TO FACE JUSTICE, WE ARE IN EFFECTIVE CONTROL OF THIS WORLD.
THERE YOU GO. EVERYONE'S AT THE TABLE.
NOW LET'S GET TO TALKING.
LET'S MAKE THIS AS PAINLESS AS POSSIBLE. YOUR LEADER SHOULD EXPECT MY CALL.
BEE BOOP
BEE BOOP

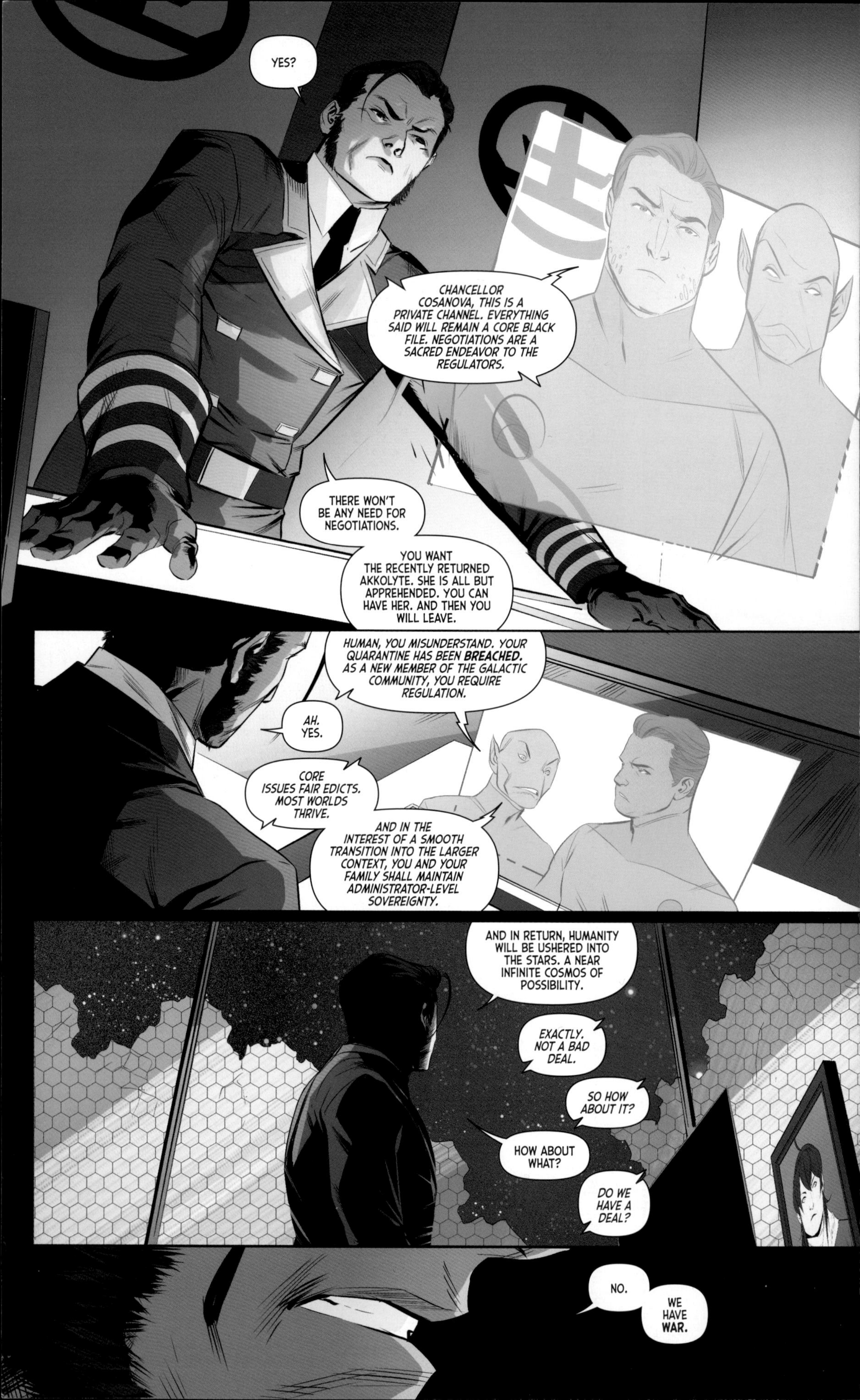

YES?
CHANCELLOR COSANOVA, THIS IS A PRIVATE CHANNEL. EVERYTHING SAID WILL REMAIN A CORE BLACK FILE. NEGOTIATIONS ARE A SACRED ENDEAVOR TO THE REGULATORS.
THERE WON'T BE ANY NEED FOR NEGOTIATIONS.
YOU WANT THE RECENTLY RETURNED AKKOLYTE. SHE IS ALL BUT APPREHENDED. YOU CAN HAVE HER. AND THEN YOU WILL LEAVE.
HUMAN, YOU MISUNDERSTAND. YOUR QUARANTINE HAS BEEN **BREACHED.** AS A NEW MEMBER OF THE GALACTIC COMMUNITY, YOU REQUIRE REGULATION.
AH. YES.
CORE ISSUES FAIR EDICTS. MOST WORLDS THRIVE.
AND IN THE INTEREST OF A SMOOTH TRANSITION INTO THE LARGER CONTEXT, YOU AND YOUR FAMILY SHALL MAINTAIN ADMINISTRATOR-LEVEL SOVEREIGNTY.
AND IN RETURN, HUMANITY WILL BE USHERED INTO THE STARS. A NEAR INFINITE COSMOS OF POSSIBILITY.
EXACTLY. NOT A BAD DEAL.
SO HOW ABOUT IT?
HOW ABOUT WHAT?
DO WE HAVE A DEAL?
NO.
WE HAVE **WAR.**

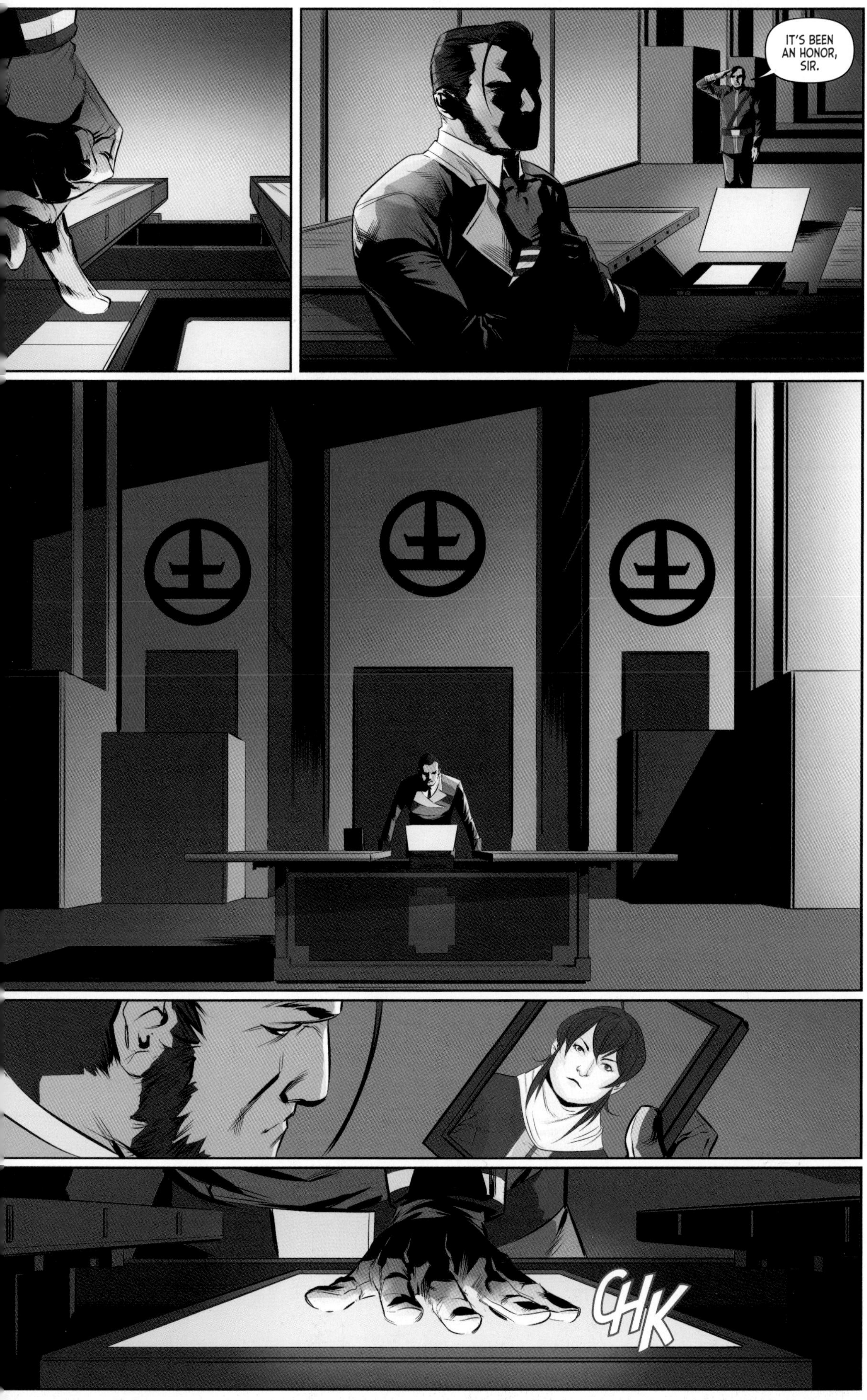
IT'S BEEN AN HONOR, SIR.
CHK

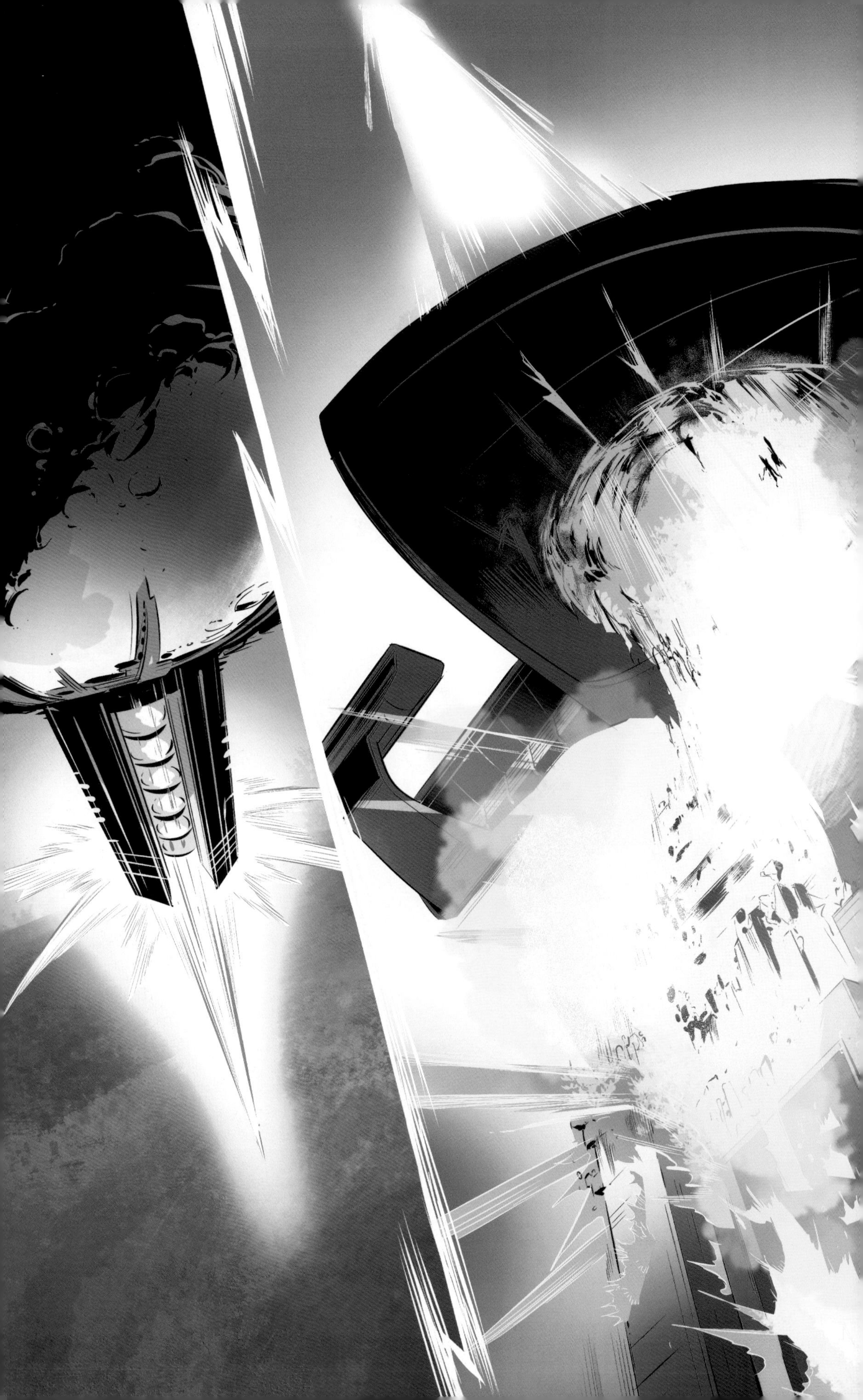

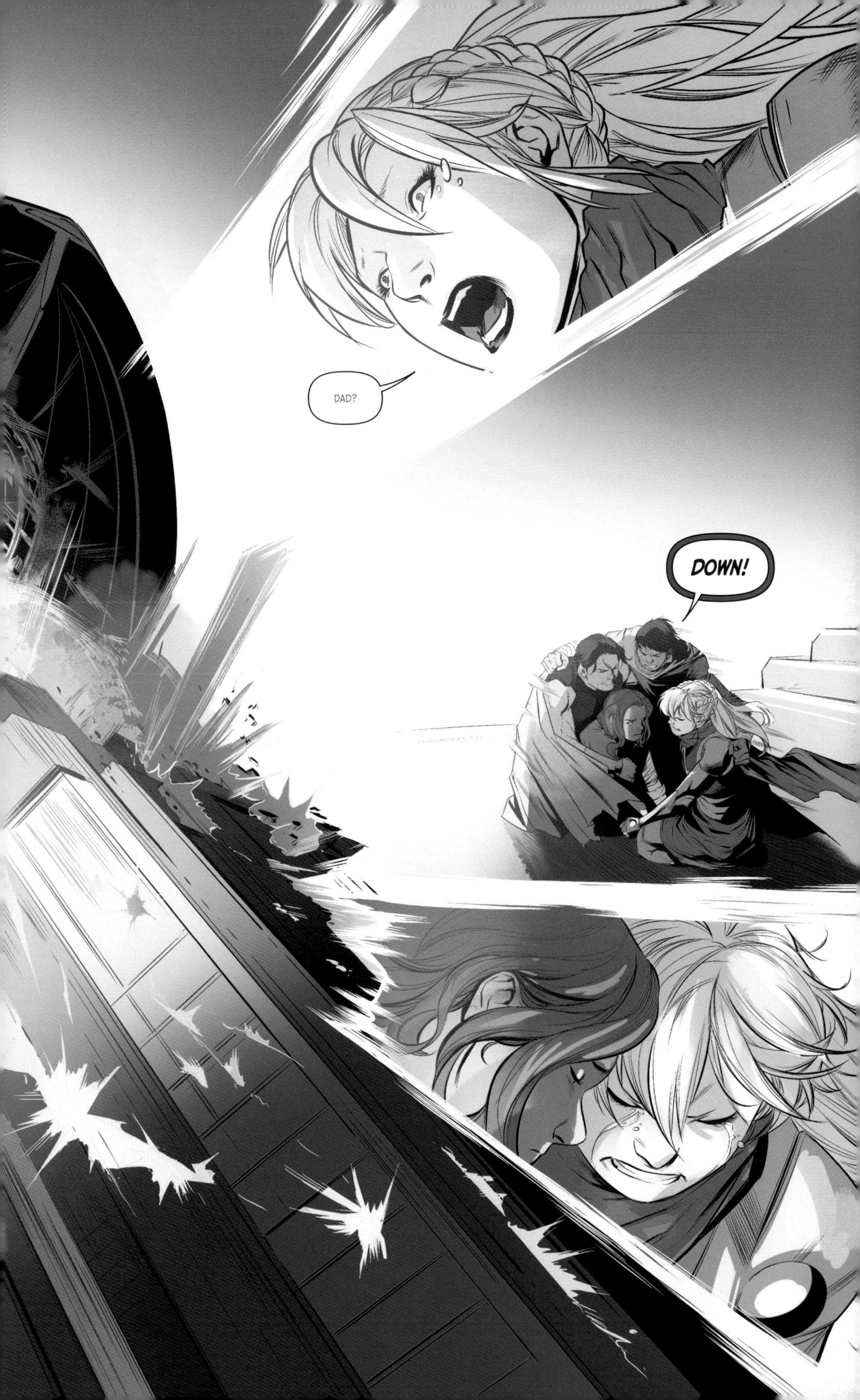
DAD?
DOWN!

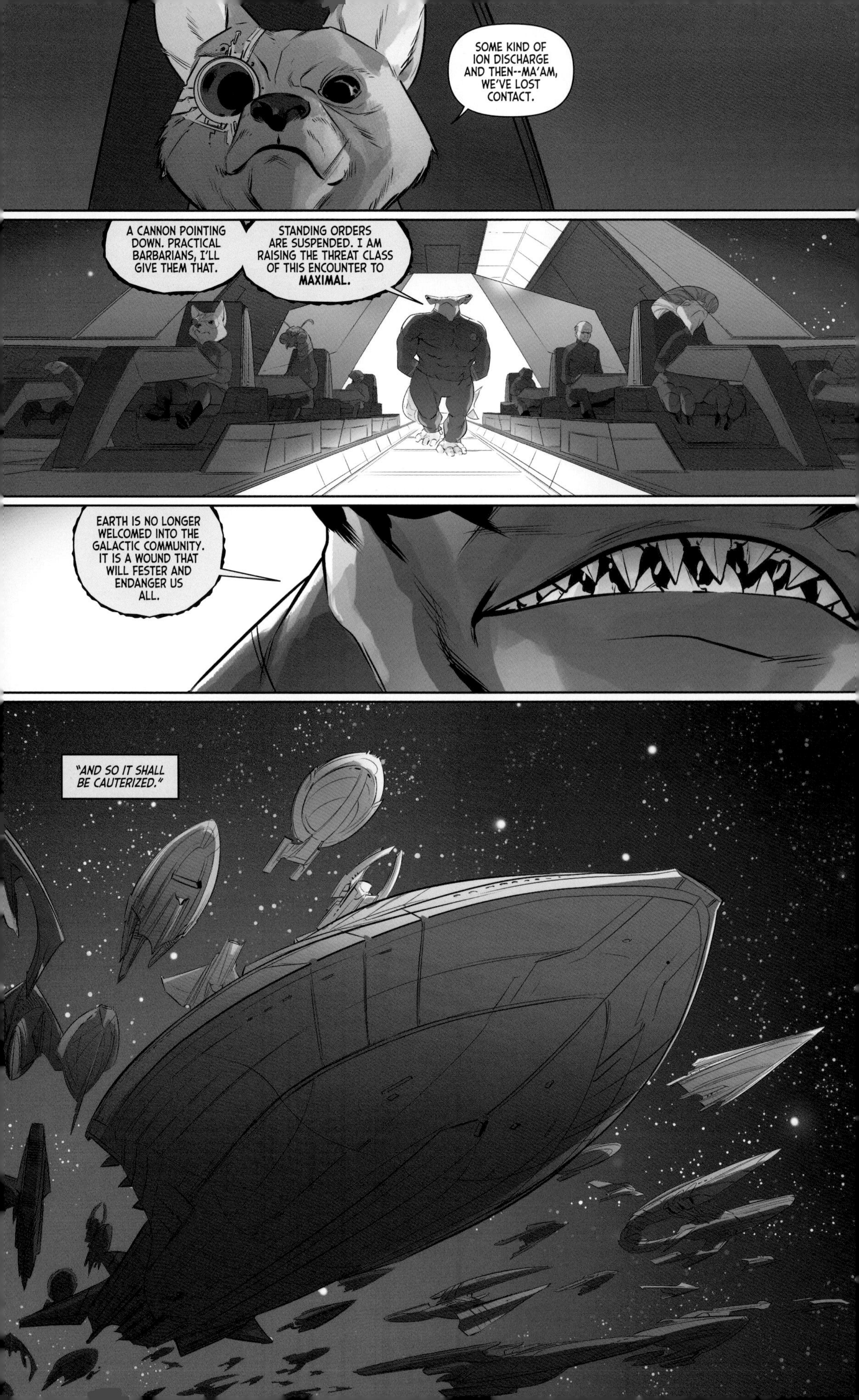
SOME KIND OF ION DISCHARGE AND THEN--MA'AM, WE'VE LOST CONTACT.
A CANNON POINTING DOWN. PRACTICAL BARBARIANS, I'LL GIVE THEM THAT.
STANDING ORDERS ARE SUSPENDED. I AM RAISING THE THREAT CLASS OF THIS ENCOUNTER TO **MAXIMAL.**
EARTH IS NO LONGER WELCOMED INTO THE GALACTIC COMMUNITY. IT IS A WOUND THAT WILL FESTER AND ENDANGER US ALL.
"AND SO IT SHALL BE CAUTERIZED."

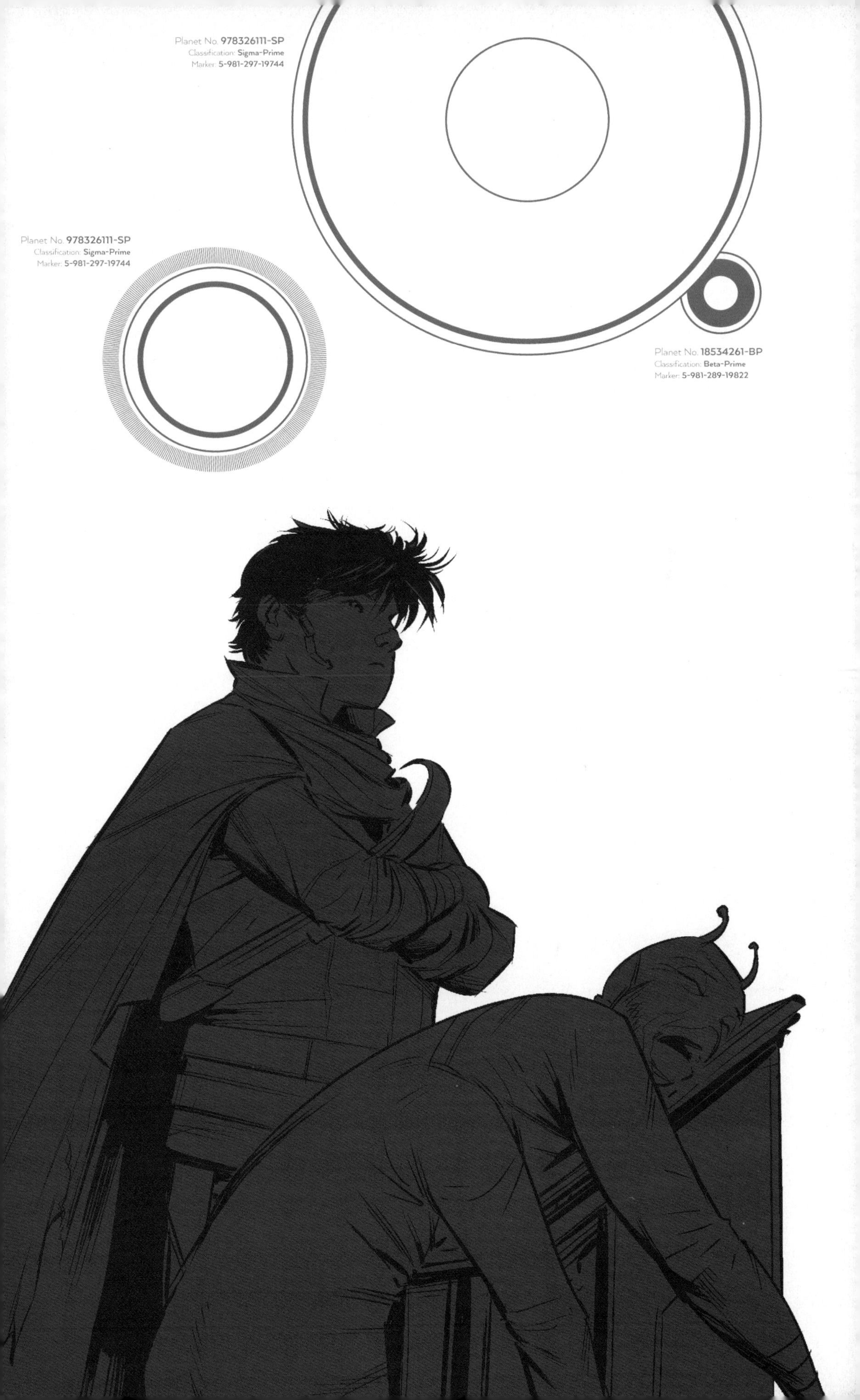

Planet No. 978326111-SP
Classification: Sigma-Prime
Marker: 5-981-297-19744
Planet No. 978326111-SP
Classification: Sigma-Prime
Marker: 5-981-297-19744
Planet No. 18534261-BP
Classification: Beta-Prime
Marker: 5-981-289-19822

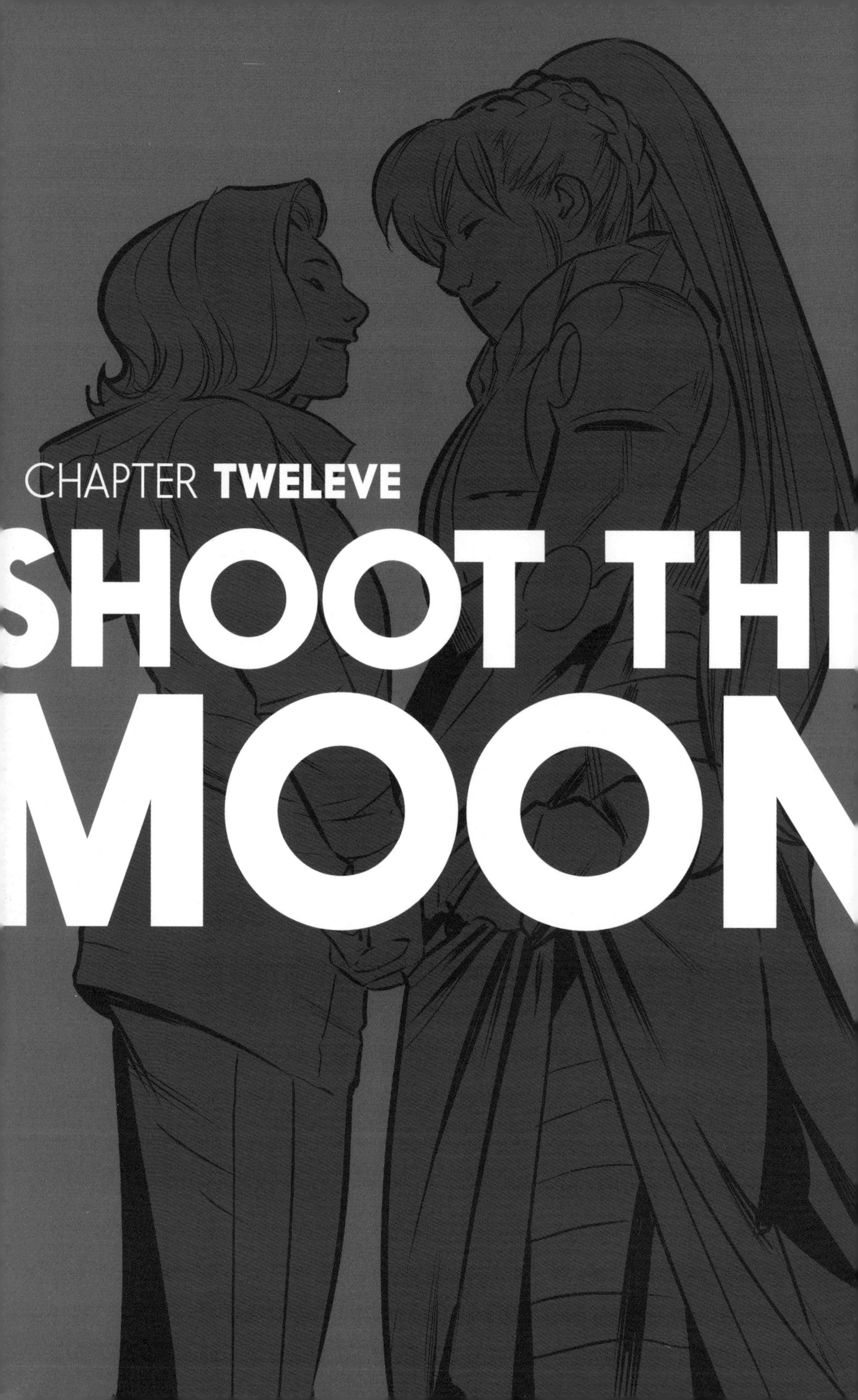

CHAPTER **TWELEVE**

SHOOT TH
MOON

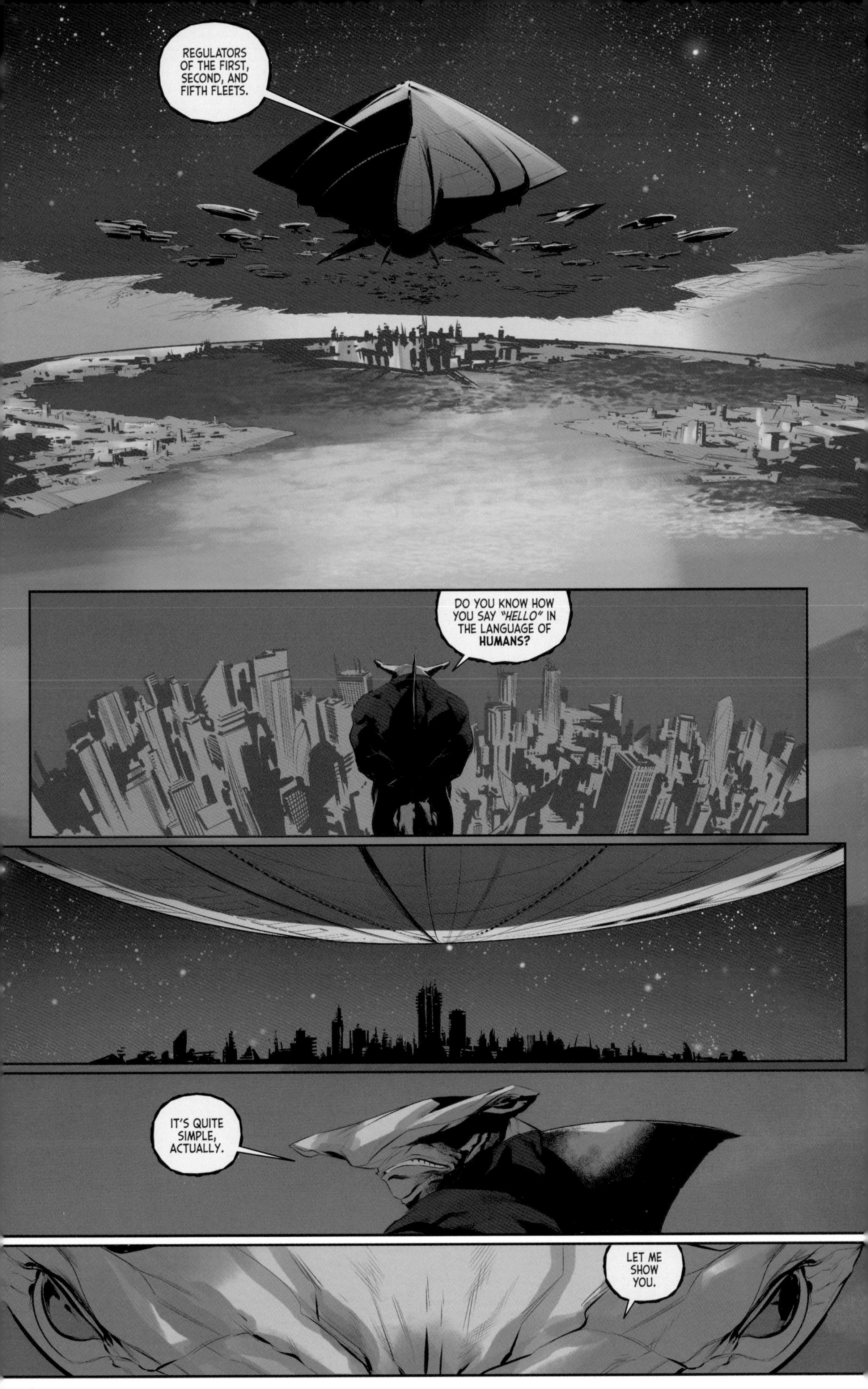
REGULATORS OF THE FIRST, SECOND, AND FIFTH FLEETS.
DO YOU KNOW HOW YOU SAY "HELLO" IN THE LANGUAGE OF HUMANS?
IT'S QUITE SIMPLE, ACTUALLY.
LET ME SHOW YOU.

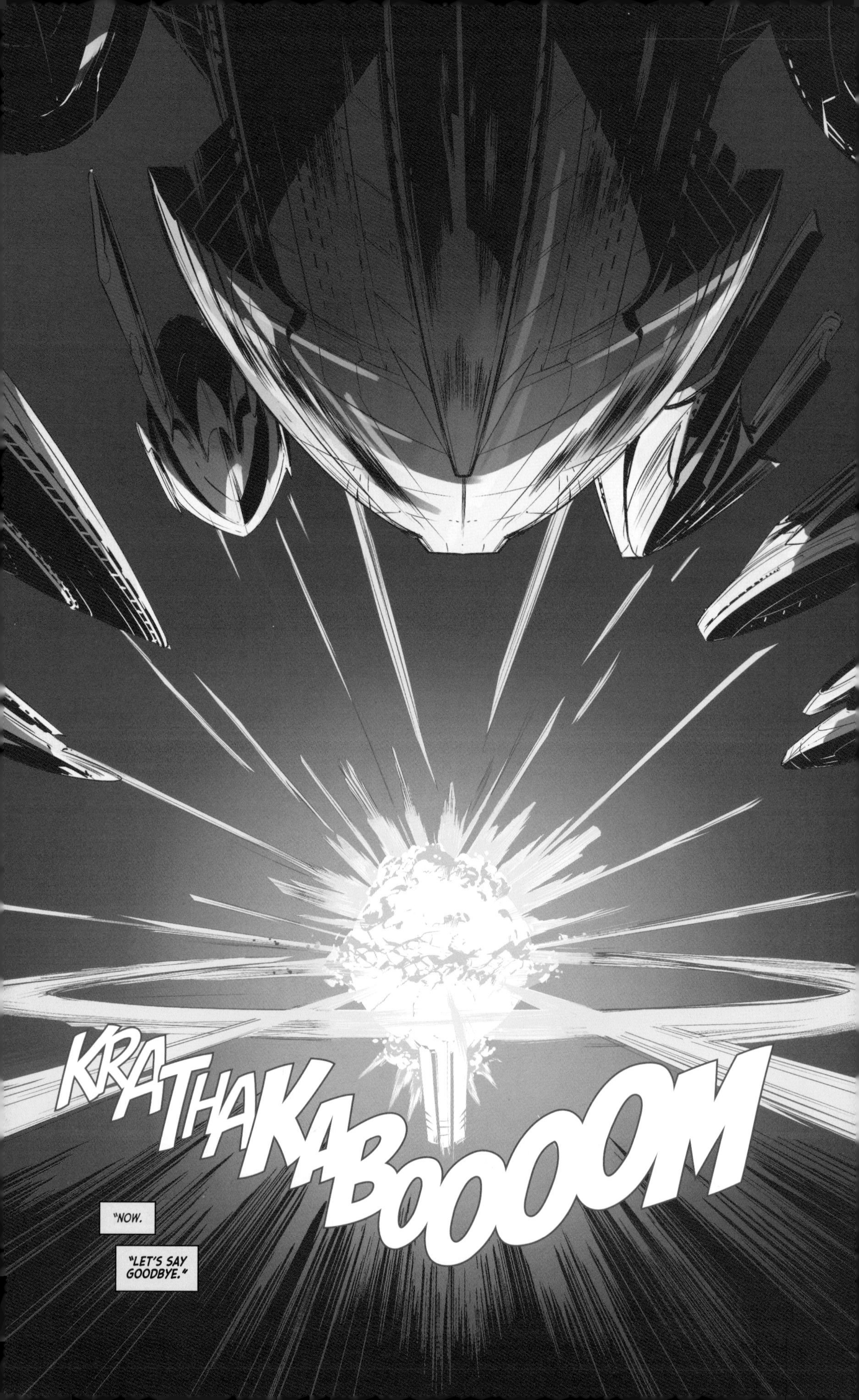
KRATHAKABOOOOOM
"NOW.
"LET'S SAY GOODBYE."

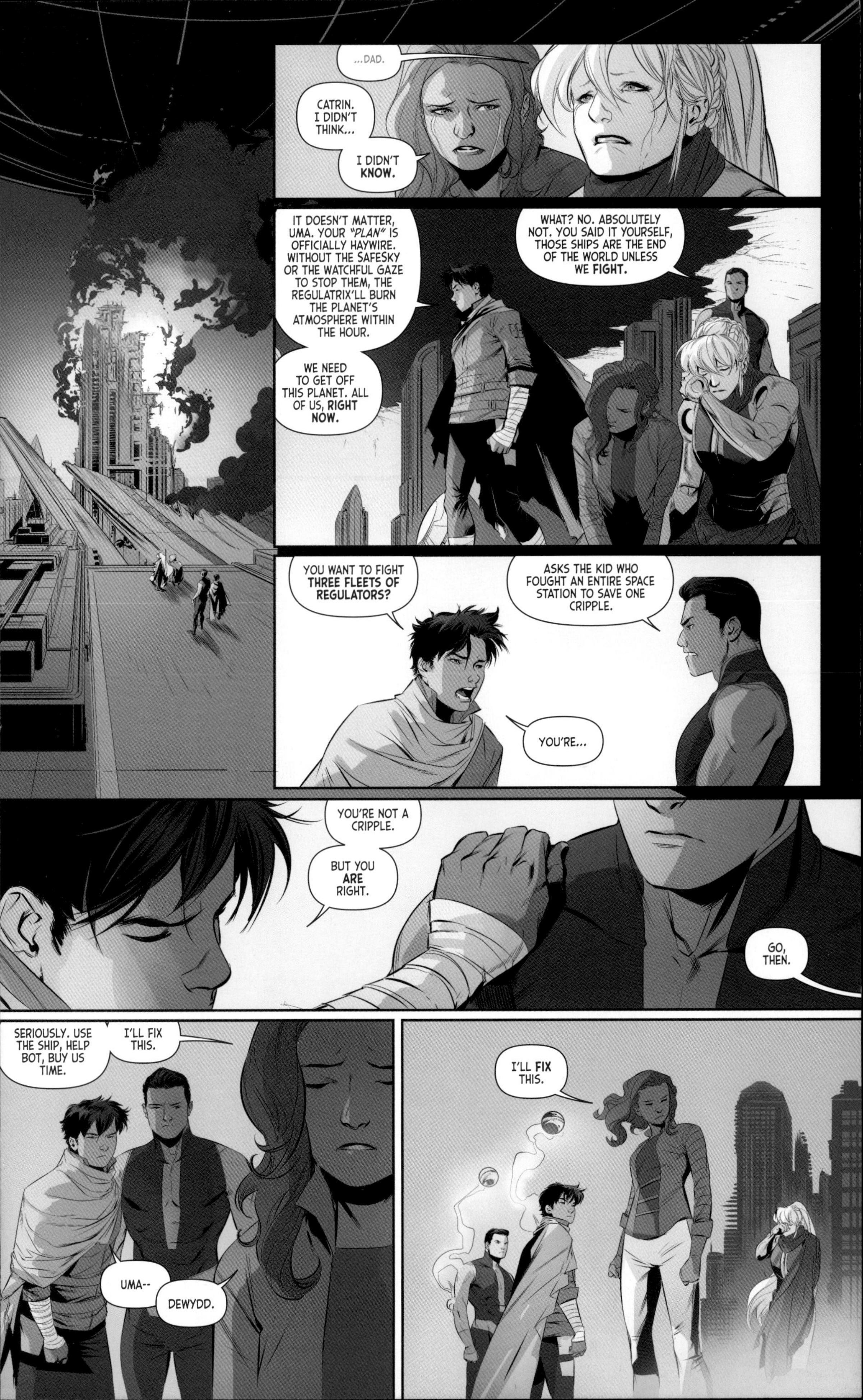
...DAD.
CATRIN. I DIDN'T THINK...
I DIDN'T KNOW.
IT DOESN'T MATTER, UMA. YOUR "PLAN" IS OFFICIALLY HAYWIRE. WITHOUT THE SAFESKY OR THE WATCHFUL GAZE TO STOP THEM, THE REGULATRIX'LL BURN THE PLANET'S ATMOSPHERE WITHIN THE HOUR.
WE NEED TO GET OFF THIS PLANET. ALL OF US, RIGHT NOW.
WHAT? NO. ABSOLUTELY NOT. YOU SAID IT YOURSELF, THOSE SHIPS ARE THE END OF THE WORLD UNLESS WE FIGHT.
YOU WANT TO FIGHT THREE FLEETS OF REGULATORS?
ASKS THE KID WHO FOUGHT AN ENTIRE SPACE STATION TO SAVE ONE CRIPPLE.
YOU'RE...
YOU'RE NOT A CRIPPLE.
BUT YOU ARE RIGHT.
GO, THEN.
SERIOUSLY. USE THE SHIP, HELP BOT, BUY US TIME.
I'LL FIX THIS.
UMA--
DEWYDD.
I'LL FIX THIS.

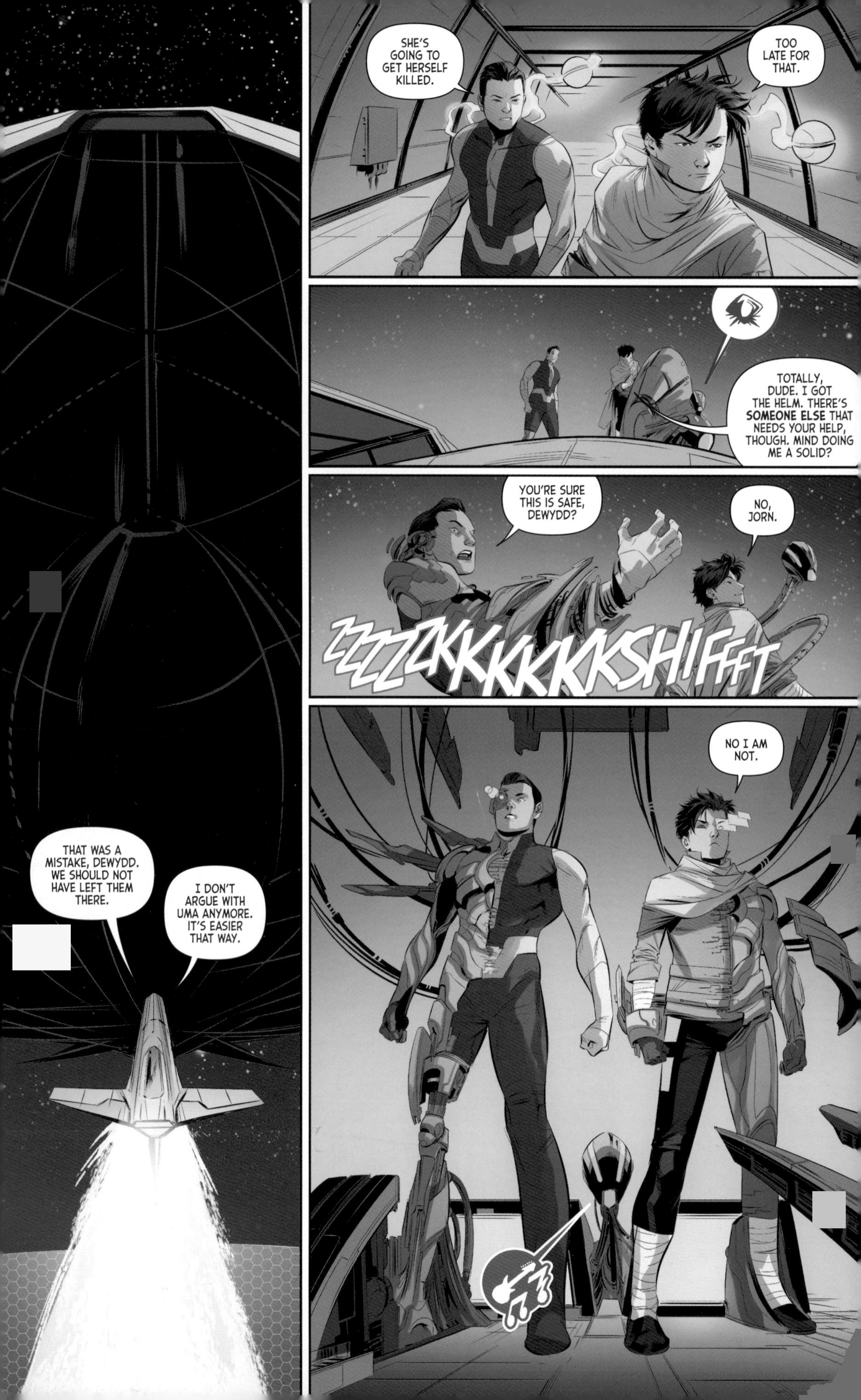
THAT WAS A MISTAKE, DEWYDD. WE SHOULD NOT HAVE LEFT THEM THERE.
I DON'T ARGUE WITH UMA ANYMORE. IT'S EASIER THAT WAY.
SHE'S GOING TO GET HERSELF KILLED.
TOO LATE FOR THAT.
TOTALLY, DUDE. I GOT THE HELM. THERE'S **SOMEONE ELSE** THAT NEEDS YOUR HELP, THOUGH. MIND DOING ME A SOLID?
YOU'RE SURE THIS IS SAFE, DEWYDD?
NO, JORN.
ZZZZKKKKKKKSHIFFFT
NO I AM NOT.

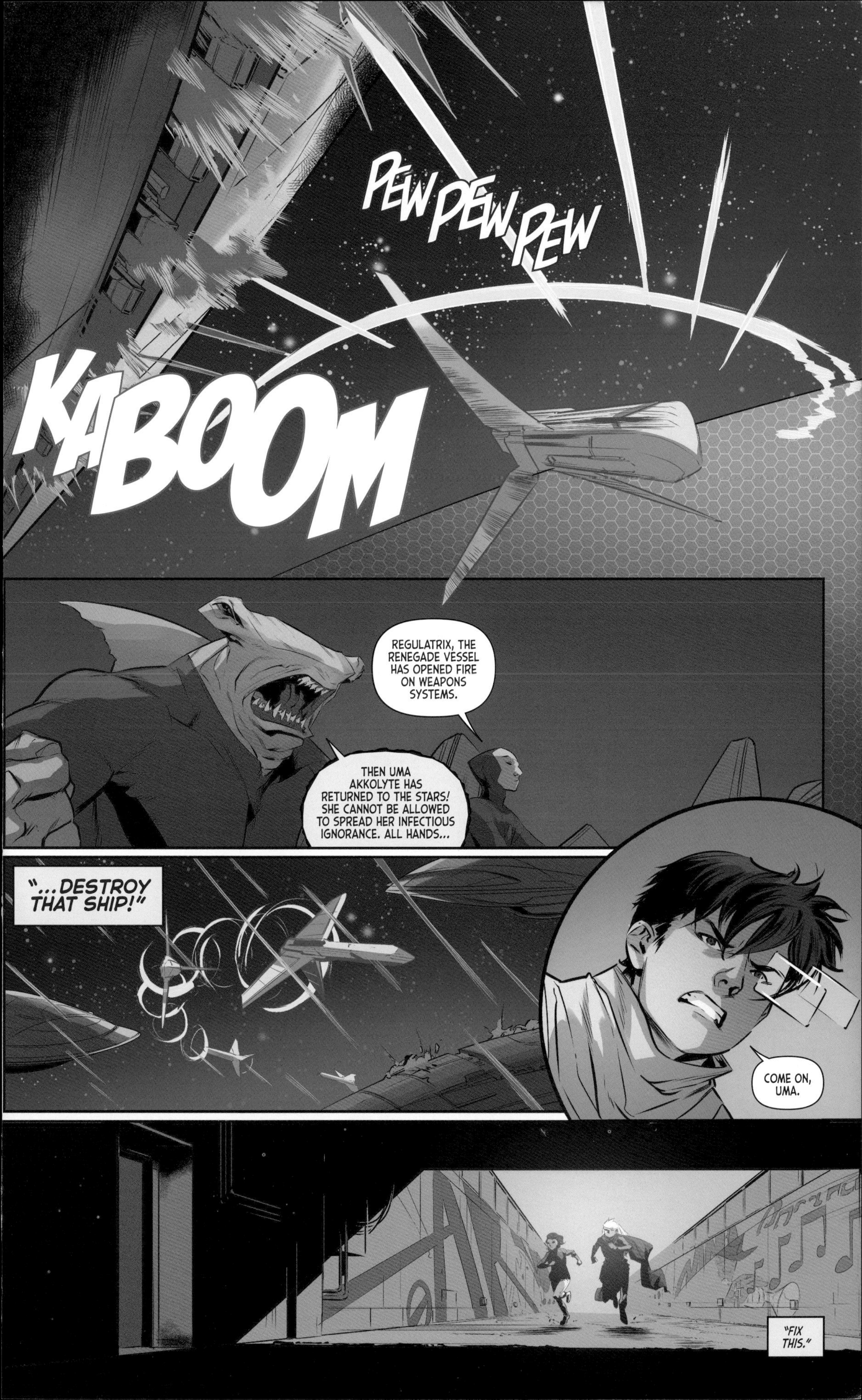
PEW PEW PEW
KABOOM
REGULATRIX, THE RENEGADE VESSEL HAS OPENED FIRE ON WEAPONS SYSTEMS.
THEN UMA AKKOLYTE HAS RETURNED TO THE STARS! SHE CANNOT BE ALLOWED TO SPREAD HER INFECTIOUS IGNORANCE. ALL HANDS...
"...DESTROY THAT SHIP!"
COME ON, UMA.
"FIX THIS."

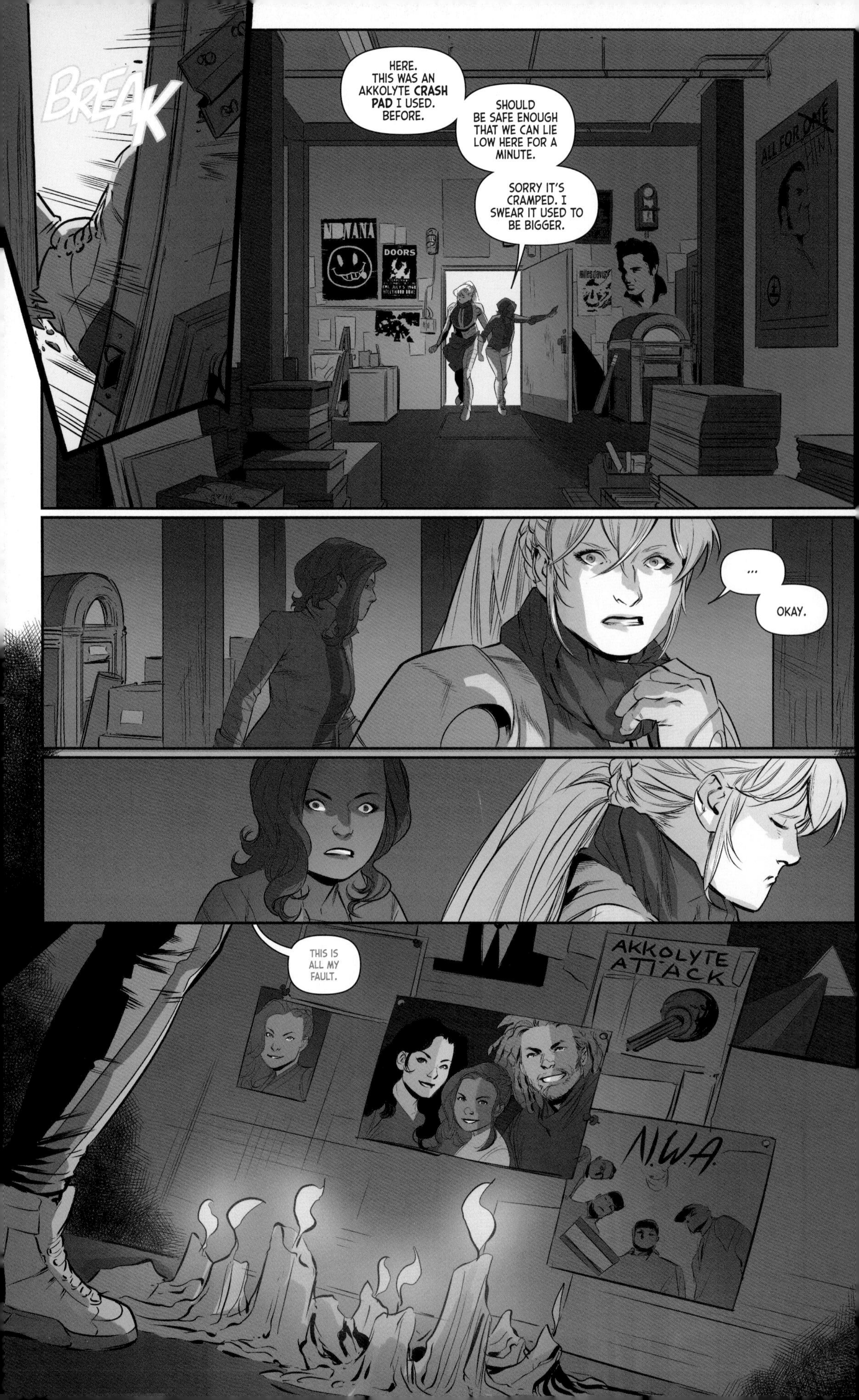
BREAK
HERE. THIS WAS AN AKKOLYTE **CRASH PAD** I USED. BEFORE.
SHOULD BE SAFE ENOUGH THAT WE CAN LIE LOW HERE FOR A MINUTE.
SORRY IT'S CRAMPED. I SWEAR IT USED TO BE BIGGER.
NIRVANA
DOORS
MILES DAVIS
ALL FOR ONE
...
OKAY.
THIS IS ALL MY FAULT.
AKKOLYTE ATTACK
N.W.A.

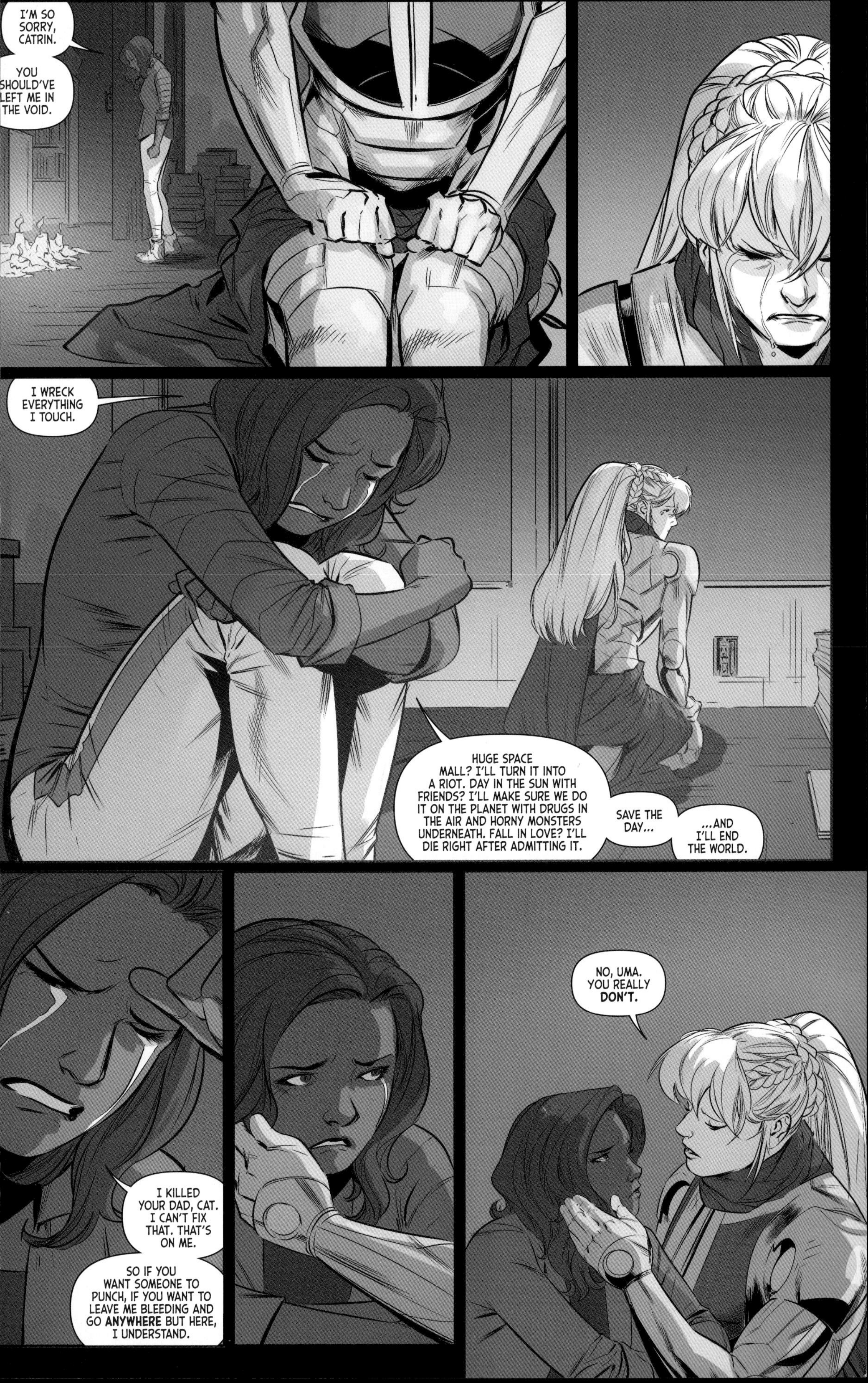
I'M SO SORRY, CATRIN.
YOU SHOULD'VE LEFT ME IN THE VOID.
I WRECK EVERYTHING I TOUCH.
HUGE SPACE MALL? I'LL TURN IT INTO A RIOT. DAY IN THE SUN WITH FRIENDS? I'LL MAKE SURE WE DO IT ON THE PLANET WITH DRUGS IN THE AIR AND HORNY MONSTERS UNDERNEATH. FALL IN LOVE? I'LL DIE RIGHT AFTER ADMITTING IT.
SAVE THE DAY...
...AND I'LL END THE WORLD.
I KILLED YOUR DAD, CAT. I CAN'T FIX THAT. THAT'S ON ME.
SO IF YOU WANT SOMEONE TO PUNCH, IF YOU WANT TO LEAVE ME BLEEDING AND GO **ANYWHERE** BUT HERE, I UNDERSTAND.
NO, UMA. YOU REALLY **DON'T.**

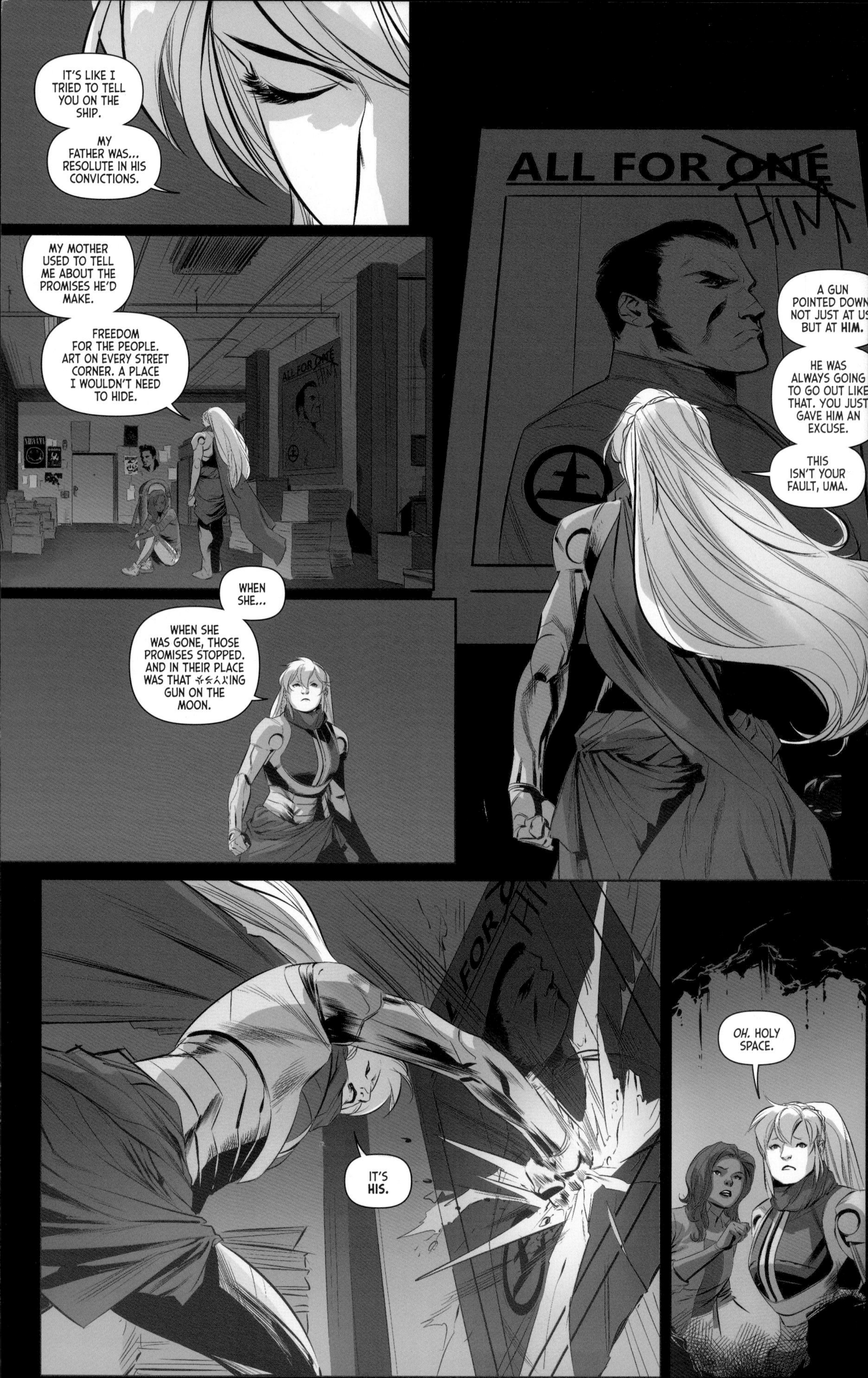
IT'S LIKE I TRIED TO TELL YOU ON THE SHIP.
MY FATHER WAS... RESOLUTE IN HIS CONVICTIONS.
ALL FOR ONE
HIM
MY MOTHER USED TO TELL ME ABOUT THE PROMISES HE'D MAKE.
FREEDOM FOR THE PEOPLE. ART ON EVERY STREET CORNER. A PLACE I WOULDN'T NEED TO HIDE.
WHEN SHE...
WHEN SHE WAS GONE, THOSE PROMISES STOPPED. AND IN THEIR PLACE WAS THAT ✱✱✱✱ING GUN ON THE MOON.
A GUN POINTED DOWN NOT JUST AT US BUT AT **HIM.**
HE WAS ALWAYS GOING TO GO OUT LIKE THAT. YOU JUST GAVE HIM AN EXCUSE.
THIS ISN'T YOUR FAULT, UMA.
IT'S **HIS.**
OH. HOLY SPACE.

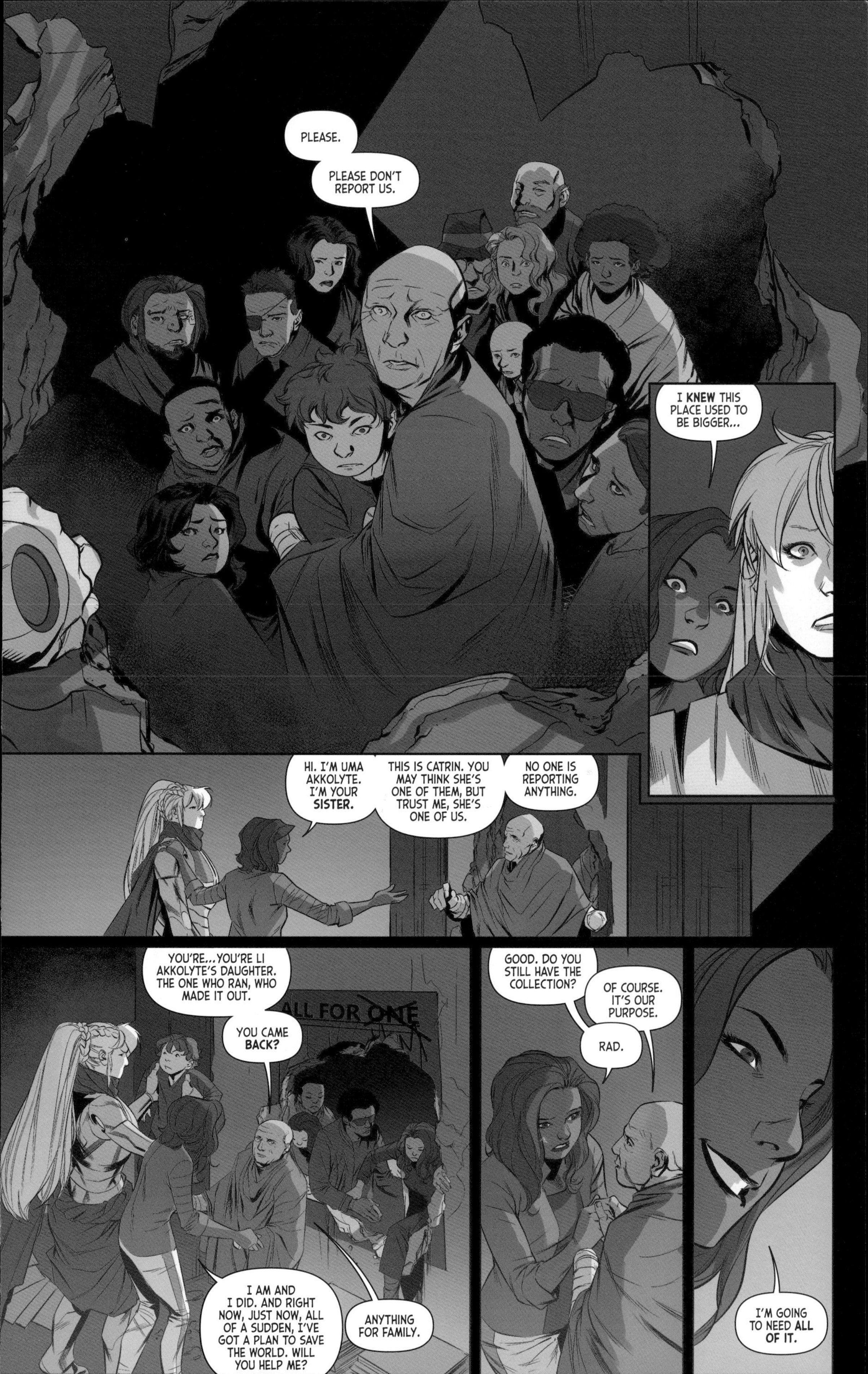
PLEASE.
PLEASE DON'T REPORT US.
I **KNEW** THIS PLACE USED TO BE BIGGER...
HI. I'M UMA AKKOLYTE. I'M YOUR **SISTER.**
THIS IS CATRIN. YOU MAY THINK SHE'S ONE OF THEM, BUT TRUST ME, SHE'S ONE OF US.
NO ONE IS REPORTING ANYTHING.
YOU'RE...YOU'RE LI AKKOLYTE'S DAUGHTER. THE ONE WHO RAN, WHO MADE IT OUT.
ALL FOR ONE
YOU CAME **BACK?**
I AM AND I DID. AND RIGHT NOW, JUST NOW, ALL OF A SUDDEN, I'VE GOT A PLAN TO SAVE THE WORLD. WILL YOU HELP ME?
ANYTHING FOR FAMILY.
GOOD. DO YOU STILL HAVE THE COLLECTION?
OF COURSE. IT'S OUR PURPOSE.
RAD.
I'M GOING TO NEED **ALL OF IT.**

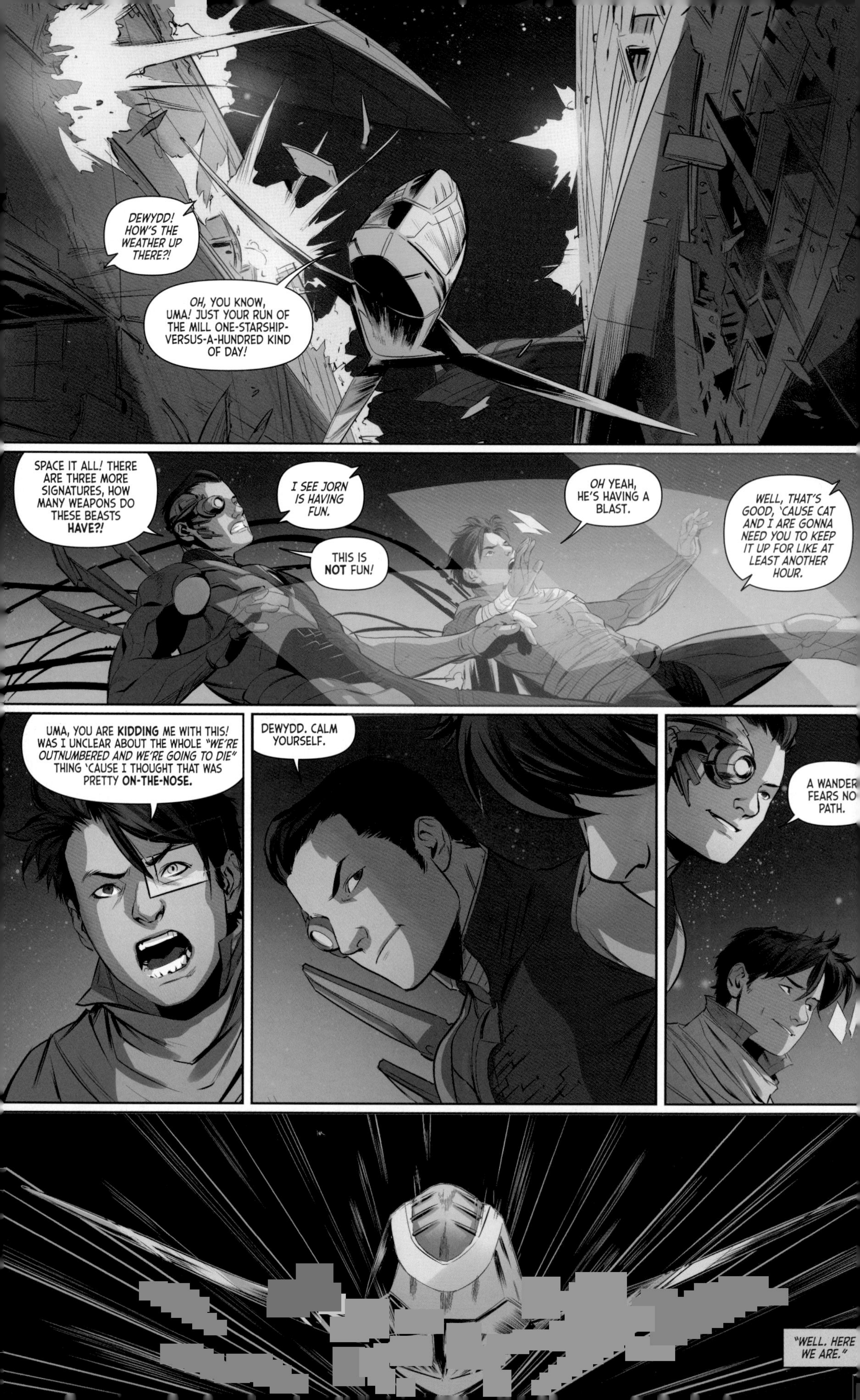
DEWYDD! HOW'S THE WEATHER UP THERE?!
OH, YOU KNOW, UMA! JUST YOUR RUN OF THE MILL ONE-STARSHIP-VERSUS-A-HUNDRED KIND OF DAY!
SPACE IT ALL! THERE ARE THREE MORE SIGNATURES, HOW MANY WEAPONS DO THESE BEASTS HAVE?!
I SEE JORN IS HAVING FUN.
THIS IS NOT FUN!
OH YEAH, HE'S HAVING A BLAST.
WELL, THAT'S GOOD, 'CAUSE CAT AND I ARE GONNA NEED YOU TO KEEP IT UP FOR LIKE AT LEAST ANOTHER HOUR.
UMA, YOU ARE KIDDING ME WITH THIS! WAS I UNCLEAR ABOUT THE WHOLE "WE'RE OUTNUMBERED AND WE'RE GOING TO DIE" THING 'CAUSE I THOUGHT THAT WAS PRETTY ON-THE-NOSE.
DEWYDD. CALM YOURSELF.
A WANDER FEARS NO PATH.
"WELL. HERE WE ARE."

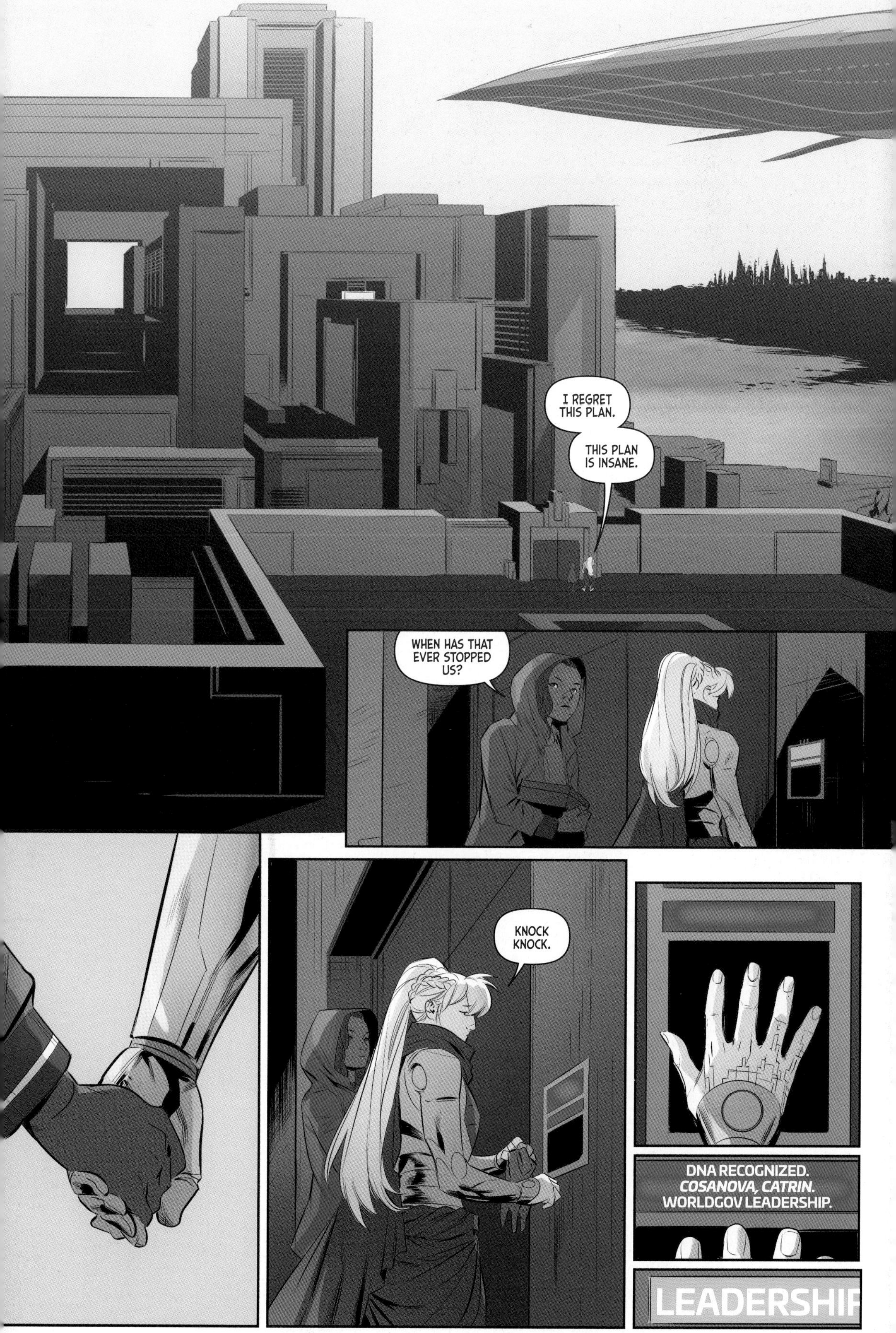
I REGRET THIS PLAN.
THIS PLAN IS INSANE.
WHEN HAS THAT EVER STOPPED US?
KNOCK KNOCK.
DNA RECOGNIZED.
COSANOVA, CATRIN.
WORLDGOV LEADERSHIP.
LEADERSHIP

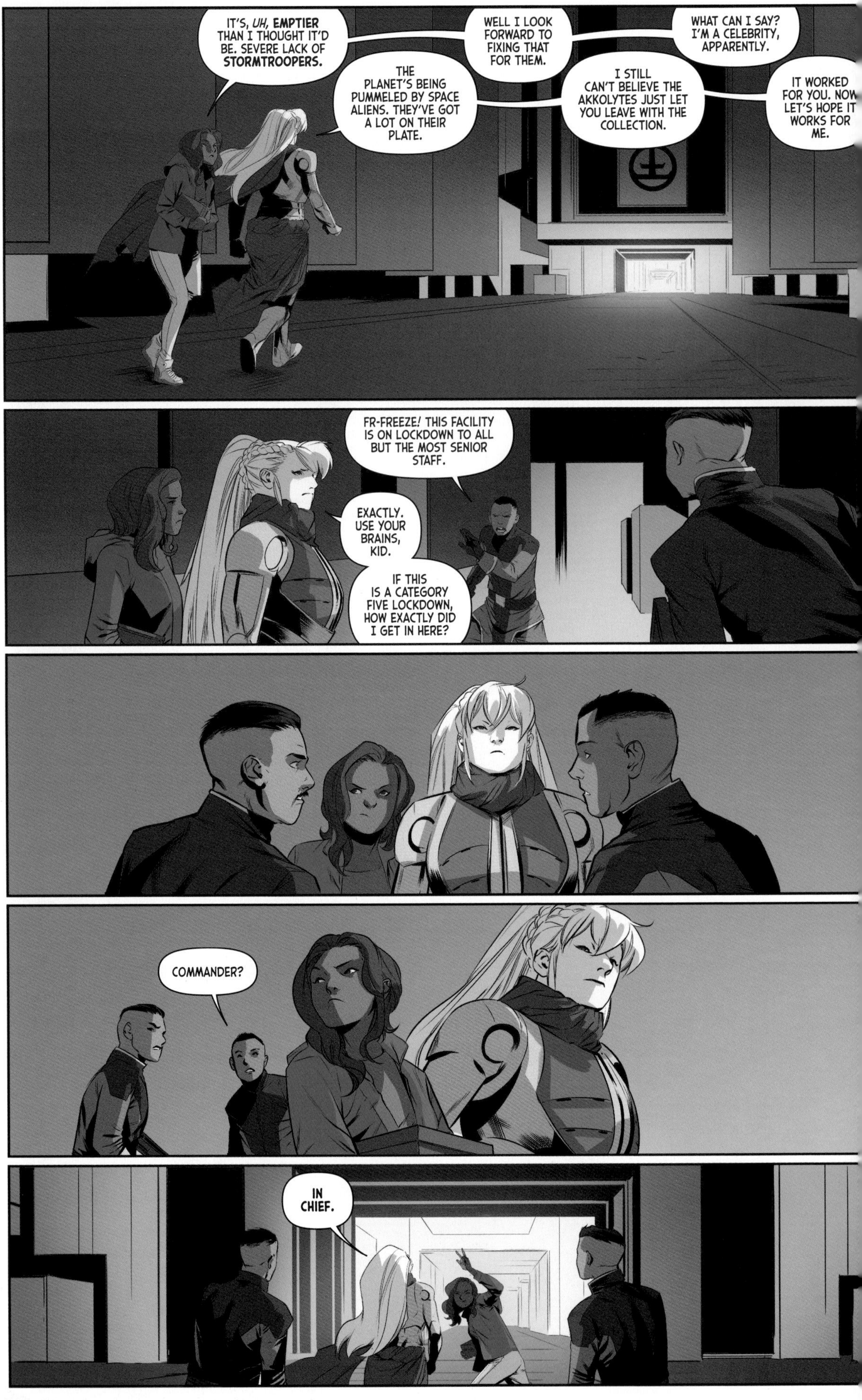
IT'S, *UH,* **EMPTIER** THAN I THOUGHT IT'D BE. SEVERE LACK OF **STORMTROOPERS.**
THE PLANET'S BEING PUMMELED BY SPACE ALIENS. THEY'VE GOT A LOT ON THEIR PLATE.
WELL I LOOK FORWARD TO FIXING THAT FOR THEM.
I STILL CAN'T BELIEVE THE AKKOLYTES JUST LET YOU LEAVE WITH THE COLLECTION.
WHAT CAN I SAY? I'M A CELEBRITY, APPARENTLY.
IT WORKED FOR YOU. NOW LET'S HOPE IT WORKS FOR ME.
FR-FREEZE! THIS FACILITY IS ON LOCKDOWN TO ALL BUT THE MOST SENIOR STAFF.
EXACTLY. USE YOUR BRAINS, KID.
IF THIS IS A CATEGORY FIVE LOCKDOWN, HOW EXACTLY DID I GET IN HERE?
COMMANDER?
IN CHIEF.

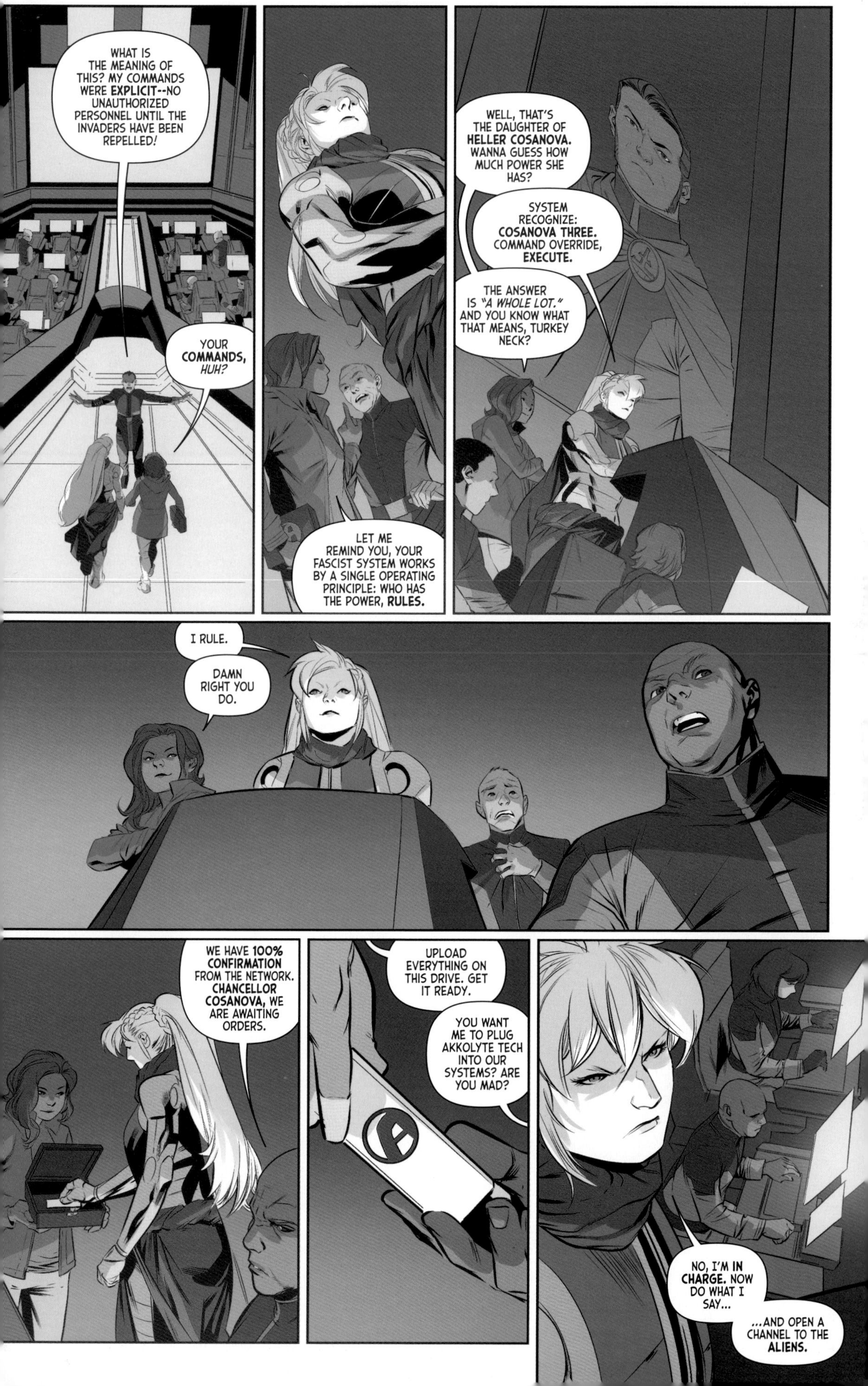
WHAT IS THE MEANING OF THIS? MY COMMANDS WERE EXPLICIT--NO UNAUTHORIZED PERSONNEL UNTIL THE INVADERS HAVE BEEN REPELLED!
YOUR COMMANDS, HUH?
LET ME REMIND YOU, YOUR FASCIST SYSTEM WORKS BY A SINGLE OPERATING PRINCIPLE: WHO HAS THE POWER, RULES.
WELL, THAT'S THE DAUGHTER OF HELLER COSANOVA. WANNA GUESS HOW MUCH POWER SHE HAS?
SYSTEM RECOGNIZE: COSANOVA THREE. COMMAND OVERRIDE, EXECUTE.
THE ANSWER IS "A WHOLE LOT." AND YOU KNOW WHAT THAT MEANS, TURKEY NECK?
I RULE.
DAMN RIGHT YOU DO.
WE HAVE 100% CONFIRMATION FROM THE NETWORK. CHANCELLOR COSANOVA, WE ARE AWAITING ORDERS.
UPLOAD EVERYTHING ON THIS DRIVE. GET IT READY.
YOU WANT ME TO PLUG AKKOLYTE TECH INTO OUR SYSTEMS? ARE YOU MAD?
NO, I'M IN CHARGE. NOW DO WHAT I SAY...
...AND OPEN A CHANNEL TO THE ALIENS.

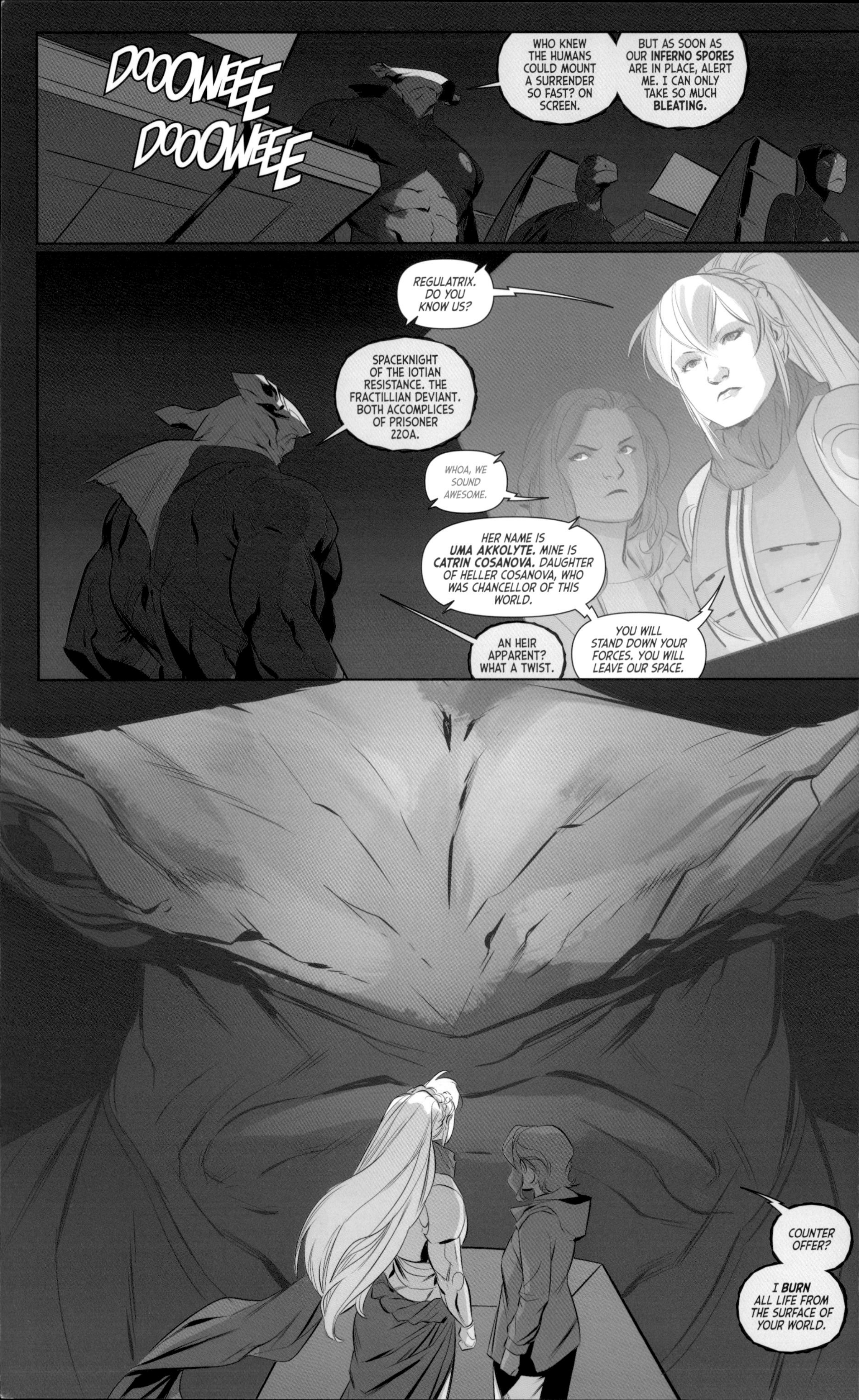
DOOOWEEE DOOOWEEE
WHO KNEW THE HUMANS COULD MOUNT A SURRENDER SO FAST? ON SCREEN.
BUT AS SOON AS OUR INFERNO SPORES ARE IN PLACE, ALERT ME. I CAN ONLY TAKE SO MUCH BLEATING.
REGULATRIX. DO YOU KNOW US?
SPACEKNIGHT OF THE IOTIAN RESISTANCE. THE FRACTILLIAN DEVIANT. BOTH ACCOMPLICES OF PRISONER 220A.
WHOA, WE SOUND AWESOME.
HER NAME IS UMA AKKOLYTE. MINE IS CATRIN COSANOVA. DAUGHTER OF HELLER COSANOVA, WHO WAS CHANCELLOR OF THIS WORLD.
AN HEIR APPARENT? WHAT A TWIST.
YOU WILL STAND DOWN YOUR FORCES. YOU WILL LEAVE OUR SPACE.
COUNTER OFFER?
I BURN ALL LIFE FROM THE SURFACE OF YOUR WORLD.

TYPICAL OVERCOMPENSATING **THUG**.

THREE KIDS PISS YOU OFF, SO YOU WIPE OUT A **PLANET**?

IT'S AMAZING THERE'S ANYTHING LEFT FOR CORE TO REGULATE.

THE HUMAN RACE IS, EASILY, THE MOST PRIMITIVE AND DISGUSTING, CLOSE MINDED, TROUBLESOME, SEETHING **ACHE** IN THIS SECTOR OF STARS.

A WART. A **CANCER**. A SMALL **WORLD** OF **SMALL HEARTS**, CONTENT TO WRITHE IN **FILTH**. AND THOSE THAT AREN'T, **BREAK** EVERY LAW WE'VE SET.

WELL THEY WERE **CRAP LAWS**. IF YOU WANT APOLOGIES, YOU'RE DIGGING IN THE WRONG DIRT. YOU'VE BEEN ON OUR PLANET, WHAT, AN **HOUR**?

WHAT YOU **SHOULD** BE SEEKING IS UNDERSTANDING.

YOU SAY THERE'S NO POINT TO US. THAT WE'RE FILTH. WE'RE TRASH. WE'RE ROTTEN.

AND YOU KNOW, SOMETIMES, WE ARE. THE SAME WAY SOMETIMES THE REGULATORS DECIDE TO DO SOMETHING STUPID LIKE WIPING OUT AN ENTIRE SPECIES WITHOUT KNOWING **JACK** ABOUT THEM.

'CAUSE SEE, YOU MIGHT THINK WIPING US OUT CLEANS A STAIN...

BUT YOU'RE ERASING THE BRIGHTEST COLOR YOU'VE GOT.

SO, YOU'RE A VERTEBRATE AFTER ALL. DYING WITH YOUR SPINE STRAIGHT. LITERALLY THE LEAST YOU CAN DO.

SIR, INFERNO SPORES ARE COMBUSTION READY.

PULL OUR PEOPLE BACK. BEGIN SYNTHETIC FUSION.

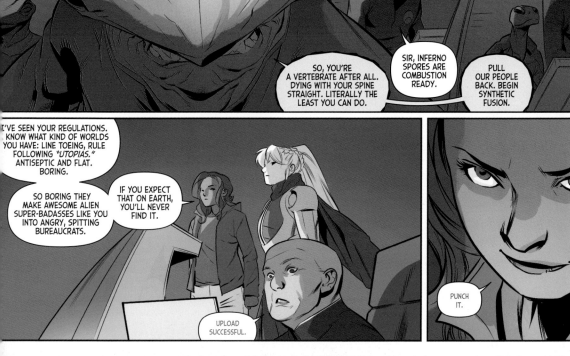

I'VE SEEN YOUR REGULATIONS. I KNOW WHAT KIND OF WORLDS YOU HAVE: LINE TOEING, RULE FOLLOWING *"UTOPIAS."* ANTISEPTIC AND FLAT. BORING.

SO BORING THEY MAKE AWESOME ALIEN SUPER-BADASSES LIKE YOU INTO ANGRY, SPITTING BUREAUCRATS.

IF YOU EXPECT THAT ON EARTH, YOU'LL NEVER FIND IT.

UPLOAD SUCCESSFUL.

PUNCH IT.

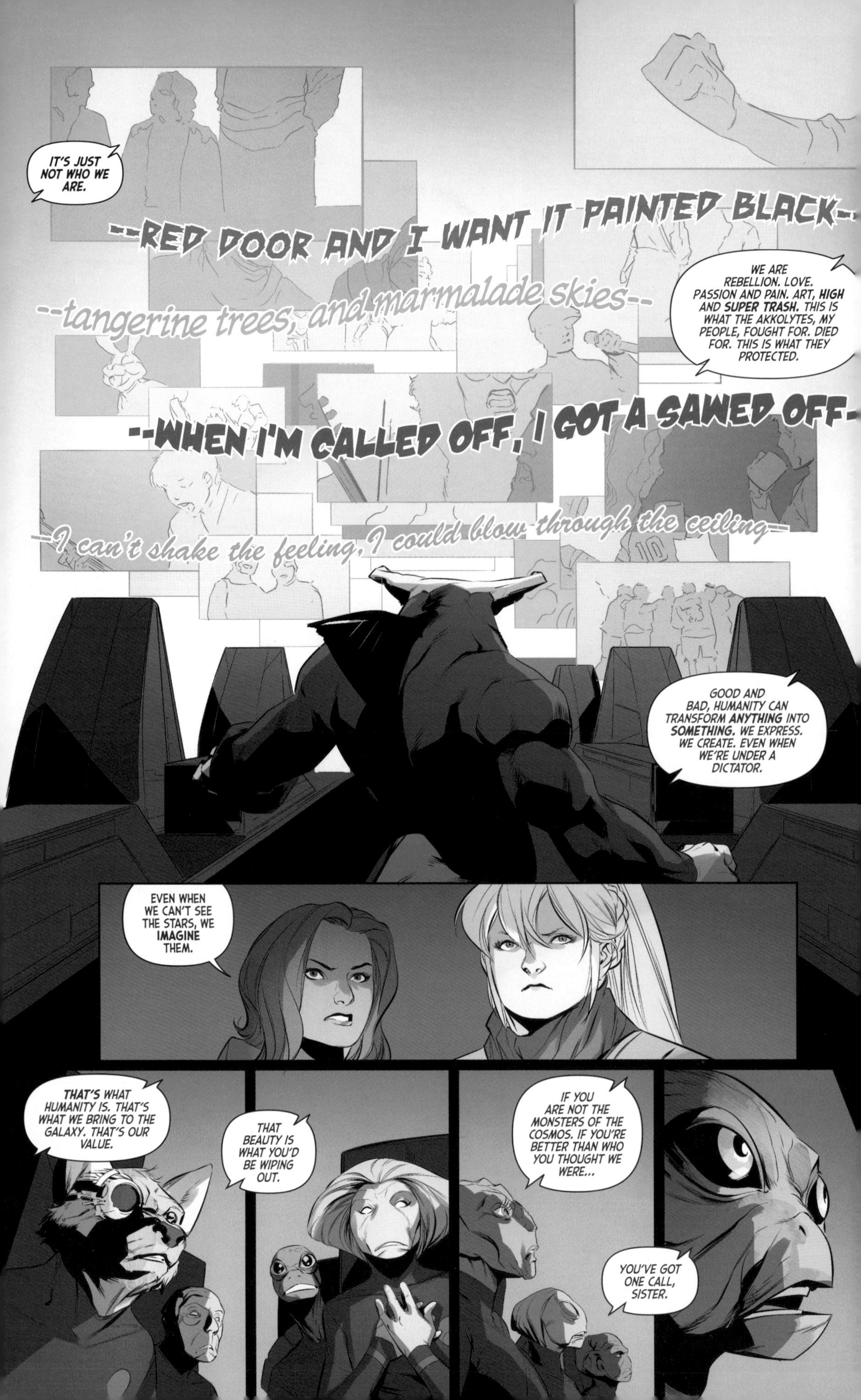

IT'S JUST NOT WHO WE ARE.
--RED DOOR AND I WANT IT PAINTED BLACK--
--tangerine trees, and marmalade skies--
WE ARE REBELLION. LOVE. PASSION AND PAIN. ART, HIGH AND SUPER TRASH. THIS IS WHAT THE AKKOLYTES, MY PEOPLE, FOUGHT FOR. DIED FOR. THIS IS WHAT THEY PROTECTED.
--WHEN I'M CALLED OFF, I GOT A SAWED OFF--
--I can't shake the feeling, I could blow through the ceiling--
GOOD AND BAD, HUMANITY CAN TRANSFORM ANYTHING INTO SOMETHING. WE EXPRESS. WE CREATE. EVEN WHEN WE'RE UNDER A DICTATOR.
EVEN WHEN WE CAN'T SEE THE STARS, WE IMAGINE THEM.
THAT'S WHAT HUMANITY IS. THAT'S WHAT WE BRING TO THE GALAXY. THAT'S OUR VALUE.
THAT BEAUTY IS WHAT YOU'D BE WIPING OUT.
IF YOU ARE NOT THE MONSTERS OF THE COSMOS. IF YOU'RE BETTER THAN WHO YOU THOUGHT WE WERE...
YOU'VE GOT ONE CALL, SISTER.

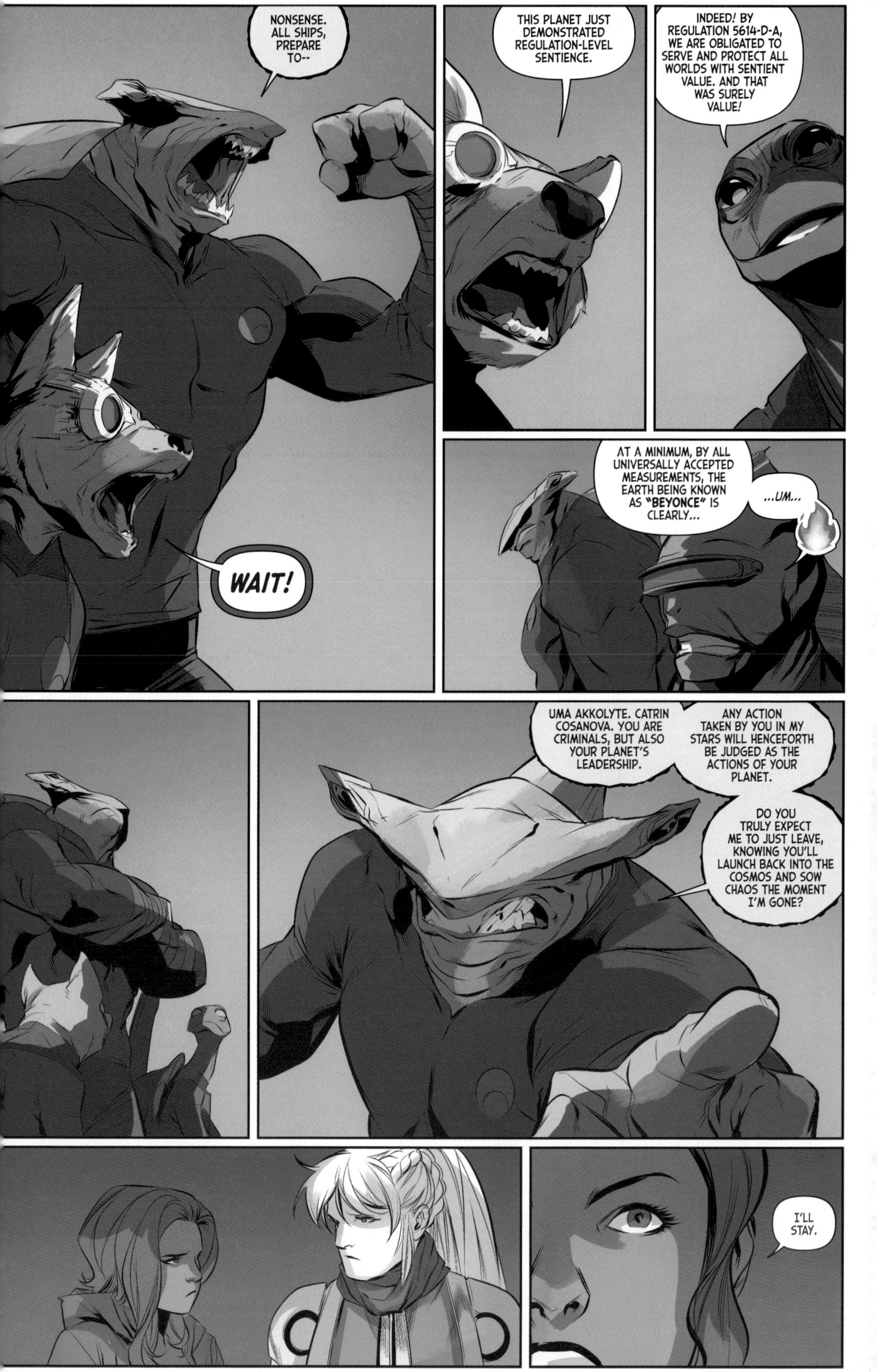
NONSENSE. ALL SHIPS, PREPARE TO--
WAIT!
THIS PLANET JUST DEMONSTRATED REGULATION-LEVEL SENTIENCE.
INDEED! BY REGULATION 5614-D-A, WE ARE OBLIGATED TO SERVE AND PROTECT ALL WORLDS WITH SENTIENT VALUE. AND THAT WAS SURELY VALUE!
AT A MINIMUM, BY ALL UNIVERSALLY ACCEPTED MEASUREMENTS, THE EARTH BEING KNOWN AS "BEYONCE" IS CLEARLY...
...UM...
UMA AKKOLYTE. CATRIN COSANOVA. YOU ARE CRIMINALS, BUT ALSO YOUR PLANET'S LEADERSHIP.
ANY ACTION TAKEN BY YOU IN MY STARS WILL HENCEFORTH BE JUDGED AS THE ACTIONS OF YOUR PLANET.
DO YOU TRULY EXPECT ME TO JUST LEAVE, KNOWING YOU'LL LAUNCH BACK INTO THE COSMOS AND SOW CHAOS THE MOMENT I'M GONE?
I'LL STAY.

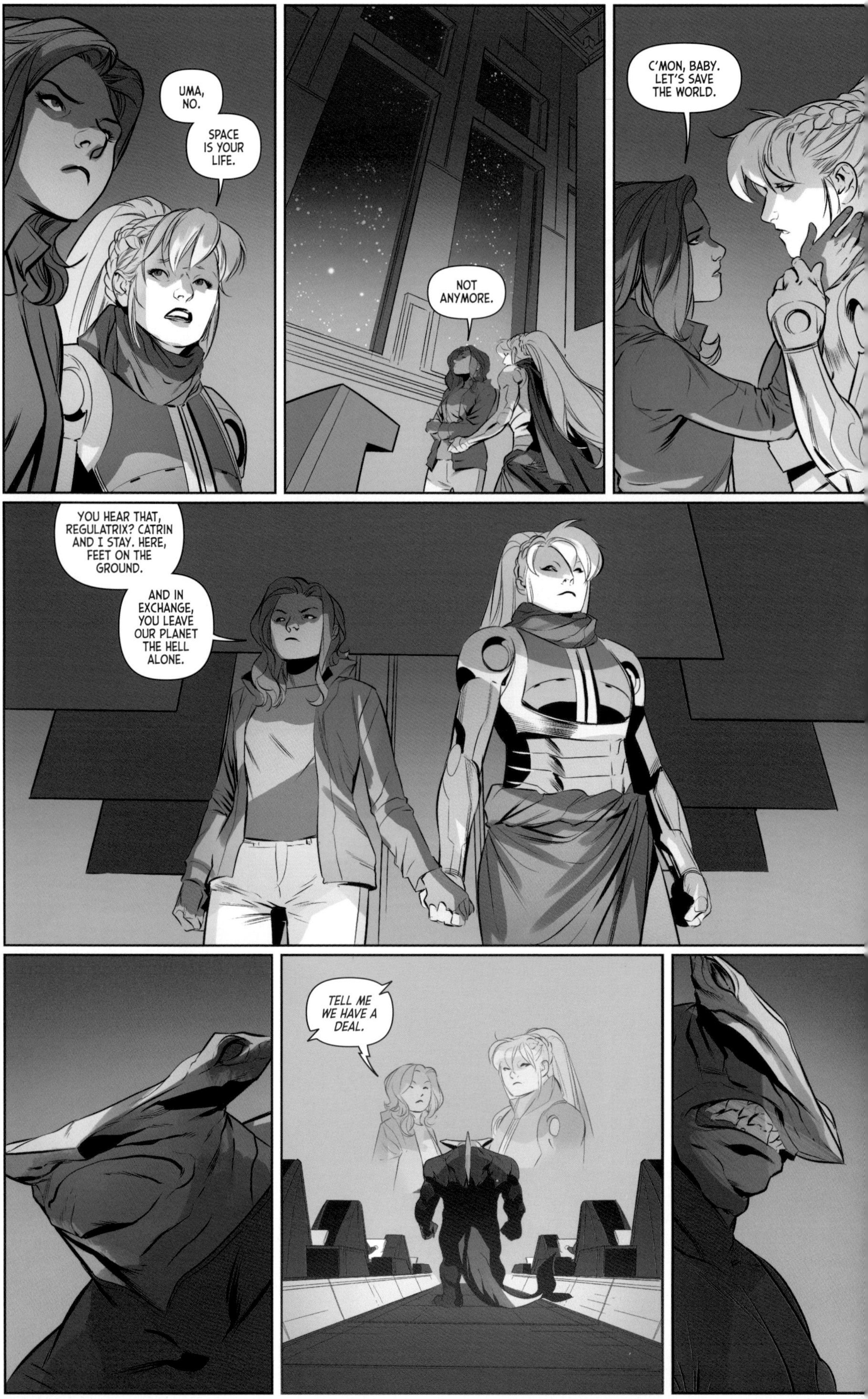
UMA, NO.
SPACE IS YOUR LIFE.
NOT ANYMORE.
C'MON, BABY. LET'S SAVE THE WORLD.
YOU HEAR THAT, REGULATRIX? CATRIN AND I STAY. HERE, FEET ON THE GROUND.
AND IN EXCHANGE, YOU LEAVE OUR PLANET THE HELL ALONE.
TELL ME WE HAVE A DEAL.

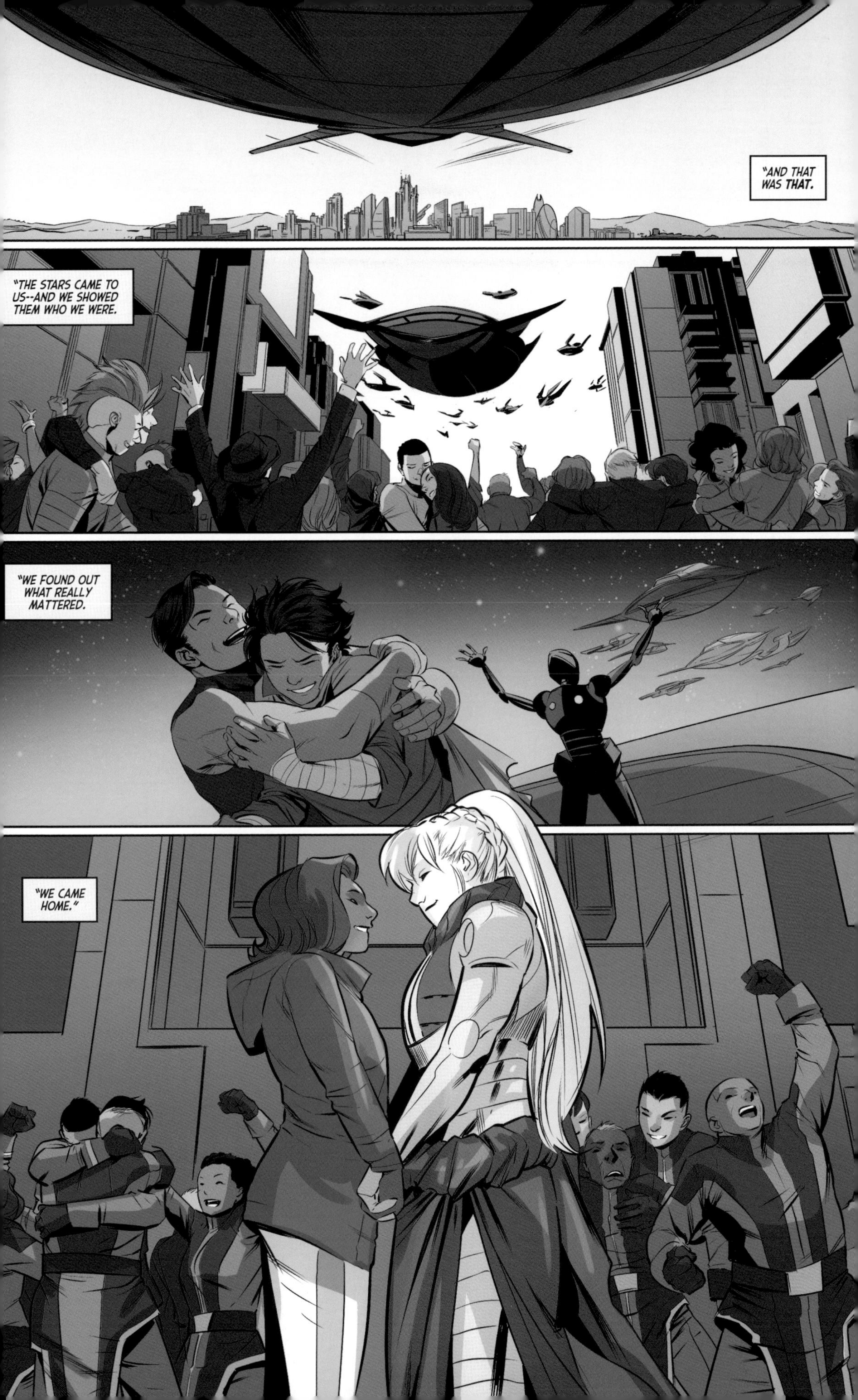
"AND THAT WAS THAT.
"THE STARS CAME TO US--AND WE SHOWED THEM WHO WE WERE.
"WE FOUND OUT WHAT REALLY MATTERED.
"WE CAME HOME."

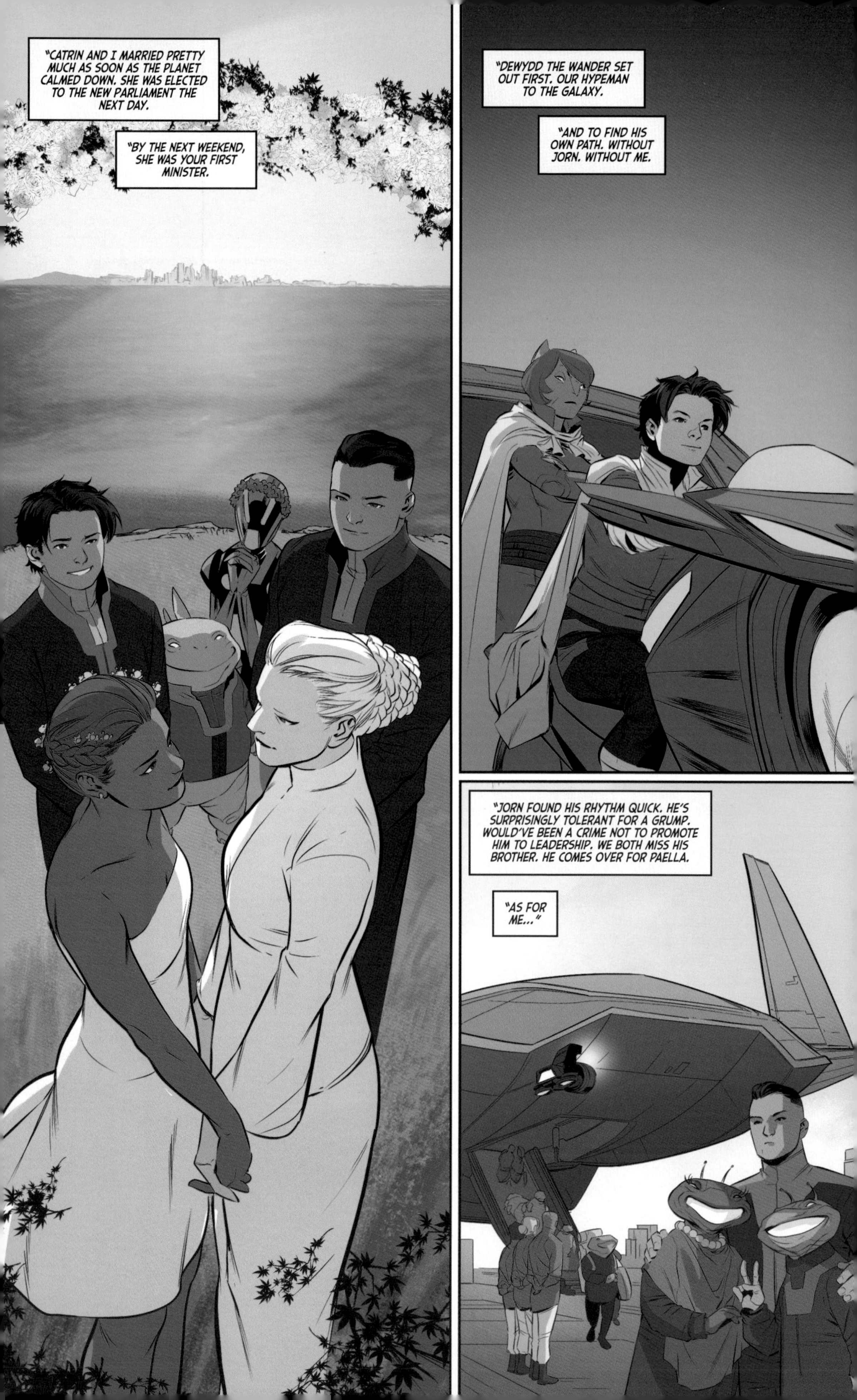
"CATRIN AND I MARRIED PRETTY MUCH AS SOON AS THE PLANET CALMED DOWN. SHE WAS ELECTED TO THE NEW PARLIAMENT THE NEXT DAY.
"BY THE NEXT WEEKEND, SHE WAS YOUR FIRST MINISTER.
"DEWYDD THE WANDER SET OUT FIRST. OUR HYPEMAN TO THE GALAXY.
"AND TO FIND HIS OWN PATH. WITHOUT JORN. WITHOUT ME.
"JORN FOUND HIS RHYTHM QUICK. HE'S SURPRISINGLY TOLERANT FOR A GRUMP. WOULD'VE BEEN A CRIME NOT TO PROMOTE HIM TO LEADERSHIP. WE BOTH MISS HIS BROTHER. HE COMES OVER FOR PAELLA.
"AS FOR ME..."

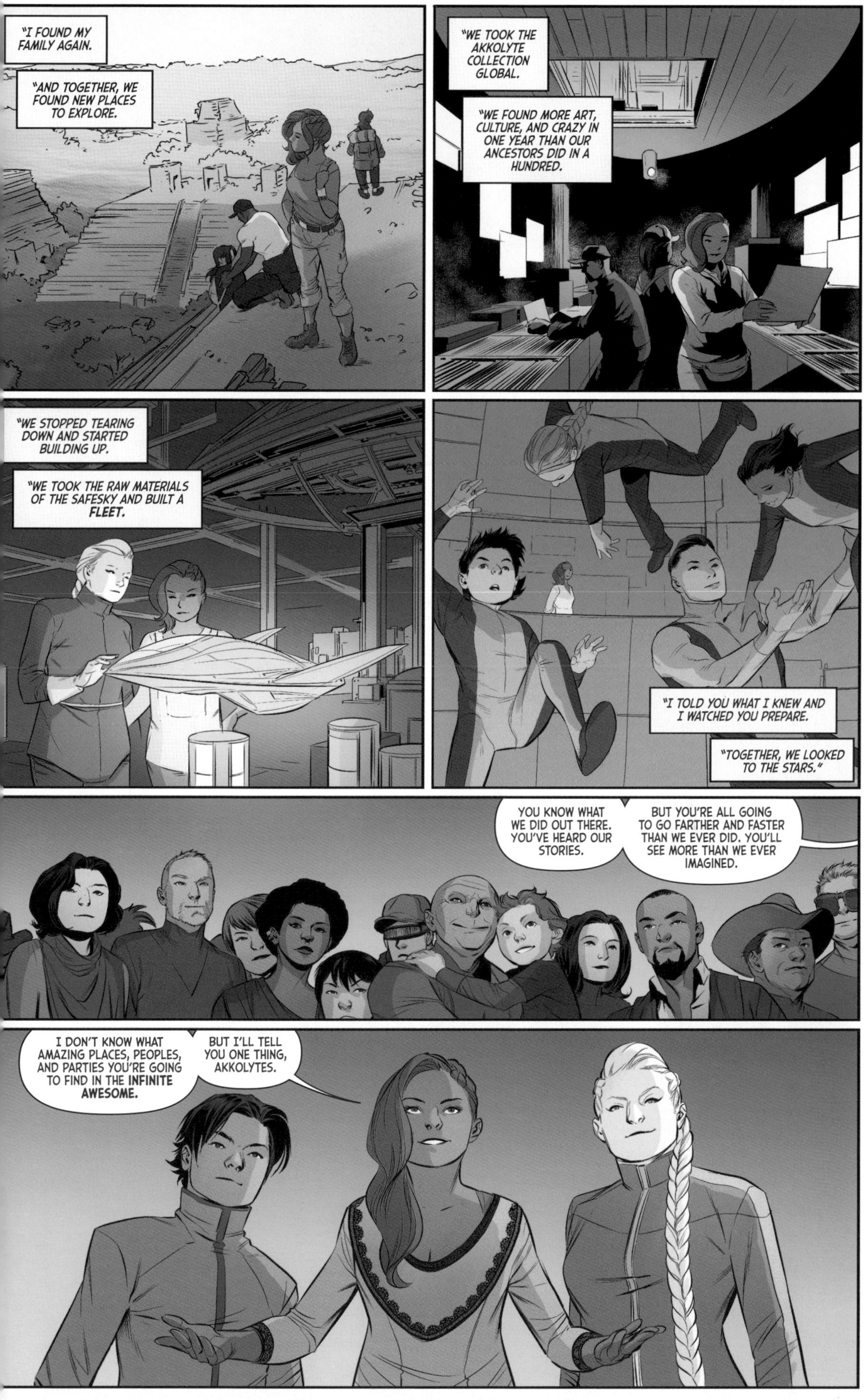
"I FOUND MY FAMILY AGAIN.
"AND TOGETHER, WE FOUND NEW PLACES TO EXPLORE.
"WE TOOK THE AKKOLYTE COLLECTION GLOBAL.
"WE FOUND MORE ART, CULTURE, AND CRAZY IN ONE YEAR THAN OUR ANCESTORS DID IN A HUNDRED.
"WE STOPPED TEARING DOWN AND STARTED BUILDING UP.
"WE TOOK THE RAW MATERIALS OF THE SAFESKY AND BUILT A **FLEET.**
"I TOLD YOU WHAT I KNEW AND I WATCHED YOU PREPARE.
"TOGETHER, WE LOOKED TO THE STARS."
YOU KNOW WHAT WE DID OUT THERE. YOU'VE HEARD OUR STORIES.
BUT YOU'RE ALL GOING TO GO FARTHER AND FASTER THAN WE EVER DID. YOU'LL SEE MORE THAN WE EVER IMAGINED.
I DON'T KNOW WHAT AMAZING PLACES, PEOPLES, AND PARTIES YOU'RE GOING TO FIND IN THE **INFINITE AWESOME.**
BUT I'LL TELL YOU ONE THING, AKKOLYTES.

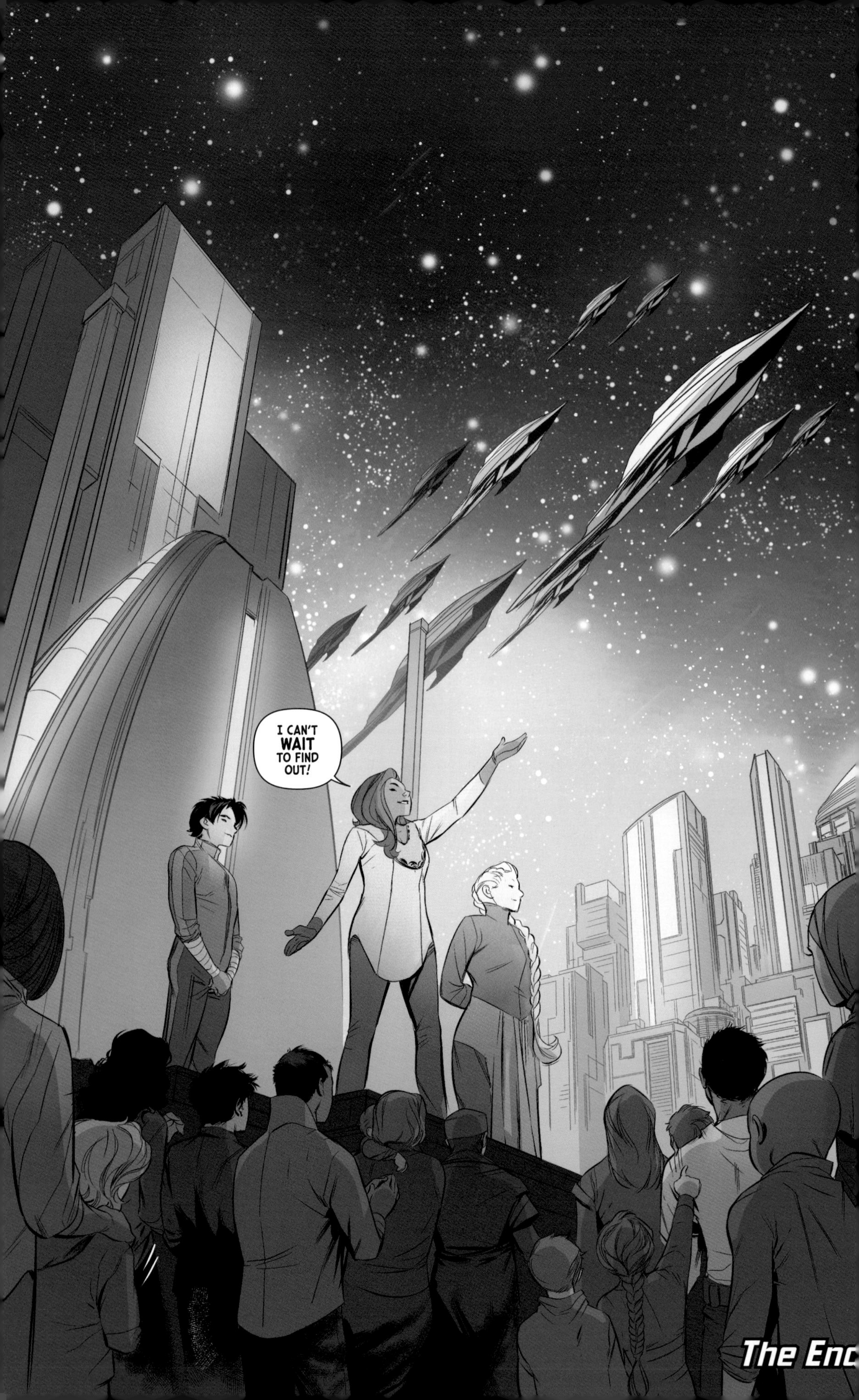
I CAN'T WAIT TO FIND OUT!
The Enc

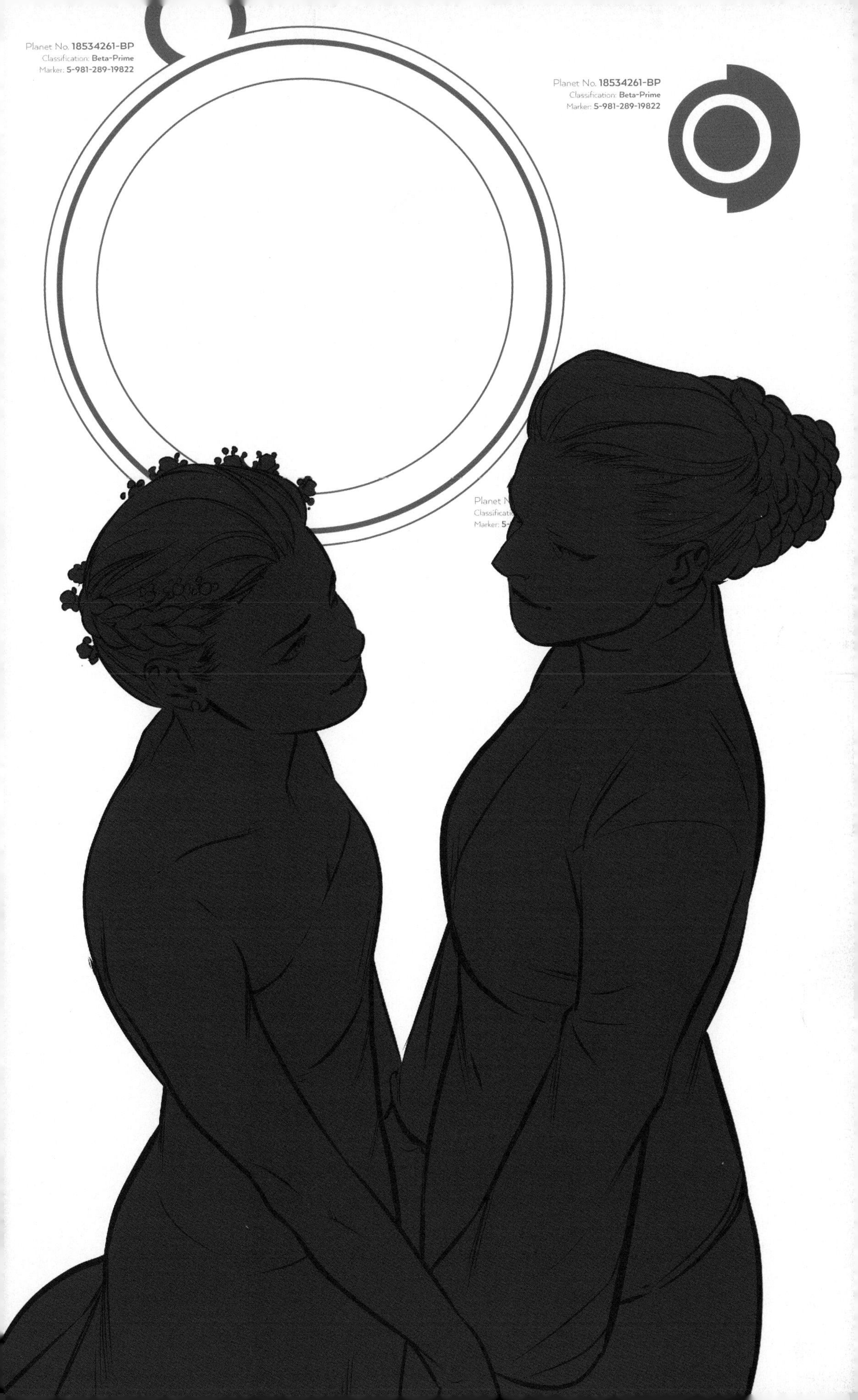
Planet No. 18534261-BP
Classification: Beta-Prime
Marker: 5-981-289-19822
Planet No. 18534261-BP
Classification: Beta-Prime
Marker: 5-981-289-19822

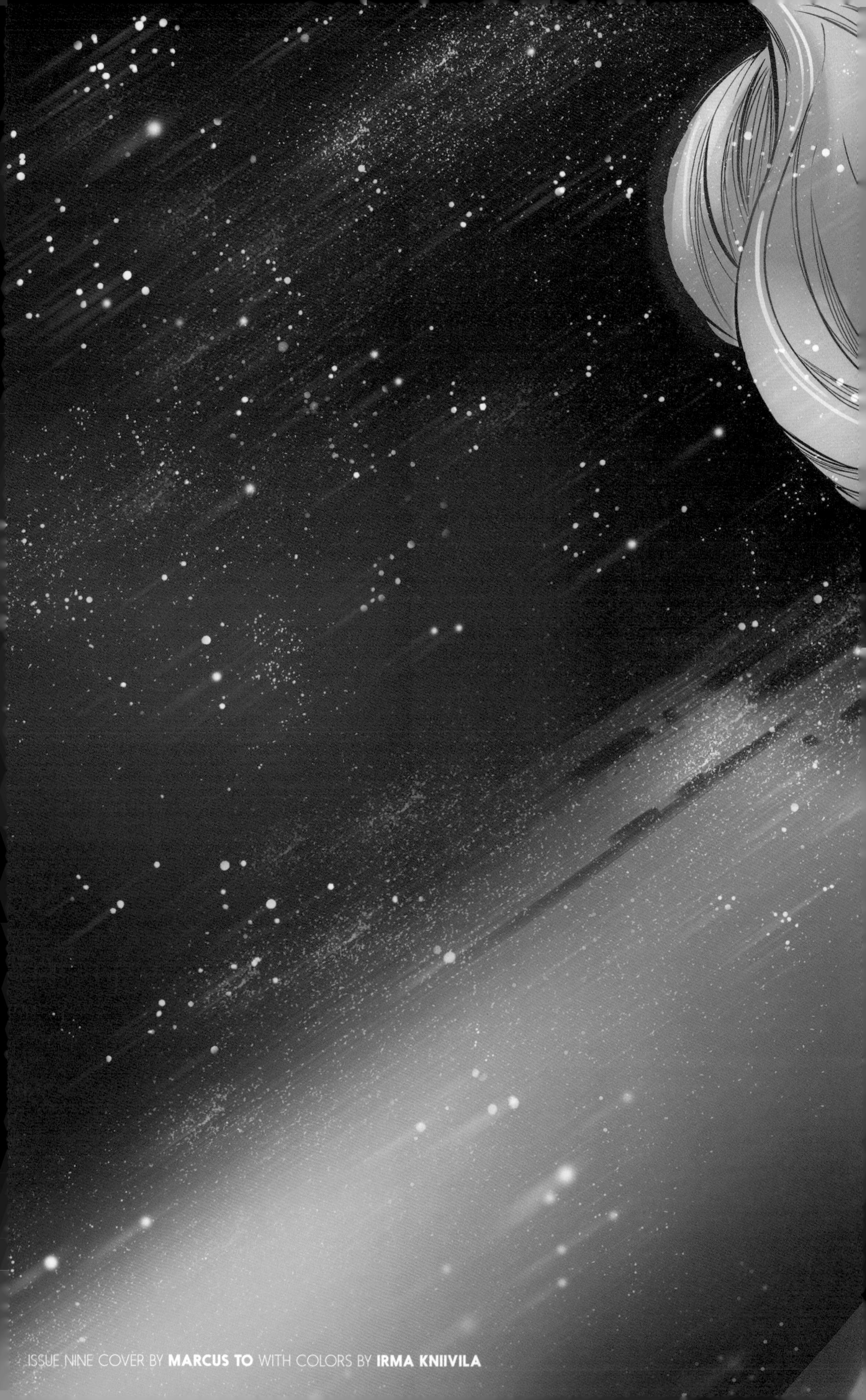

ISSUE NINE COVER BY **MARCUS TO** WITH COLORS BY **IRMA KNIIVILA**

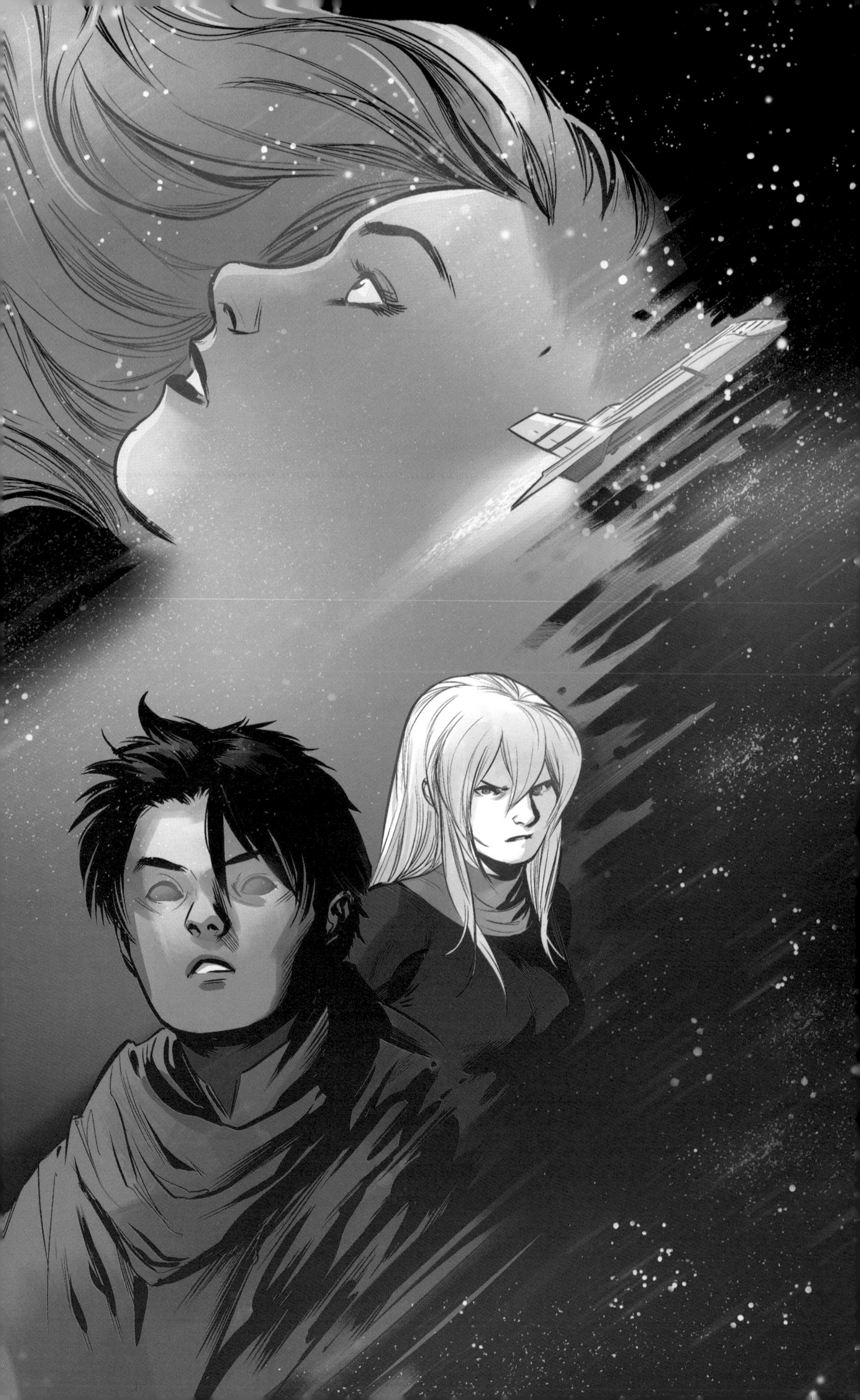

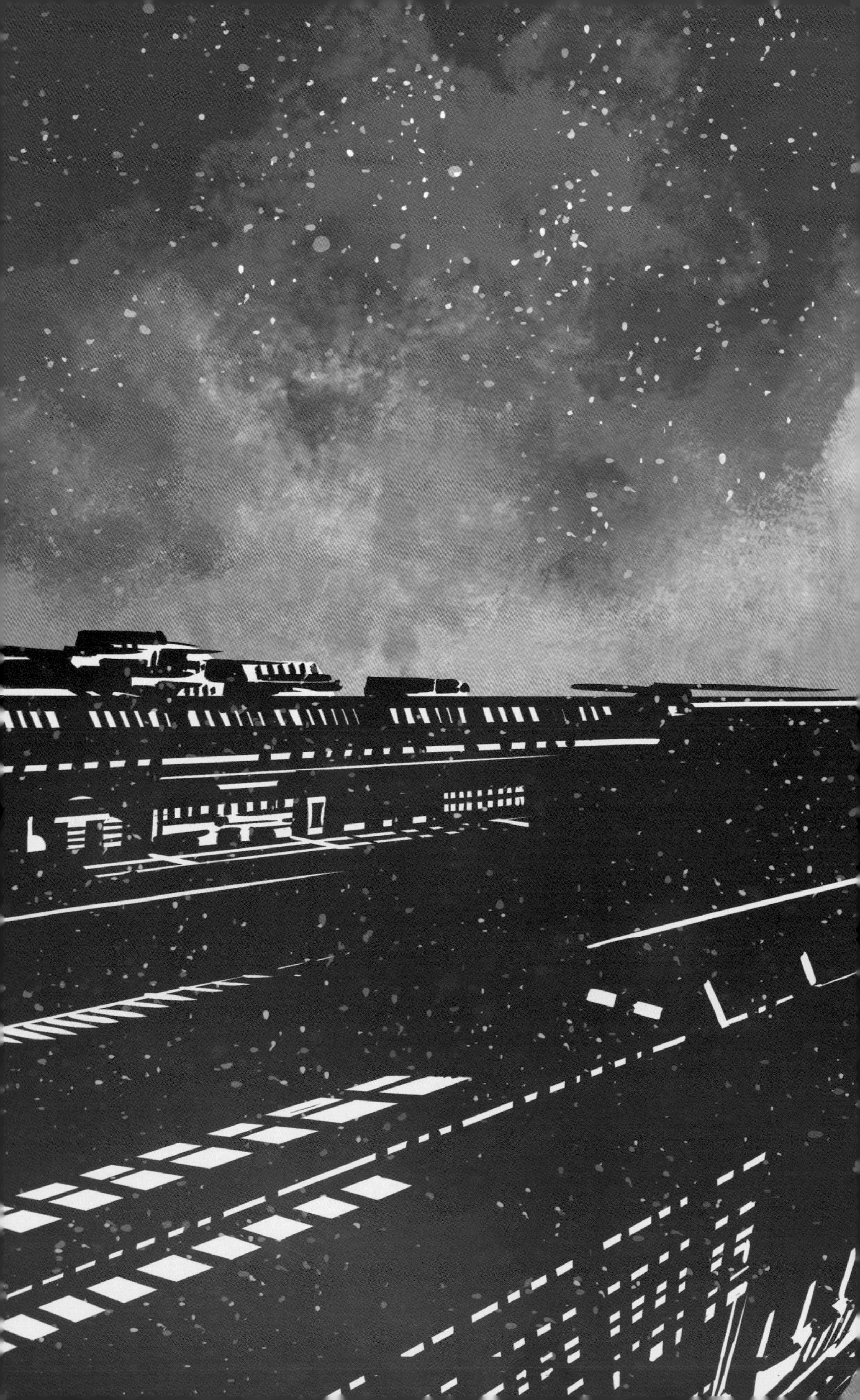

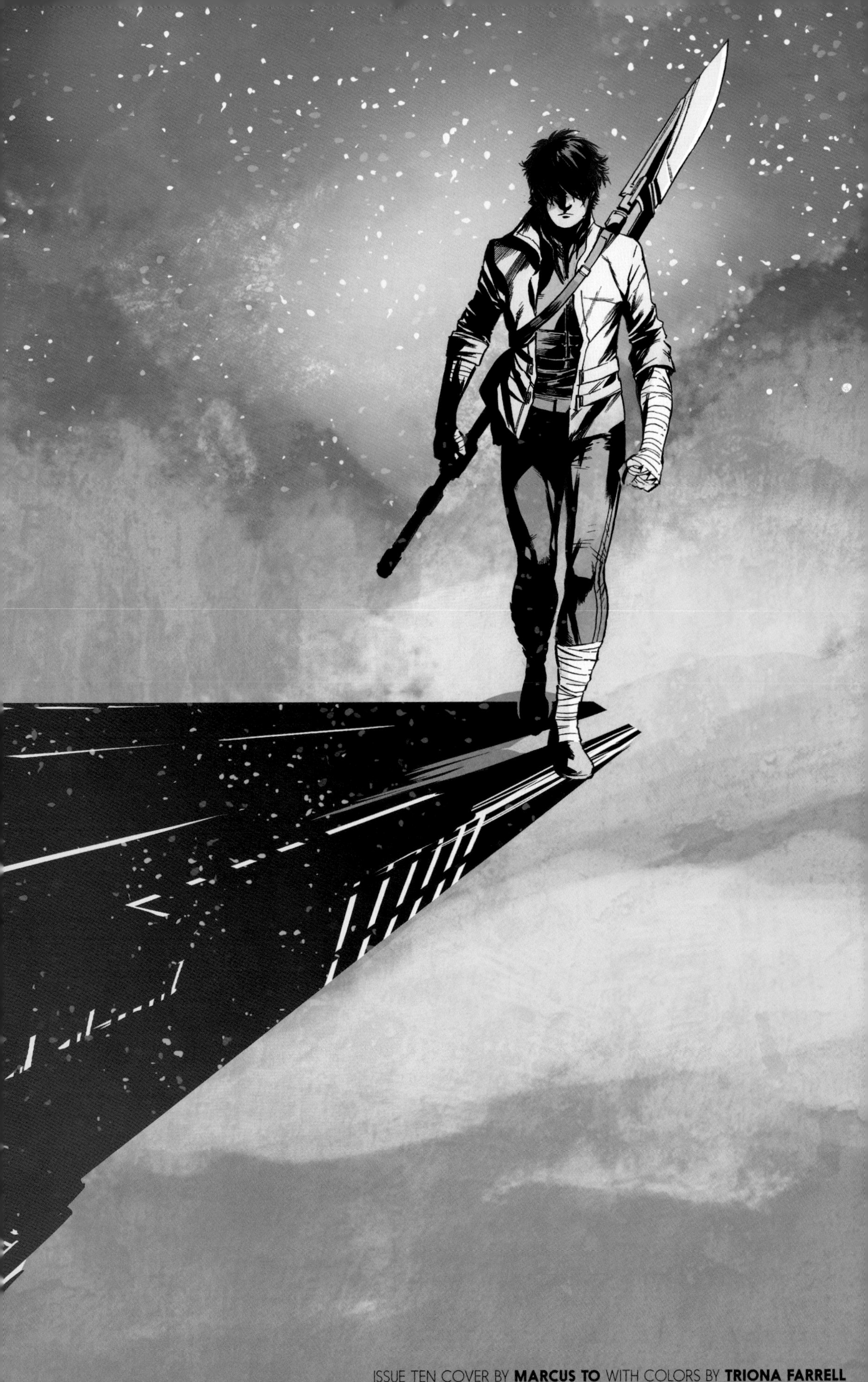

ISSUE TEN COVER BY **MARCUS TO** WITH COLORS BY **TRIONA FARRELL**

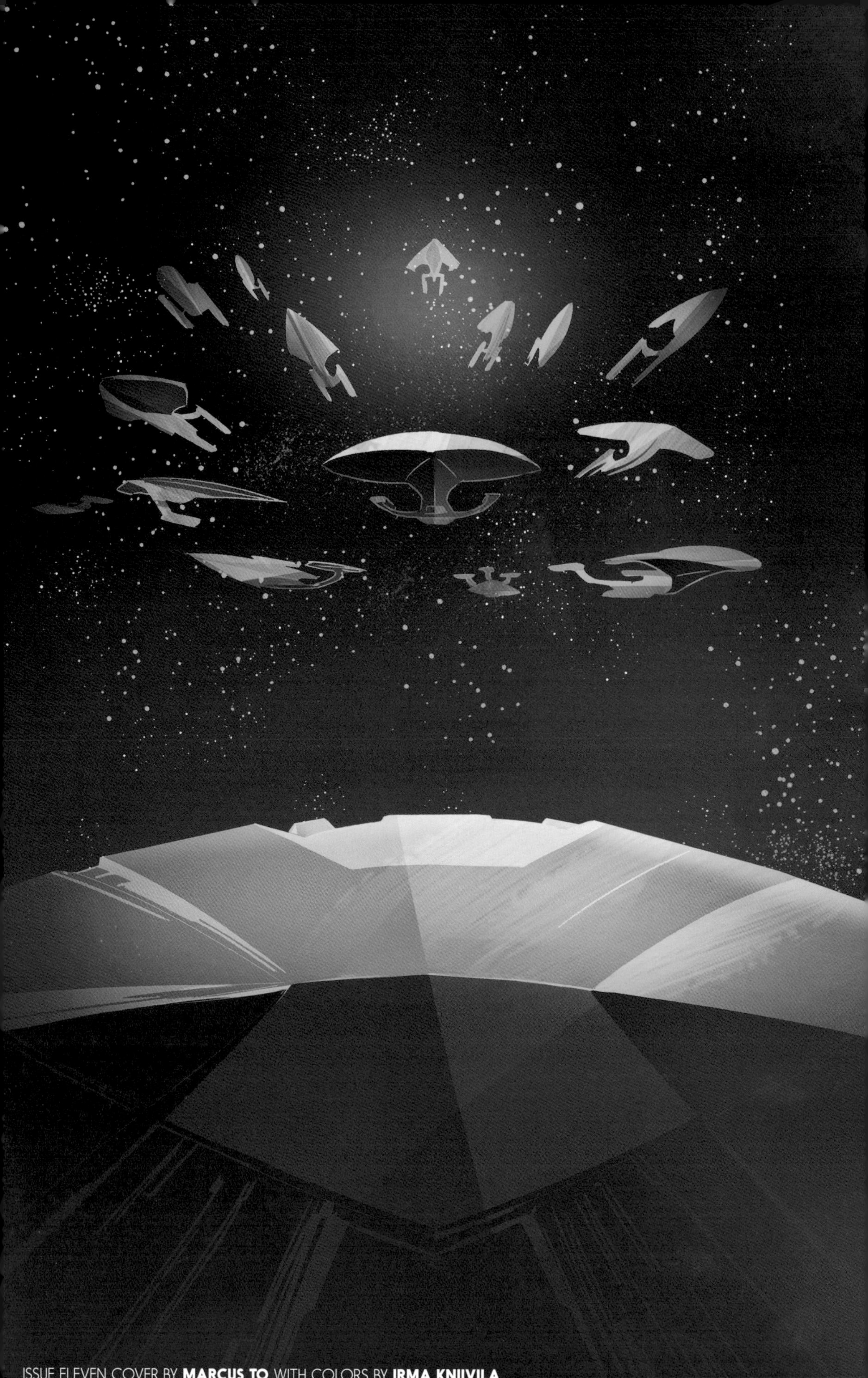

ISSUE ELEVEN COVER BY **MARCUS TO** WITH COLORS BY **IRMA KNIIVILA**

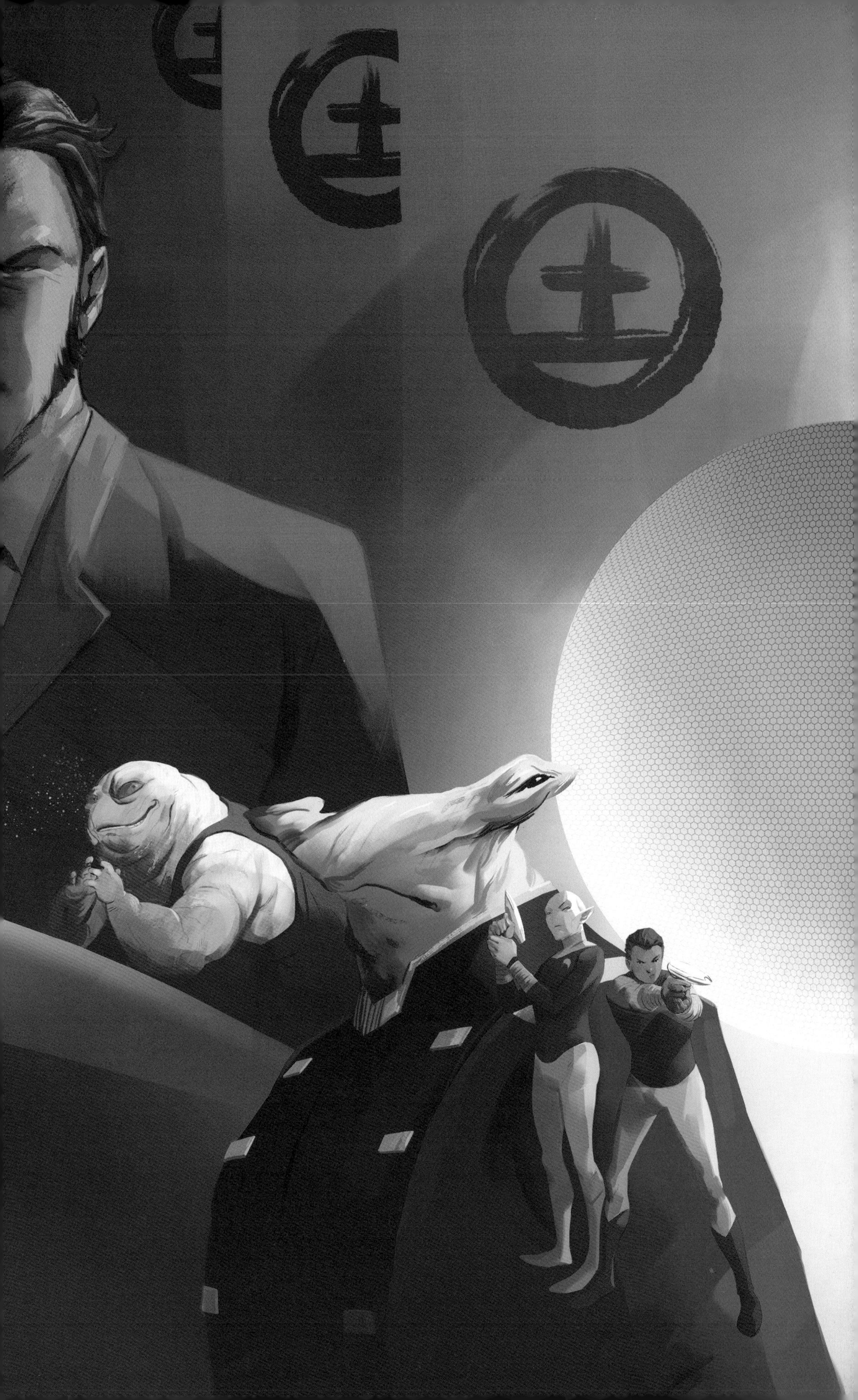

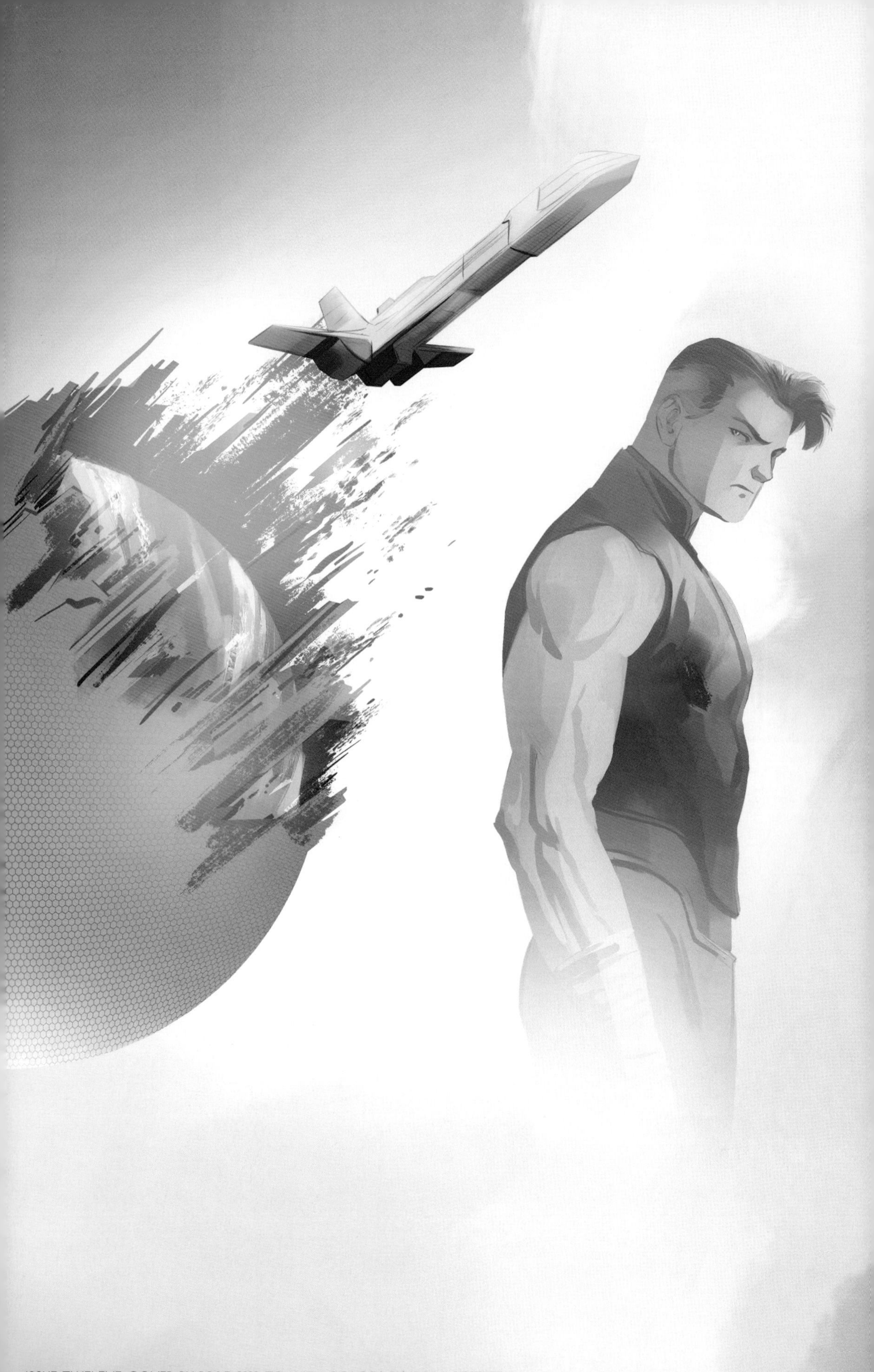

ISSUE TWELEVE COVER BY **MARCUS TO** WITH COLORS BY **IRMA KNIIVILA**

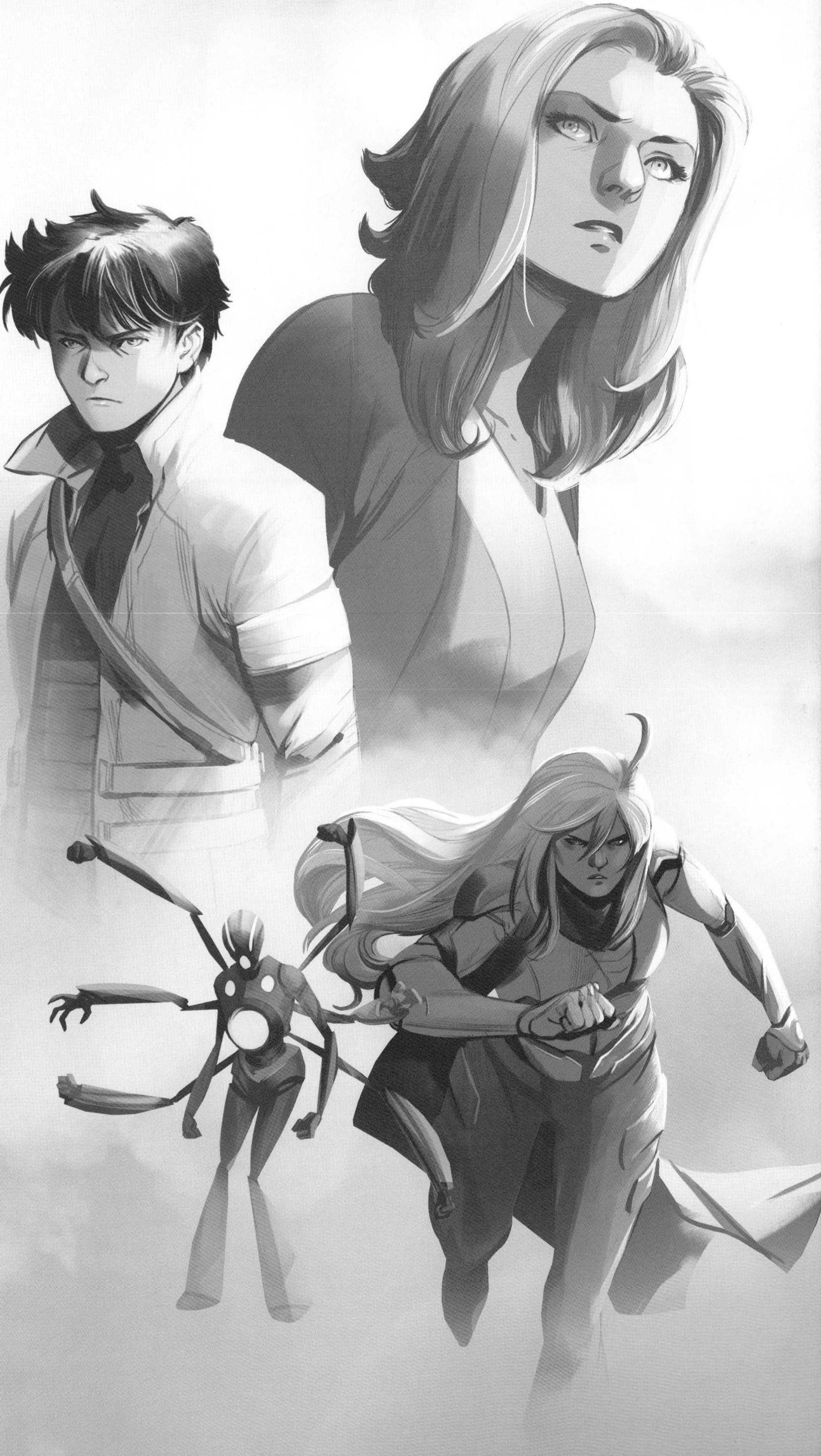

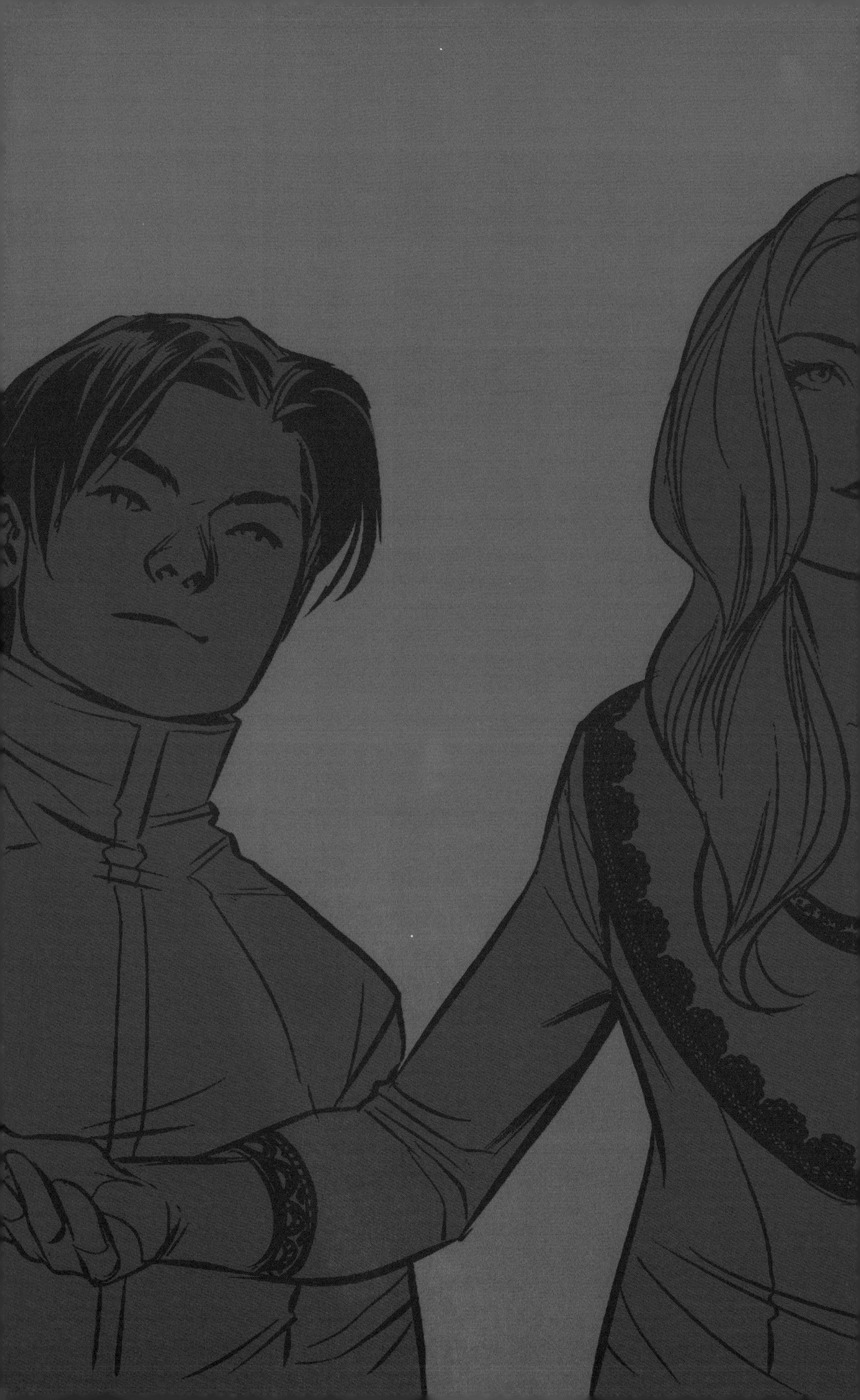

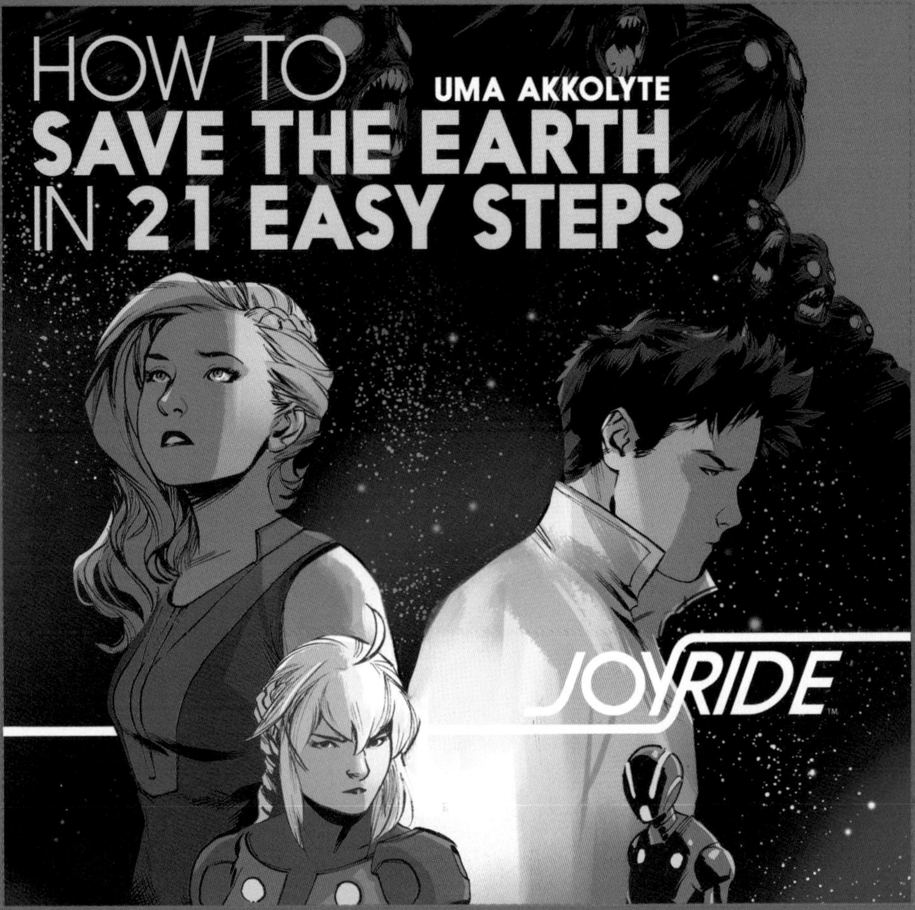
HOW TO
SAVE THE EARTH
IN 21 EASY STEPS
UMA AKKOLYTE
JOYRIDE

JOYRIDE HOW TO SAVE THE EARTH IN 21 EASY STEPS UMA AKKOLYTE

Final Song MØ
A 1000 Times Hamilton Leithauser + Rostam
True Love Waits Radiohead
Where Is My Mind Pixies
Back To Me Allison Weiss
What Went Down Foals
Werewolf Gimmick The Mountain Goats
Don't Get Captured Run The Jewels
Radio of Lips The Joy Formidable
One Day I Will Sin No More Ezra Furman
Needed Me Rihanna
Space Exploration Disaster Sunflower Beam
Funk The Fear Esperanza Spalding
Touch The Sky Kanye West ft Lupe Fiasco
Two Coffins Against Me!
Queen Perfume Genius
(You Gotta) Fight For Your Right (To Party) Beastie Boys
Redemption Song Bob Marley & The Wailers
Single Ladies (Put A Ring On It) Beyoncé
Mountain Top Bedouin Soundclash
Dog Days Are Over Florence + The Machine

WHAT I AM IS **FREE**

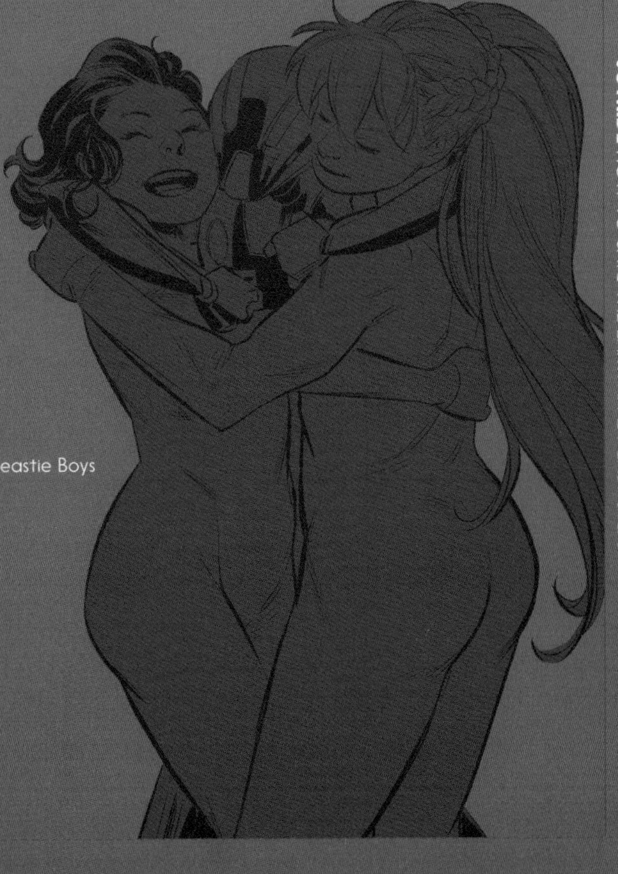

JOYRIDE HOW TO SAVE THE EARTH IN 21 EASY STEPS UMA AKKOLYTE

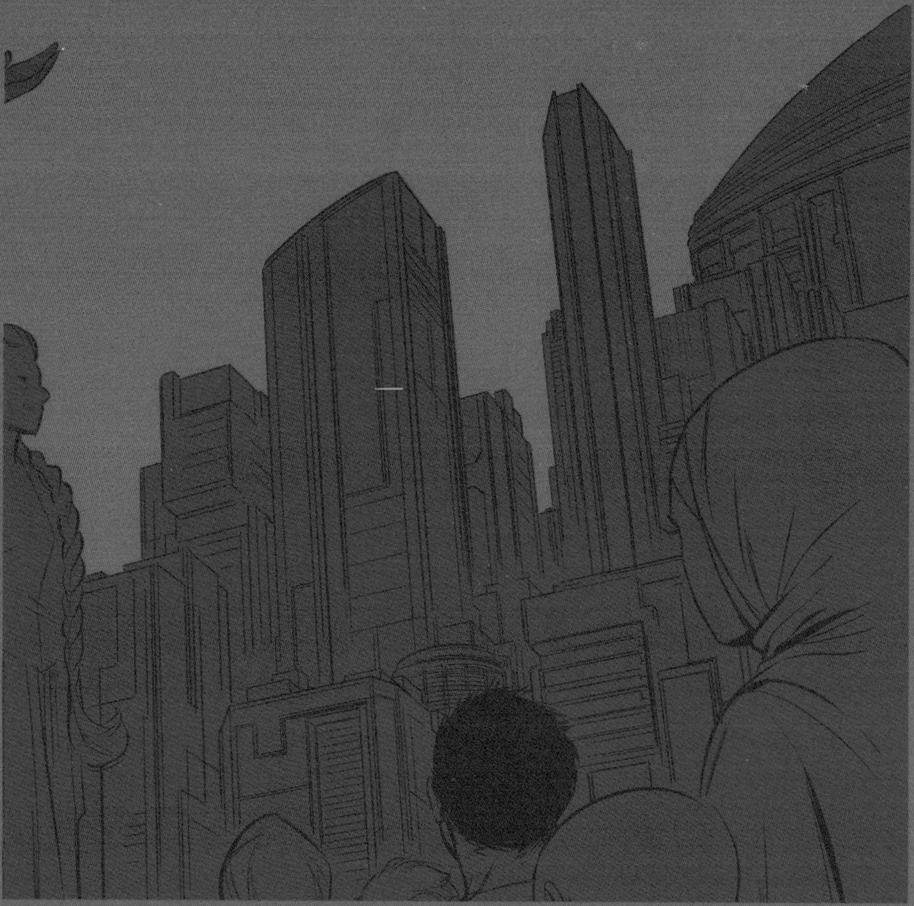

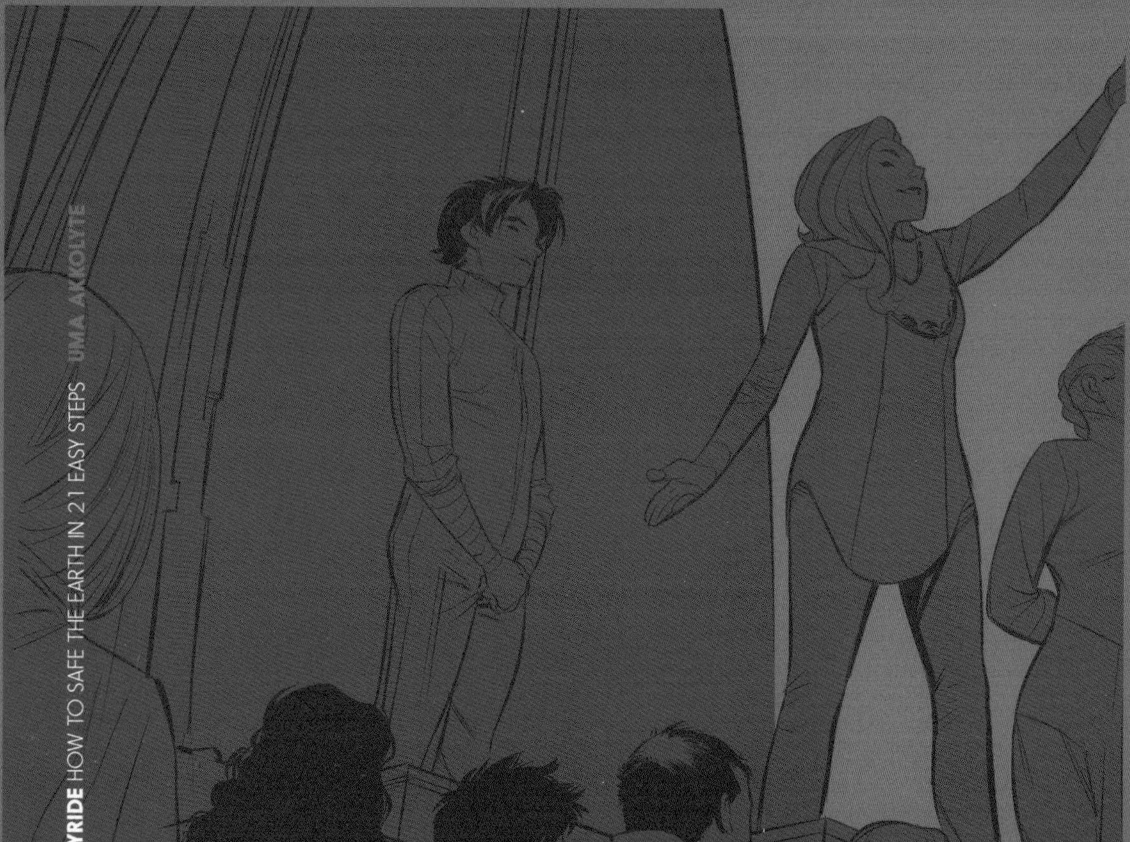